Dawn M. Hadley   Julian D. Richards

THE VIKING GREAT ARMY
AND THE MAKING
OF ENGLAND

FRONTISPIECE The camps and other places visited by the Viking Great Army as mentioned in the *Anglo-Saxon Chronicle,* AD 865–78.

First published in the United Kingdom in 2021 by Thames & Hudson Ltd, 181A High Holborn, London WC1V 7QX

First published in the United States of America in 2021 by Thames & Hudson Inc., 500 Fifth Avenue, New York, New York 10110

The Viking Great Army and the Making of England
© 2021 Thames & Hudson Ltd, London
Text © 2021 Dawn M. Hadley and Julian D. Richards

Maps and hand-drawn illustrations by Drazen Tomic
© 2021 Dawn M. Hadley, Julian D. Richards and Thames & Hudson Ltd, except where specified on p. 294

British Library Cataloguing-in-Publication Data
A catalogue record for this book is available from the British Library

Library of Congress Control Number 2020940907

ISBN 978-0-500-02201-6

Printed in China by Reliance Printing (Shenzhen) Co. Ltd

Be the first to know about our new releases, exclusive content and author events by visiting
thamesandhudson.com
thamesandhudsonusa.com
thamesandhudson.com.au

Contents

Heroes and Villains

It was an autumnal morning in the year AD 872. The longships cut through the water and were carried upriver on the incoming tide. The rustle of leaves in the trees along the riverbank and the occasional cry of a moorhen, startled by the intrusion, seemed to be the only sounds, but an alert listener would also have heard the splash of oars upon the water and the flapping of the sails in the gentle breeze. The fog was rising from where it had been hanging over the river and an observer cautiously watching from the riverbank would have seen a whole fleet emerging from the morning mist. The oarsmen were tired; they had been travelling for weeks. They had already sailed all the way from London to York earlier that year and now they were heading back south, crossing the Humber estuary and continuing up the River Trent. They were in hostile territory deep within the Anglo-Saxon kingdom of Mercia, heading for a safe place where they could camp for the winter, where they could rest, melt down the gold and silver they had plundered from Northumbrian monasteries and sell the slaves they had acquired. They did not need extra mouths to feed over the winter, although they had been told that the barns where they were heading were stuffed with grain and salted meat. They had been sailing since dawn. A mile back, when they passed the causeway where the ancient Roman road still crossed the Trent, a cry had gone up from the steersman of the lead boat. Now, as they rounded a bend in the river, they spotted the campfires of the advance party on the higher land on the left bank. Sails were rapidly furled and scores of longships were steered into the marshes and beached on the flood-plain alongside the river. At last they had reached their home for the winter months – Turc's Island or, as we know it today, Torksey.

From AD 865 to 878 a Viking army wreaked havoc on the kingdoms of Anglo-Saxon England, leading to military and political conquest, settlement on a substantial scale and extensive Scandinavian cultural and linguistic changes in eastern and northern England. Previous Viking raids in England had largely been coastal hit-and-run affairs, but this period saw a change in tactics, as the raiders penetrated deep into the countryside, moving rapidly by road and river, exploiting Anglo-Saxon internal divisions and overwintering at strategic locations. While Viking raids on the British Isles had begun in the 790s as a quest for portable wealth in the form of silver and slaves, by the 860s and 870s the aims of Viking armies had shifted to land seizure and political conquest. This critical period for English history led to revolutionary changes in land ownership, society and economy, including the growth of towns and indus-try, while transformations in power politics would ultimately see the rise of Wessex as the pre-eminent kingdom of Anglo-Saxon England. In the countryside, estates were broken up, farmsteads were abandoned and new settlement patterns emerged. Yet despite the pivotal role of the so-called Great Army (*micel here* in Old English) in these events, little was known of it until recently; the available documentary sources provide few insights into its activities and intentions, and archaeological evidence for the presence of the Great Army had remained largely elusive. Nonetheless, the Great Army loomed large in late medieval imaginings of the Viking Age, from which some of the most dramatic accounts of Viking atroci-ties derive. The Army still captures the imagination today and has inspired numerous novels, including Bernard Cornwell's *The Last*

Kingdom series (2004–20), first televised for the BBC in 2015, as well as the History Channel's historical drama *Vikings* (2013–). In 2018 *Thrones of Britannia – The Great Viking Army* became the latest addition to the *Total War* series of computer games.

Like all good stories, this book has plenty of heroes and villains, although it is not always clear which is which. There are Viking leaders: some, fearsome warriors such as Ivar the Boneless and Ubba, who martyred the Anglo-Saxon King Edmund; others, such as Guthrum, who were baptized and became kings according to the Christian model. There are Anglo-Saxon kings such as Ælla and Osberht of Northumbria, Burgred of Mercia and Alfred of Wessex who fought amongst themselves as much as against the Vikings. There are Christian clerics too: some who died hiding their treasure from the Vikings; others who were persuasive publicists, writing propaganda that would eventually create Victorian heroes out of their patron-kings, as Asser did in his biography of Alfred the Great, while hiding the achievements of others. There are also 21st-century heroes and villains in the story: the metal-detectorists whose work has uncovered – or sometimes selfishly concealed – the activities of the Great Army and early medieval Scandinavian immigrants in England. The story this book tells could not have been written ten years ago. In the last decade, our understanding of the Great Army has been transformed by a wealth of newly recovered archaeological evidence, largely derived from metal-detecting, and this is also the story of those discoveries.

While the Army's winter camps are documented in contemporary sources, new evidence has recently enabled us, for the first time, to identify their precise locations and immense scale. Moreover, we now know that the activities that took place at these camps extended far beyond the purely military, to include trade, manufacturing and craft-working. The new evidence provides fresh insights into a period during the 9th and 10th century that was crucial to the emergence of a unified English kingdom, and that saw the development of urban centres in northern and eastern England and the start of its first industrial revolution. Traces of the newly identified archaeological signature of the Great Army are starting to emerge beyond the winter camps, across the rural landscape of northern and eastern England. Here they tell a story of major changes in the countryside, too, with attacks on Anglo-Saxon settlements by elements of the Great Army, resulting in the abandonment of some Anglo-Saxon sites and the appearance of new types of Anglo-Scandinavian farmsteads, which ultimately led to the settlement patterns that we see today over much of eastern England.

Our research into the Viking Great Army has taken us on an archaeological journey of discovery. We have endeavoured to capture some of that excitement by interspersing conventional discussion of the archaeological and historical evidence with creative accounts based on that evidence. We have also included narratives about present-day discoveries and the people who made them, as it is important to acknowledge their role in rewriting history. Many of the modern heroes in this story are not university-educated archaeologists, but local enthusiasts who have spent months of their lives in the wind and rain, eyes on the ground and ears tuned to listen for the tell-tale beep – not solely in the hope of monetary gain, but because of a genuine interest in the past and the thrill of unearthing something that no one has touched since it was lost by a Viking warrior over a thousand years ago. Will it be yet another shotgun cartridge or, this time, an Anglo-Saxon coin? But we shall also meet some 21st-century villains: the nighthawks who metal-detect illegally and fail to report their finds, and some of whom are now languishing in prison for their theft of everyone's heritage.

First, however, we must travel back in time, to the mid-9th century, in Scandinavia and Anglo-Saxon England.

PART I

The Vikings and Their World

1

Warrior-Chiefs and Kings

Major changes were underway in southern Scandinavia in the 9th century AD. The region had lain beyond the northern frontiers of the Roman Empire and so had never had the substantial walled towns seen in western Europe and England – nor experienced the military, economic and social changes that were needed to support them and to pay taxes to Rome. Nonetheless, while the inhabitants of southern Scandinavia still effectively lived in the Iron Age, the region had not entirely escaped Roman impact. To protect its own borders, the Roman Empire had sought to make alliances with what its rulers viewed as the barbarian tribes beyond them. Diplomatic gifts of Roman silver plate, bronze flagons and glass beakers, as well as weapons, turn up in Scandinavian graves and treasure hoards. Such prestige items must have reinforced the power and status of the local chiefs, whose control of imports of precious metals and other luxuries allowed them to buy the loyalty of their followers. Scandinavian leaders typically took tribute from those who were in a weaker position and passed on these gifts to others to acquire status and support. If gifts were not forthcoming then they could be extracted by force instead. The emergence of these Scandinavian social elites and their quest for wealth underpinned the transition from the Iron Age to the Viking Age.[1]

The Viking diaspora also needs to be set against a background of an ideology based upon warfare. The spoils of battle were given as offerings to the gods in great bog deposits of slaughtered enemy warriors and captured weapons of defeated Iron Age armies, such as those excavated at Illerup Ådal in Jutland. Hoards of gold offerings and exotic treasures were another sign of the establishment and legitimation of an elite, who now communicated with the gods on behalf of the community. Since literacy and book production would be later Christian developments in the region, we lack any contemporary Scandinavian written sources, but in the 13th- and 14th-century Norse saga literature strong leaders are characterized as 'ring-givers' because they bestow silver arm-rings on their followers to secure and reward their allegiance. As access to portable wealth became essential, but supplies from the Roman Empire dried up, Viking chieftains began to turn their attention overseas, trading or raiding as seemed best.

By the 8th and 9th centuries there are occasional references in continental sources to individuals described as kings, who apparently controlled territories, although the modern countries of Denmark, Norway and Sweden did not yet exist. There is also archaeological evidence for early stages of state formation, including monumental military works such as the Danevirke, a system of fortifications *c.* 35 km (22 miles) long, closing the Schleswig pass between the Schlei fjord, which cuts in from the east, and the marshy areas around the rivers that flow into the North Sea to the west. The first phases of construction are now thought to be as early as the 6th century AD, but the ramparts were heavily reinforced in the 8th century and in 808 they were extended under a ruler named in the *Frankish Royal Annals* as King Godfred.[2] It would be a mistake, however, to take this as evidence for an 8th-century state that corresponded to modern Denmark. From the 8th century major trading sites with wide-ranging connections also began to emerge and, while at first temporary, they soon developed a settled, urban character. The foundation of these international trading ports was intrinsically linked to the growth of royal power and the establishment of the early Scandinavian states. These trading sites must have been hubs

The North Sea in the 9th century.

that conveyed news about opportunities for wealth abroad.[3] In the 8th and 9th centuries traders from many nations found their way to these sites. A late 9th-century traveller and trader, Wulfstan, source of a contemporary Old English account of the Baltic and North Sea trading sites, testifies to the presence of Anglo-Saxons in the region, but the predominant non-Scandinavians were a people known as the Frisians.[4] Frisia was a coastal territory in what is today a large part of the Netherlands as well as northern Germany. The people were a maritime nation and important traders, with their own major trading site at Dorestad, near Utrecht, which had been established on the site of a Roman fortress in the 7th century.

One of the earliest Scandinavian towns, founded in the early 8th century at Ribe in southern Jutland [pl. 2], was clearly modelled on Frisian sites. Excavations have revealed a network of regular plots, surrounded by wattle fences and separated by small ditches. These plots were already laid out when the first merchants arrived and have been taken as direct evidence for royal patronage and organization. Ribe was first thought to have been a seasonal market town for generations before people started to settle there more permanently, but excavations in 2018 demonstrated that solid houses existed in Ribe only a few years after the earliest activities in the area, no later than the 720s. Specialized metalworkers were casting a range of jewellery types, while others were making glass beads from reused Roman and Byzantine mosaic tiles. There were also imported lava querns (grindstones), pottery from the Rhineland, whetstones and reindeer antler from Norway. From the 8th century, silver coins known as sceattas were minted in Ribe. Although these coins appear to have been used only in towns, the evolution of a monetary economy was essential in the development of early medieval states: it facilitated trade, removing the reliance on barter and reciprocity, and it allowed taxes to be paid in coin. By the mid-9th century Ribe was surrounded by a town ditch. However, as this ditch was only 2 m (6 ft) wide and 1 m (3 ft) deep it cannot have had a defensive function and appears, instead, to have denoted a mercantile zone, possibly under royal protection and tax jurisdiction.[5]

Hedeby, in what is now northern Germany, developed as a major town thanks to its commanding position at the foot of the Jutland peninsula at one end of the Danevirke, which enabled it to control east-west trade. The earliest activity dates to the 8th century, when the first jetties were built and a number of workshops came into use. During the 9th century streets were laid out at right angles, parallel to a stream, defining fenced building plots of regular size. The town was enclosed by a semi-circular rampart and defended by a small fort, while the harbour was protected by a semi-circular arrangement of piles. There were over 10,000 graves in Hedeby, of which c. 1,350 have been excavated; it has been estimated that the town had a population of *c.* 1,500, including both traders and craftworkers. Imported materials supported a range of industries: ironworking with Swedish ore; the dressing of lava querns; bronze jewellery production; antler-, bone-, leather- and woodworking; and the manufacture of glass and amber beads. From the early 9th century Hedeby also minted its own sceattas.

The earliest town in Sweden lay at Birka, situated on the island of Björkö in Lake Mälaren, near modern Stockholm. On the neighbouring island of Adelsö, separated from Björkö by a narrow strait, stand the remains of a royal estate centre. It is tempting to see this as the power base from which Birka was controlled and taxed, from a

The trading site at Hedeby, at the neck of the Jutland peninsula. The trees follow the line of the semicircular ramparts.

Selection of artefacts from the trading site at Kaupang,
in southern Norway.

distance. Birka was fortified, on land and water, from its foundation
in the mid-8th century. Like Hedeby, the first town was enclosed
by a semi-circular rampart, which at its northern end extended
out into the harbour in Lake Mälaren as a series of piles. Like Ribe,
Birka appears to have been permanently occupied from the start.

The first Norwegian town was at Kaupang (literally, 'marketplace'),
on the west side of the Oslo fjord. Excavations have revealed that
the laying-out of individual plots was preceded by a very short-lived
phase of itinerant craft production. Permanent buildings, for year-
round use, were then constructed on each of the plots, probably in
the early 9th century. Kaupang had wide-ranging trading connections. The traded goods include German wine in Rhenish pottery,
accompanied by glass drinking-vessels also from the Rhineland,
Danish or Slavonic honey and Norwegian whetstones. The inhabitants of Kaupang were also melting down precious metals and the
excavated finds include ingot moulds and pieces of gold and silver

jewellery that may have arrived as the result of raiding activity. There are at least eight cemeteries, including both inhumation and cremation burials, many under mounds, and over 60 high-status boat burials. It has been suggested that the cremation graves reflect the local burial rite, but that the boat burials may indicate Danish merchants. Tree-ring dating of the jetty proves that it was erected after 803. It is therefore argued that, like Hedeby, Kaupang may have been founded by Godfred in the early 9th century, as southern Norway was under the control of Danish kings at this time.

Towns at this time would have been quite small by modern standards, with perhaps 500–1,500 inhabitants. The majority of the Scandinavian population still lived in the countryside in farming settlements, although there were also aristocratic residences, such as Tissø on western Sjælland in Denmark. Here an exceptional settlement has been discovered on the shores of a lake, 7 km (c. 4 miles) from the coast and accessible from the sea via river.[6] Tissø was not an agricultural estate – there are few stalls for cattle and it must have been supplied with food by dependent farms in the area. Instead it was sustained by tribute, trade and manufacture. By the 9th century there was a substantial bow-sided timber hall set within an enclosure and a craft and market area with workshops and small booths in which goods may have been traded under the lord's protection. Here goldsmiths and silversmiths worked, and bronze was cast into costume brooches, while other craftsmen made combs, as well as glass and amber beads. Over 100 coins have been found at the Tissø settlement, including 8th-century Scandinavian and Frankish coins, although most are later Islamic issues; their distribution suggests that trading was taking place on-site. A mid-9th-century Byzantine lead seal bears the name of Theodosius, head of the Byzantine armoury and recruiting office in Constantinople (now Istanbul). It is known that Theodosius travelled overland to the Frankish court in Ingelheim on the River Rhine, where he was seeking assistance against Arab attacks on Byzantium.[7] The Tissø seal is identical to examples from Ribe and

Some of the weaponry deposited as offerings in the lake at Tissø, on western Sjælland in Denmark.

Hedeby, and it has been suggested that he may have been buying iron or recruiting mercenaries from Scandinavia. Viking trade routes extended throughout Scandinavia and western Europe, but also eastwards through the Russian river systems to the Black Sea, linking with the Silk Road.

Tissø may be an example of an aristocratic or even royal residence. Weapons and riding gear, including spurs, bridles and a large number of arrowheads and sword mounts are concentrated in the enclosure. Frankish and Carolingian drinking vessels were also found around the central halls. Miniature amulets, including Thor's hammers and tiny lances, recovered from this part of the site may indicate a small enclosed cultic area. Tissø means 'Týr's Island' and was named after the war god Týr. In the 19th century some 50 swords, axes and lances were found on the lake bottom. They date back to the start of the settlement, but continue into the 9th century and probably represent offerings to Týr. Tissø demonstrates that Viking Age lords had several functions: they were responsible for military protection of the local area; they controlled trade and crafts in the marketplace; and they were responsible for heathen cult ceremonies, including feasting in the great hall.

In trading or raiding Scandinavians were aided by a strong seafaring tradition and their skills in shipbuilding and ocean navigation. In the islands and steeply sided coastal fjords on the Norwegian coastline it was easier to travel by boat than by land. One contemporary written account of this way of life comes from a Norwegian merchant called Ottar (Ohthere in Old English) who visited the English King Alfred in the late 9th century; Alfred asked Ottar about his travels and had them recorded.[8] Ottar's homeland was in the far north of Norway, above the Arctic Circle, in *Halgoland*. His land was poor, however, and much of his income came from exploiting the reindeer. He also went whaling and walrus-hunting, and took tribute in kind (presumably walrus ivory and furs) from the neighbouring Lapps. Ottar had his own ship and travelled south to the markets of northern Europe. He told Alfred that no one lived north of him, except for a few places where the Lapps had their camps, but that there was a market town to the south called *Sciringes heal* in Old English (probably *Skiringssal* in Old Norse), which is thought to be Kaupang. He said that it took at least a month to get there under sail if he laid up at night and had a favourable wind every day, sailing at all times along the coast. From Kaupang he said he sailed five days to the trading town at Hedeby.[9]

The Vikings are renowned for their dragon-headed ships. In 1904 the grave of a Norwegian princess was discovered at Oseberg on the Oslofjord. She had been buried in *c.* 834 in an elaborately deco-rated plank-built ship constructed some fifteen years earlier. Such vessels combined the use of a sail, which allowed them to reach high speeds under favourable winds, with oars for manoeuvring or for when they were becalmed. They also had a shallow hull, which would allow them to sail far upriver, as well as a mast that could be taken down to pass under bridges. The Oseberg ship was a broad vessel, 21.5 m (70 ft) long by 5 m (16 ft) wide, with space for 30 oarsmen; it was probably only intended for use in coastal waters. Much larger ships have since been discovered, including the remains of one in the harbour of the trading site at Hedeby and another found in advance of an extension to the ship museum at Roskilde in Denmark. The 10th-century Hedeby 1 vessel had a crew of 60, while Roskilde 6, built after 1025, was 36 m (120 ft) long by 3.5 m wide. It had 78 rowing stations and probably held a crew of around 100; it is the largest Viking warship yet found. These are the types of ships that were depicted on the Bayeux Tapestry and that brought Scandinavian armies to England. The communication and teamwork needed to sail a Viking longship would also have made its crew an effective fighting unit on land.[10]

What, then, were the causes of the Viking Age and Scandinavian expansion overseas? Factors ranging from climate change to selective female infanticide and the quest for marriageable women have all been invoked. Nevertheless, Viking raids on England had their roots in growing networks of trade and in the quest for wealth – whether in the form of portable luxuries or land for settlement – underpinned by a militarized society in which an emerging elite had the capacity to raise an army and to transport it across the sea.[11] While most discussions of the causes of the Viking Age have sought to explain the documented raids on western European monasteries in the late 8th century, there is growing evidence that Scandinavians had been travelling east long before this in search of trading opportunities. For example, two Scandinavian boat burials dating to the early 8th century have been excavated recently at Salme in Estonia, while Scandinavian settlers can be identified from their burials and craftworking at Staraya Ladoga in Russia by the mid-8th century.[12] Wherever traces of Scandinavian settlement can be identified we also invariably find Islamic silver coins, or dirhams, suggesting that the lure of silver was a major factor in this expansion out of the Scandinavian homelands. To the east lay trading opportunities, but to the west were concentrations of wealth to be looted and, in that context, trading began to spill over into raiding.

England in the 9th century had much in common with Scandinavia and was part of the same northern European trading network. Yet its society and institutions were very different. Unlike Scandinavia, it had been part of the Roman Empire and while the legions were long departed, their traces remained in ruined cities and serviceable roads. Its rulers were in regular contact with continental Europe; one important source of that connection was the Church. England, unlike Scandinavia, was Christian, with many wealthy churches and monasteries, and literate clerics who left detailed written accounts that inform us about its political geography. By the mid-9th century England comprised four independent kingdoms – East Anglia, Wessex, Mercia and Northumbria – all of which were relatively new and faced internal challenges. Lindsey, formerly a separate kingdom, was now a contested region between Mercia and Northumbria. Mercia was the strongest military power, extending west to Offa's Dyke – the great earthwork constructed along its frontier with Wales – and south to the Thames. Northumbria was divided by internecine feuding between the rulers of the former sub-kingdoms of Bernicia in the north and Deira in the south. Beyond its northern borders were the Strathclyde Britons and other small kingdoms, which only appear very dimly in the historical record, as was also the case in Ireland. Under King Ecgberht (r. 802–39) Wessex was growing in power, absorbing first Devon and then Cornwall in the south-west, and subsequently the kingdoms of the East Saxons, South Saxons and Kent. Ecgberht conquered Mercia in 829 and was recognized as *bretwalda*, literally 'wide ruler', or 'ruler of Britain', although this was short-lived.

Some 500,000 to 1 million people lived in England in the 9th century. The population structure was probably comparable to that of a developing country in the modern world. In other words,

The Anglo-Saxon kingdoms and their neighbours, *c.* 800.

life expectancy was worse than it is in England today, but better than it was during the 19th-century Industrial Revolution. Twelve seems to have been widely recognized as the age of maturity; the laws of Æthelstan (r. 924–39) decreed that any man over twelve years old could be killed if found guilty of theft. Poor hygiene and nutrition were probably the most common causes of death. Childbearing females were most at risk; in the Anglo-Saxon community at Raunds in Northamptonshire men were much more likely than women to reach their late thirties, and there were also high levels of child mortality. Anglo-Saxon society was rigidly hierarchical; a small aristocracy lived off the labour of a great many peasants. At the top was the king and his *ealdormen*, with control over specific regions of the kingdom, often called *scirs*, rather smaller territories than the modern shires. They came together periodically in an assembly called the *witan* to issue laws and grant land. Then there were the *thegns*, or landholders, who were the local lords. Next there were various grades of agricultural workers, including free peasant farmers (*ceorls*), and finally a substantial slave class, possibly up to a quarter of the population.[13]

As in Scandinavia, most of the population in Anglo-Saxon England lived in the countryside, where the mixed-farming economy would have been familiar to Viking travellers. Most people lived and worked in wooden buildings; stone was reserved for churches. Much of the land was organized in large estates, owned directly by the king or the Church, but broken down into smaller administrative and territorial units, sometimes known as *vills*. The nucleated villages that became familiar features of the medieval landscape did not emerge until at least the 10th century. Instead, the normal settlement pattern on the eve of the Viking raids was of clusters of farms, probably with outfields surrounding stock enclosures, and intensively cultivated fields immediately around the homesteads. Indeed, this pattern survives over much of Denmark to this day.[14]

Churches and monasteries were important features of the landscape. Monastic sites were particularly vulnerable to attack.

Anglo-Saxon monasteries were frequently major landowners and by the 8th century many had also amassed considerable portable wealth of their own, as well as often being entrusted with royal treasures. The origins of monastic life among reclusive hermits meant that many early monasteries were sited on isolated coastal sites, with no effective defence against attack from the sea. In Northumbria the exposed coastal sites at Tynemouth, Hartlepool, Whitby, Monkwearmouth, Jarrow and Lindisfarne were all to fall prey to Viking raids. Inland, a network of minster churches covered the country by the mid-9th century. These included major buildings in former Roman towns, such as King Edwin's minster in York, and smaller churches attached to rural aristocratic sites. Minster churches frequently originated as monastic communities; the Old English *mynster* is derived from the Latin *monasterium*. By the 9th century their function may have evolved into that of a church serving a congregation, with a community of clergy responsible for the pastoral care of a large area. Priests may have been sent out to preach to local communities and the laity would come for baptism and burial. Minster churches may also have been founded by the aristocracy in the middle of their estates. There are several sites which, from the range of finds (including styli indicating literacy), appear to have had some ecclesiastical function, but which are otherwise indistinguishable from aristocratic settlements.[15] However, few communities would have had their own church as there was as yet no parochial system, and on the eve of the 9th-century Viking raids going to church would have been an infrequent activity for most people.

At the end of the Roman Empire, urban life had largely collapsed in Britain by the 5th century, but in the lowland zone of southern and eastern England it started to re-emerge from the 7th and 8th centuries. As in northern Europe and southern Scandinavia, international trading sites were being established, apparently under royal patronage, and described as *wics* in Old English. In Wessex, the key site was *Hamwic*, the predecessor of the modern

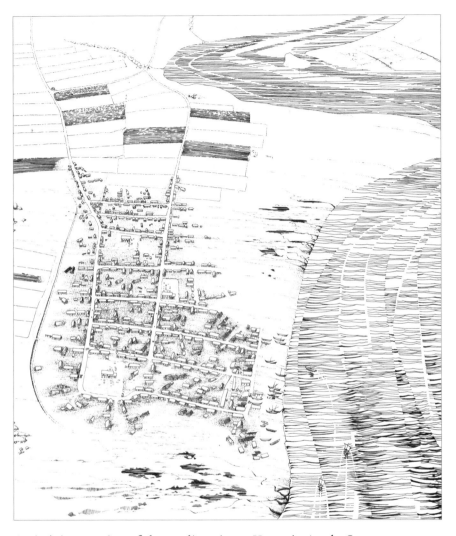

Artist's impression of the trading site at *Hamwic*, Anglo-Saxon Southampton.

port of Southampton. Here there is evidence for a 45 ha (110 acre) trading site during the period *c*. 700–850, sheltering a population of 2,000–3,000 people, enclosed by a bank and ditch (probably to define the trading zone as much as for defence), with properties laid out on a regular street system. A number of sites have been excavated within the Saxon town. At the Six Dials some 68 houses and workshops, 21 wells and 500 pits have been recorded.[16] A major north–south road was constructed first, followed by the digging of the boundary ditch 3 m (10 ft) wide and 1.5 m (5 ft) deep, before the houses and properties were laid out. *Hamwic* had trading contacts with northern France and the Rhineland; many of its inhabitants made their living from processing imports and exports, and by manufacturing goods from imported raw materials.[17] From the 8th century silver sceattas were being minted there.

In East Anglia, settlement at *Gippeswic* (Ipswich) began along the waterfront in the early 7th century. A cemetery was established on heathland to the north in what became the Buttermarket, but this was incorporated into the expanding settlement from the early 8th century, just a generation or two after it had been closed for burials.[18] Rubbish pits cut through some of the graves, and a metalled road ran across the site, with buildings on the street frontage. The grave goods suggest a society with wide-ranging connections; one man who was buried in a coffin with weapons and imported glass cups appears to have come from the Continent and could have been directly involved in the control of overseas trade. Imports of Frankish pottery demonstrate the wide trading links.[19] Around 720, and to the north-east of the settlement, Ipswich started to develop its own unique pottery industry, supplying a large hinterland. The *wic* expanded rapidly in the early 9th century to cover an area of about 50 ha (125 acres) on both sides of the River Gipping.

London (Roman *Londinium*) had been founded in the 1st century AD, but had fallen into disrepair after the collapse of the Roman Empire. The southern Mercian port of *Lundenwic*, first mentioned in a royal charter of 672–74, was located in London's West End, where excavations in 1996 at the site of the Royal Opera House have revealed that as *Lundenwic* expanded beyond the waterfront market on the Strand it was built over a mid-7th-century cemetery associated with a small settlement close to the foreshore. In the late 7th or early 8th century a 3 m- (10 ft-) wide metalled road was laid out, with narrow drains on either side. It was well maintained and so frequently resurfaced that by the mid-9th century, at the end of its use, the successive layers of gravel were nearly a metre thick. The first buildings were erected alongside this street and as further buildings were added the arrangement of building plots became more formalized and firmly established, as did a network of roads and alleys. By the early 8th century *Lundenwic* had probably grown to its full extent, covering an area of up to 60 ha (150 acres) between what is now Trafalgar Square and Aldwych.[20]

By the mid to late 8th century the area was densely occupied as new buildings were constructed in previously open areas, sometimes over backfilled rubbish pits. In total the remains of 63 rectangular timber buildings were identified. The average building was nearly 12 m (40 ft) long and just over 5.5 m (18 ft) wide, much the same as medieval peasant houses, and roughly comparable to the ground floor area of an average Victorian terraced house. Doorways were generally placed in the long sides of the buildings, and a few had porches. In many cases the vertical wall posts were set directly in the ground, although some rested upon horizontal sill-beams. Between the posts there were wattle panels, covered with daub made from the local brickearth, sometimes mixed with chaff or straw; occasionally the daub walls were whitewashed. The earthen floors were sometimes reinforced with gravel around the thresholds. Enclosed clay ovens or open hearths were probably used for cooking and heating, but deposits of slag indicate that some may have been used for smithing. Changes in floor surface sometimes indicate individual rooms separated by internal partitions, with wall benches in the living areas.

Evidence for trade, industries, crafts and daily life is provided by household rubbish in pits and surface middens. Long-distance trade with the Continent is demonstrated by pottery imported from northern France and Flanders, and Badorf ware from the Rhineland. Trading connections are also indicated by fragments of lava querns and glass vessels. The archaeological evidence reflects

Bede's description of the settlement as a 'mart of many nations coming to it by land and sea'.[21] In addition to metalworking there is evidence for other crafts and industries. Weaving is indicated by large numbers of loom weights; a complete row of weights was discovered where they had fallen from a loom or a shelf in a burnt-out building. A large quantity of horn cores and antler waste from the manufacture of such items as combs, spindle whorls, pins and needles shows that boneworking was also important.[22]

We can gain an idea of ancient diets from archaeological finds of plant remains and animal bones. Evidence for plants had been preserved by charring, and included the seeds of pea, sloe and apple or pear, hazlenut shells, and cereal grains for bread and soup. The animal bones show there was butchery on the site, and it is likely that livestock may have been brought on the hoof for slaughter. The diet of the inhabitants of *Lundenwic* seems to have been rather limited; beef was the main meat, but pork and mutton were also quite common. The lack of variety seen in the animal-bone assemblages from *Lundenwic* and other *wics* has led to the suggestion that these settlements were supplied with foodstuffs levied by kings through 'food-rents'. In the countryside the diet would have been varied by hunting of wild game although this was a rarity in towns. Nonetheless, as might be expected at a riverside settlement, the inhabitants supplemented their diet with fish from the sea and the river. Some of the freshwater fish and eels consumed in *Lundenwic* would probably have been caught in traps such as those found on the Thames foreshore at Chelsea and Barn Elms. Shellfish, particularly oyster, were also popular, and nearly 2,000 shells were recovered from one midden.

From the early 9th century, however, the *Lundenwic* settlement was in decline. Fewer buildings were erected and there was generally less activity, possibly indicating, as in other *wics*, a gradual reduction in trade due to the disruption being caused by Viking raids.

The *wics* never really developed major urban industries, with the exception of the Ipswich pottery industry, which flourished between the 7th and 9th centuries. In Northumbria, the trading site of *Eoforwic* was the predecessor of Viking *Jorvik*, modern York (see Chapter 8), but it may have been established after 700 and seems to have been much smaller than the other *wics*. Finally, given its role later in our story, it is worth mentioning the possible *wic* at Lincoln, in Lindsey. The upper city around the medieval cathedral was already an ecclesiastical enclave, but the lower city has produced evidence for 8th- to 9th-century settlement, particularly in and immediately outside its south-east quarter. Facing this across the River Witham was the settlement of Wigford ('ford by/to the *wic*').[23]

The Anglo-Saxon *wics* appear very similar to their Scandinavian counterparts, with suggestions of town planning, and royal foundation with continued royal oversight. However, during the 9th century they were all abandoned, some going into decline even from the start of the century. Given that this period saw increasing Viking raids on the Continent and, as we shall see in the next chapter, the first raids on England, it is hard to escape the conclusion that the vulnerability of the *wics* to attack by Viking raiders was the cause of their decline.

2

The Raids Begin

In the reign of Beorthric, king of Wessex (r. 786–802), three ships of 'Northmen' (*Norðmanna*) landed at Portland on the Dorset coast. The king's local agent was a man called Beaduheard, who was probably based at Dorchester. Beaduheard was the 'shire-reeve', the predecessor of the medieval 'sheriff', and his duties included tax collection, controlling the ports and escorting visitors, as required by the laws of Wessex. Seaborne traders were not an unusual sight off the southern English coast: Frisian merchants from the emporia of northern Europe were regular visitors to *Hamwic* (Southampton). On this occasion, however, Beaduheard, perhaps summoned to the shore by clifftop beacons lit by the locals, discovered that these new arrivals spoke a different tongue. It transpired they were from Hordaland, the region surrounding Bergen in western Norway. They also appeared not to know the rules: traders were meant to use the king's ports so he could control their commerce and take his rightful share. Beaduheard admonished the Norwegians and attempted to force them to go with him to the king's residence, 'against their will'.[1] They turned on him, slaughtering him and all his men. The *Anglo-Saxon Chronicle*, with the benefit of hindsight, reports that 'Those were the first ships of Danish men which came to the land of the English.'[2]

Over the next hundred years the Viking onslaught on western Europe evolved from periodic attacks on vulnerable coastal sites, mainly monasteries, to sustained raiding. Viking raiders sailed up the major European river systems and took full advantage of the shallow draught of their longships to penetrate deep into hostile territory, appearing where they were least expected. They established camps, where their forces overwintered, and the warriors became increasingly embedded in the societies in which they were spending years at a time. In this chapter we trace the trajectory of Viking activities *c.* 800–900, looking at the evidence for the forerunners of the Great Army in Ireland, Frisia, and what is now northern France, but which from 800 to 888 was part of the Carolingian Empire of the Frankish ruler Charlemagne and his descendants. A consistent pattern emerges across these regions, revealing the extent to which Viking activity was interconnected. We will see how royal courts and monastic communities were well-informed about the raiders, how rapidly news spread of the murder and mayhem they inflicted, and how chroniclers sought to make sense of, and even to justify, the raids and the responses of their fellow Christians. Viking armies did not, however, present a unified force; they came together and went their separate ways as it suited them, and rivalries frequently emerged between their leaders. These Viking internal divisions were sometimes exploited by local rulers in the areas attacked, to help in their own disputes. While not downplaying the threat that the Viking armies posed, this chapter also explores how they accommodated themselves to the communities they encountered, engaging in trade and political negotiations, and beginning to settle permanently.

We will never know whether the men of Hordaland who landed in Dorset had originally planned to trade and simply lost their cool when challenged by the local taxman, or whether they were in search of silver and slaves and were reconnoitring the area for easy pickings. The closing decades of the 8th century certainly witnessed multiple coastal raids, mainly on islands containing monastic communities, including Iona in the Hebrides, *Rechru* or

Rathlin Island off the Antrim coast in Ireland, St Patrick's Isle near Dublin, and Noirmoutier in the mouth of the River Loire in France. The most infamous raid occurred in 793 off the north-east coast of England, as reported in the *Anglo-Saxon Chronicle*:

> In this year dire portents appeared over Northumbria and sorely frightened the people. They consisted of immense whirlwinds and flashes of lightning, and fiery dragons were seen flying in the air. A great famine immediately followed those signs, and a little after that in the same year, on 8 June, the ravages of heathen men miserably destroyed God's church on Lindisfarne, with plunder and slaughter.[3]

A letter written shortly afterwards to the king of Northumbria, Æthelred, corroborates this graphic account of the raid and provides further gory details. Alcuin, a Northumbrian scholar at the court of the Frankish king Charlemagne, describes the church of St Cuthbert on Lindisfarne as being 'spattered with the blood of the priests of God, despoiled of its ornaments'. However, he also used the attack as an object lesson in the consequences of lax behaviour:

> Consider the dress, the way of wearing the hair, the luxurious habits of the princes and people. Look at your trimming of the beard and hair, in which you have wished to resemble the pagans. Are you not menaced by terror of them whose fashion you wished to follow?[4]

This letter reveals not only that news of the raid spread rapidly, but also that there had been previous contact with Scandinavians. However, something had changed; Alcuin wrote that 'never before has such terror appeared in Britain'.[5] Viking raiders had now become a significant threat to the peace and security of western Europe.

Terrifying and occasionally fatal as the raids undoubtedly were, religious communities managed to survive, although in some cases this simply left them open to further attack. St Columba's monastery on Iona survived the raid of 794 only to be burnt in 802; 86 members of its community were then killed in 806 and, most shockingly, its abbot, Blathmac, was killed in an attack of 825. An account of how he met his death was written in the monastery at Reichenau, on Lake Constance in southern Germany, a few years later:

> To this island [Iona] came Blathmac, wishing to endure Christ's scars, because there many a pagan horde of Danes is wont to land, armed with malignant greed .... See, the violent cursed host came rushing through the open buildings, threatening cruel perils to the blessed men; and after slaying with mad savagery the rest of the associates, they approached the holy father, to compel him to give up the precious metals wherein lie the holy bones of St Columba; but [the monks] had lifted the shrine from its pediments and had placed it in the earth .... This booty the Danes desired; but the saint remained with unarmed hand, and with unshaken purpose of mind ... 'I know nothing at all of the gold you seek ....' Therefore the pious sacrifice was torn limb from limb .... Thus [Blathmac] became a martyr for Christ's name.[6]

Perhaps St Blathmac, as his continental hagiographer insisted, had indeed sought out a place vulnerable to Viking attack in order to achieve martyrdom, where he went 'but armed with the shield of faith and the helmet of salvation'; more likely, he was just unlucky. Nonetheless, the account gives us other useful information about the impact of a Viking raid. Firstly, it appears that in a futile attempt to protect the church silver, including Columba's reliquary, the monks had buried it underground. Secondly, this is another example of how widely, and how quickly, tales of Viking atrocities travelled across early medieval Europe. Even remote monasteries that had never seen a Viking were hearing about their violence and willingness to kill men who had given their lives to religious devotion.

The early 9th century saw Viking raiding intensify, especially in Ireland. The *Annals of Ulster*, which survive in a 15th-century manuscript but were based on much earlier accounts, now lost, report the slaughter of local communities of the Conmaicne in 812 and the Umaill in 813. According to legend the Conmaicne were descended from a mythical ancestor known as Conmac, and settled in Connacht, while the Umaill held territory in what is now Co. Mayo. There was also an attack on Howth (Co. Dublin) in 821, in which large numbers of women were taken captive. The monastery at Bangor (Co. Down) was raided in both 823 and the following year when the shrine of St Comgall was smashed and bishops and scholars were killed, and in the same year the abbot of the remote island monastery on Skellig Michael (Co. Kerry) was kidnapped and subsequently died of hunger and thirst.[7] We get an impression of a spate of 'hit-and-run' raids on religious communities, although their increasing frequency makes it likely that Viking armies were already based somewhere in the British Isles by the early 9th century.

The chroniclers have little to say about secular communities, but it is unlikely that they were unaffected; the taking of hostages and cattle implies that the raiders remained in the vicinity. This became ever more likely in the 830s and 840s when Viking forces began to raid further inland: in 836 they caused 'a most cruel devastation of all the lands of Connacht' in western Ireland, and 'carried off many prisoners and killed many and took many captives' in Brega (Co. Meath).[8] The holding of hostages became increasingly common, as detailed in the late 9th-century *Life of St Findan*. It describes how Findan, an Irish nobleman from Leinster in eastern Ireland, was captured while negotiating the ransom of his sister from Viking raiders. He was released, because 'the more sensible of them ... argued that men who had come to ransom others ought not themselves to be held by force'. But some years later, in the 840s, Findan was taken captive again by Vikings who arrived while he was attending a feast, helped, it is alleged, by his enemies. Findan

Ireland, showing approximate domains of Irish dynasties in the 9th century.

was sold on multiple times and the *Life* recounts that during his journey with one set of captors another group boarded the ship and enquired about Ireland and how his captors had fared there, providing one indication of how Viking forces shared intelligence about locations to target. This encounter also led to a bloody fight between these two Viking bands after it was discovered that a member of the group who came aboard had previously killed the brother of one of Findan's captors. Findan nonetheless made it alive to the Orkneys, where he escaped, and eventually travelled to the monastery of Reichenau, where his *Life* was written.[9]

We have far less information about Viking raids in Britain. While the impression emerges from the number of raids recorded in Irish sources that Ireland was the main focus in the early 9th century, it is clear that a similar intensification of raiding was taking place in Britain. The *Annals of Ulster* record that in 839 the 'pagans' defeated 'the men of *Fortriu*', which is the central part of the Pictish territory in eastern Scotland.[10] The account of St Findan's enslavement and transportation to Orkney also reveals Viking activity in the northern isles of Scotland in the mid-9th century. Meanwhile, the *Anglo-Saxon Chronicle* reports raids on the monastic island of Sheppey (off the north-east coast of Kent) in 838; on *Hamwic* and Portland in 841, when the local ealdorman was killed; and on Lindsey, East Anglia and Kent in 841. The Northumbrians were heavily defeated by Viking raiders in 844 and their king, Rædwulf, was killed. In 850, the *Chronicle* reports, 'for the first time, heathen men stayed through the winter on Thanet' off the coast of Kent.[11] This brief sentence sets the scene for the devastation that would be enacted upon England for the next half-century.

By 850, however, the overwintering of Viking armies was not a new strategy. In the 840s the Viking raiders were already becoming a year-round presence in Ireland. In 840 a group spent the winter on Lough Neagh, the largest lake in Ireland, while in the following year the *Annals of Ulster* record the establishment of Viking bases at Linn Duachaill (Annagassan in Co. Louth) and Dublin.[12] These bases were described as *longphuirt* (singular *longphort*), a word derived from two Latin loan-words, [*navis*]*longa*, meaning [war]ship, and *portus*, a harbour or haven. They were located close to accessible harbours but also near the borders between Irish kingdoms, suggesting that the local political geography was an influential factor.[13] Indeed, the year after the construction of the *longphort* at Linn Duachaill the local abbot 'was fatally wounded and burned by heathens and Irish', in just one of many recorded examples of Vikings finding allies among the Irish kingdoms.[14] The raiders had a skill for finding strategic targets, such as royal estates and churches housing the relics of prominent saints, and they often attacked on feast days and festivals, suggesting that they had good local intelligence and an understanding of the traditions of their victims.[15] By the 840s Ireland had been swamped by the raiders, as captured in the Frankish *Annals of St Bertin*. These *Annals* provide a chronicle for the period 830–82, and despite the name (which reflects only where the earliest known manuscript survives) they were written from the perspective of a secular court rather than a monastery. In the entry for 847 they record that 'The Irish, who had been attacked by the Northmen for a number of years, were made into regular tribute-payers. The Northmen also got control of the islands all around Ireland, and stayed there without encountering any resistance from anyone.'[16] This may have been an exaggeration, but it reveals the contemporary perception in another country that found itself on the receiving end of Viking raids in the 9th century.

Whether the *longphuirt* should be regarded as a specific type of settlement has been extensively debated, and there have been attempts, based on the form of early Scandinavian trading sites, to identify their locations on maps and aerial photographs by seeking out traces of semicircular enclosures (often described as D-shaped) facing onto watercourses.[17] Since these are undated they are at best inconclusive, and more recent excavation and

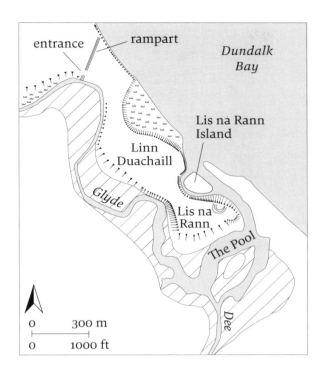

Plan of the *longphort* of Linn Duachaill, Annagassan, Co. Louth, showing the rivers and tidal flood plain (hatched).

survey work has begun to identify a wider suite of morphological and locational characteristics of *longphuirt*.[18] For example, in 2010 geophysical survey and excavation at Annagassan revealed the form of the Linn Duachaill *longphort*, where a peninsula over 1 km long between the River Glyde and the sea was defended by a rampart *c.* 245 m (800 ft) long. Evidence for industrial activity was identified in the form of burning and metalworking debris; other traces of the Viking camp included ship rivets (or clench nails), a fishing weight and an iron knife, as well as evidence for trade in the form of cut pieces of silver (known as hacksilver), a lead weight, and what has been interpreted as a balance arm for a weighing scale.[19] For a long time the *longphort* at Dublin was thought to have been located around 2 km (1.25 miles) west of the city centre, where excavation since the late 18th century had uncovered furnished graves containing weaponry. The 10th-century town was thought to have developed further east, on the west bank of the River Poddle

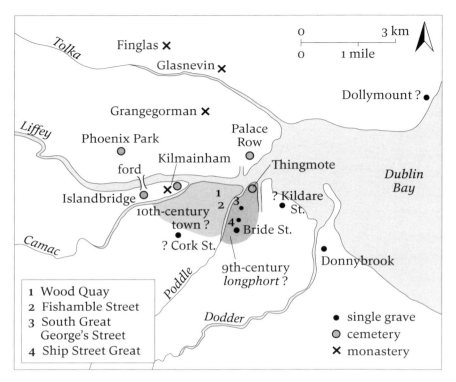

Dublin, showing known areas of Viking activity.

where excavations in the Wood Quay and Fishamble Street areas had identified numerous buildings and streets of that date. However, more recent excavations to the east of the Poddle have identified burials and occupation layers of the earlier 9th century in South Great George's Street and Ship Street Great, which may be the site of the *longphort*, and perhaps even pre-date its first recorded mention in 841.[20]

The most important insights into a *longphort* have, however, come from the excavations at Woodstown (Co. Waterford). This part of Ireland is poorly represented in surviving documentary sources, and Woodstown is not specifically recorded as a *longphort*, but it was clearly the base for a Viking army over many decades, perhaps from the mid-9th to the early 10th century. The site was discovered on the banks of the River Suir during the construction of the

N25 Waterford City bypass between 2003 and 2007. Geophysical survey revealed two adjacent D-shaped enclosures encompassing *c.* 2.91 ha (7.2 acres). Although ploughing had destroyed many archaeological features, traces of a rectangular building were uncovered, along with 47 crucible fragments (for the melting of metals). Fragments of furnace linings and bases were also found, as well as woodworking tools, sharpening stones, knives, dress accessories, and 41 lead weights. A single grave was found outside the eastern end of the enclosure, where sometime during the second half of the 9th century a Viking warrior had been buried with a sword, spear, shield and axe, as well as a sharpening stone. His cloak had been held in place by a copper-alloy ringed pin, of a type that the raiders had adopted from Irish communities, and iron clench nails and copper-alloy mounts were found nearby. No human skeletal remains survived, although there were burnt animal bones at one end of the grave, which was covered by a stone cairn.

The Viking camp at Woodstown, Co. Waterford.

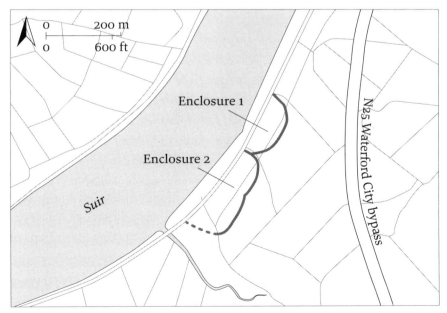

Further insights into the activities within the Woodstown camp came from the use of metal-detectors. Although amateur metal-detecting is illegal in the Republic of Ireland, it is permissible for archaeologists. Its value can be seen by comparing the number of finds recovered from excavated layers with those retrieved by metal-detecting. Excavation recovered *c.* 500 finds but another 4,019 items were recovered by metal-detecting of topsoil by the archaeologists, including 566 clench nails indicative of ship maintenance, 41 dress accessories and 15 weapons. There were also fragments of two dirhams, which must have travelled along the long-distance slave and silk trade routes and been brought to Ireland by a Viking trader or warrior. Twenty-three silver ingots and 174 lead weights also reflect bullion exchange.[21]

By the mid-9th century the Viking raiders sometimes met with powerful opposition. In 845, for example, a raiding group was routed in Donegal by a force led by the king of Tara, Niall Caille, while in 847 a force led by the king of Osraige reputedly killed 1,200 Vikings. Several major Irish victories are recorded the following year, with the slaying of 700 Vikings near Skreen (Co. Meath) by the new king of Tara, Mael Sechnaill.[22] Far away in northern France, this change of fortunes came to the attention of the authors of the *Annals of St Bertin* who recorded that 'the Irish attacked the Northmen, won a victory with the aid of our Lord Jesus Christ, and drove them out of their land', although this claim was something of an exaggeration and raids continued for the remainder of the century.[23] Throughout written accounts of these 9th-century raids, it is apparent that the Viking raiders were not operating as a unified force. For example, the *Annals of Ulster* record that the newly arrived *Dub-Gaill* ('dark foreigners') attacked the *longphuirt* at Dublin and Linn Duachaill in 851, while a group the *Annals* call *Gallgoídil* ('foreign Gaels') supported Mael Sechnaill against Viking raiders in 856. The *Gallgoídil* were of mixed Gaelic and Scandinavian ancestry.[24] Alliances between

Viking raiders and local rulers were not uncommon and, though often short-lived, were probably sometimes sealed by marriage: two Irish kings in the early 850s had the Norse name Bróðir, perhaps because their mothers were of Scandinavian stock.[25]

While it is difficult to discern the motivations of Viking armies, it appears that during the 850s and 860s there was a concerted effort to join forces and to carry out the political conquest of parts of Britain and Ireland. In 853 the *Annals of Ulster* record the arrival in Ireland of Olaf (Irish: Amlaíb), 'son of the king of Lochlann' (thought to refer to a Scandinavian colony in the western isles of Scotland) and that 'the foreigners of Ireland submitted to him, and he took a tribute from the Irish'.[26] In 859 Olaf and another Viking leader called Ivar (Irish: Imar) joined forces with the Irish king of Osraige, Cerball mac Dúngaile, and they raided the southern territory of the Uí Néill. This has all the hallmarks of deriving from internecine disputes among Irish kings, because Cerball was subject to the over-lordship of the increasingly powerful Mael Sechlainn, who subsequently gave Cerball greater autonomy and the two allied against Ivar and Olaf thereafter.

In 863, after plundering ancient tumuli at Knowth, Dowth and Brug na Bóinne (the Bend in the Boyne), Olaf, Ivar and a third Viking leader called Auisle were joined by the king of Meath in an attack on the lands of Flann.[27] The Vikings were clearly now a permanent fixture in Ireland, and useful allies for the rival Irish kings, although allegiances changed rapidly. As we will see in Chapter 3, the ambitions of these three Viking leaders, claimed by later sources to have been brothers, were not limited to Ireland. In 866 Olaf and Auisle led an army into *Fortriu* and 'plundered the entire Pictish country', while four years later Olaf and Ivar spent four months besieging Dumbarton Rock, the stronghold of the Strathclyde Britons, and Ivar also spent some time raiding with the Great Army in England. Viking armies and their leaders operated across multiple political regions and it would be a mistake to view their activities in England in isolation. The chroniclers inevitably lose sight of particular raiders once they depart, but by piecing together historical and archaeological evidence we can trace the wider impact of the raiders.

From the early 9th century there were also major Viking raids on continental Europe. While archaeological evidence is sparse, written sources allow us to trace a pattern of activity similar to that in Ireland. The *Frankish Royal Annals*, which provide an account of the Carolingian realm between 741 and 829, record an attack on Frisia in 810 by 200 ships of 'the Northmen called Danes', prompting the Franks to build more ships to protect themselves. A few raids were recorded in 820, when a village in Aquitaine was plundered, but attacks intensified in the 830s, with annual raids on the emporium at Dorestad (Netherlands) from 834 to 836. Frankish sources generally refer to the raiders as 'Northmen' (*Nortmanni*) and it has been suggested that this derived from a prophecy in the Old Testament Book of Jeremiah that the punishment for the Chosen People would one day come from the north.[28] Indeed, in many of the contemporary sources the Vikings are depicted as a manifestation of the wrath of God.[29] However, Frankish interactions with Danes were not limited to raids, and we can see some early attempts at diplomacy between them. In 815, the Emperor Louis the Pious (r. 814–40), the son of Charlemagne, welcomed to his court a Danish exile called Harald Klak, who had been ousted as king by a rival. Harald raided Saxony on behalf of Louis and then returned to Denmark, but was driven out again ten years later and for a second time sought the help of Louis. This time Harald and his wife came to Mainz (Germany) and in 826 along with 'a great number of Danes' – as many as 400 according to one source – they were baptized as Christians, and Harald was then granted land in Frisia.[30] Scandinavian leaders were useful in controlling territory on behalf of a Frankish ruler, and in protecting it from other Viking raiders. This is also the first example of baptism being used as a

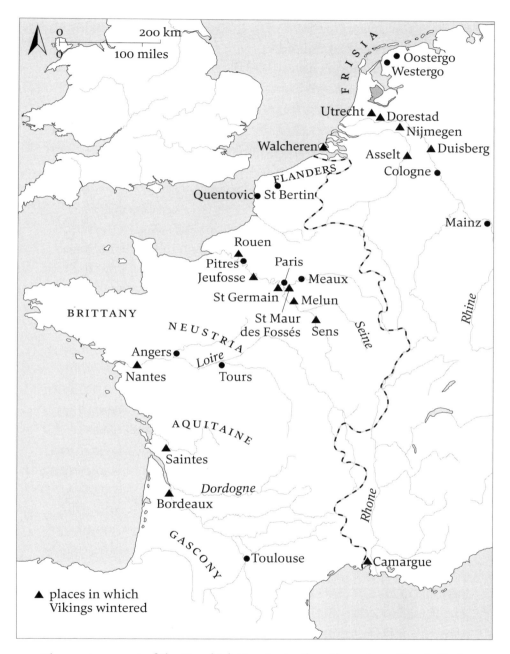

The western part of the Frankish Empire in the 9th century. The dotted line indicates the boundary between the kingdoms of Charles the Bald and Lothar agreed in AD 843.

political tool in interactions with the Danes, a tactic that would later be employed in England.

In the 820s the monk Anskar, the future archbishop of Hamburg-Bremen, joined the newly converted Harald Klak on his return to Denmark with the intention of introducing Christianity to the region. The *Life of St Anskar*, written in the late 9th century by Anskar's successor Archbishop Rimbert, reports on the achievements of Anskar and his fellow missionaries, who were probably based in Hedeby:

> many were converted to the faith by their example and teaching, and the number of those who should be saved in the Lord increased daily. They themselves, being inspired by divine love, in order to spread their holy religion, made diligent search for boys whom they might endeavour to educate for the service of God. Harald also gave some of his own household to be educated by them; and so it came about that in a short time they established a school for twelve or more boys.[31]

Whatever successes Anskar had in converting the Danes did not last, however, and he left Denmark following Harald's latest expulsion in 827. Nonetheless, this tale reveals the complexities in the interactions of western European rulers with Scandinavia during the early 9th century, and their attempts to find a means of dealing with the pagans.

The continental chronicles provide some of the most detailed accounts of Viking activity in the mid-9th century and include useful insights into the tactics of the raiders, their involvement in local politics and trade, and the alliances they made. They also describe some of the places where Vikings set up their camps when raiding along the river systems of northern France and the Low Countries, as well as what happened to them while they were encamped. This is important information to bear in mind as we look at the less well-documented camps of the Great Army in England later in this book. It is highly likely that many members of the Great Army that raided England from 865 had come from the Continent and the remainder of this chapter introduces us to the sorts of experiences that they may have had there.

When Louis the Pious died in 840, the kingdom of the Franks was divided between three of his sons – Louis the German, Lothar and Charles the Bald – who were each on the receiving end of numerous Viking attacks. They came up with two main strategies to deal with the raiders: allying with them by giving them land within their kingdoms; or paying them to go away.

Viking raids on Frisia had been frequent in the 830s, and the measure of granting land there to Harald Klak had clearly not been sufficient to protect this part of the Frankish territory. In 841, therefore, Lothar, 'to secure the services of Harald' who had been 'imposing many sufferings on Frisia and the other coastal regions of the Christians', decided to grant him the island of Walcheren, now in the Netherlands, at the mouth of the River Scheldt.[32] There are signs that this was not Lothar's first dealings with Harald, with the *Annals of St Bertin* criticizing the move as 'an utterly detestable crime'. The earlier raids are said to have been against the interests of Lothar's father and to 'the furtherance of his own', so this appears to be an early example of a Frankish king using Viking raids for his own political ends.[33] But within a decade Lothar found himself having to deal with the latest fallout from rivalries for the Danish throne, as Harald's nephew Roric raised an army and began to raid Frisia. Lothar concluded that he could not defeat Roric and so instead 'received him into his allegiance and granted him Dorestad and other counties'. By installing Roric in Dorestad, Lothar was seeking to protect these territories, over which he maintained some authority as coins continued to be minted there in his name.[34]

A turn of events in 845 saw Lothar's brother Charles the Bald adopt a different method of dealing with Viking raiders, as the *Annals of St Bertin* record:

In March, 120 ships of the Northmen sailed up the Seine to Paris, laying waste everything on either side and meeting not the least bit of opposition. Charles made efforts to offer some resistance, but realized that his men could not possibly win. So he made a deal with them: by handing over to them 7,000 pounds [of silver] as a bribe, he restrained them from advancing further and persuaded them to go away.[35]

The Franks were to use this tactic on many occasions as the 9th century progressed. For their part, the Vikings were beginning to realize that they could exploit conflicts between Frankish rulers. Their raid on Toulouse in 844, for example, followed an incident when Charles the Bald had besieged the city, in a move that had grown out of disputes about control over this region.[36] Clearly the Viking leaders were knowledgeable about the places they raided, and they could also apparently rely on local informants. It was a pattern to be repeated two decades later, in England.

The continental chronicles also reveal something of the death and destruction caused by the Viking raids in France. On the whole, they provide only brief details, and while we should be wary of some of the gorier embellishments, they clearly reflect the stories about Viking atrocities that were circulating at the time. For example, we have several broadly contemporary accounts of the activities of Viking raiders on the Seine in 845. The raiders were described by Hildegarius, the bishop of Meaux as:

harsh and cruel, as greedy and insatiable as the Fates and Furies, and from the river mouth onwards they devoured with their impatient swords all the beauty of that paradisiacal region which is watered throughout by the River Seine, and gave up everything to a devouring flame.[37]

Such lurid, apocalyptic accounts of Viking attacks were undoubtedly exaggerated, particularly when their authors used the events for moralizing purposes. In the *Translatio of St Germain*, written about five years after the event, the Viking raiders who attacked Paris in 845 were alleged to have executed 111 prisoners by hanging them in full view of the local Christians. In this account such atrocities were seen as acts of divine retribution and blamed on the Franks, particularly those who ran away, and on their failure to resist the Vikings. The Vikings next attacked the church of St Germain-des-Prés on the outskirts of Paris, but fortunately for the Franks they were immediately struck down by dysentery. The intervention of St Germain was claimed to be the decisive factor in this, and also in the Vikings agreeing to leave the kingdom of Charles the Bald; the large payment the king made them to go away is not mentioned here![38]

The late 9th-century Latin poem *Bella Parisiacae Urbis*, written by Abbo, a monk of St Germain-des-Prés, describes a Viking attack on Paris in 885 in dramatic terms. As the raiders overran the nearby countryside:

> Then, the cruel ones, both on horseback and on foot overran
> The hills, the fields, forests, open pastures, and the villages.
> All infants, boys and girls, youths, and even those hoary
>   with age,
> The father and the sons and even mothers – they killed
>   them all.
> They slaughtered the husband before the very eyes of
>   his wife;
> The children perished right before the eyes of their parents.

The Franks were not entirely helpless against the Viking raiders, nor purely reliant on saintly intervention or paying them off. Control over rivers and bridges was crucial to the Franks' defence. Three examples from consecutive decades demonstrate their tactics. In 852, Viking raiders on the Seine were stopped by the combined forces of Lothar and Charles the Bald by blockading them from either bank of the Seine. While this move succeeded, what happened next reveals how difficult dealing with Vikings could be. It was Christmas, and Charles's men did not want to fight, so he had no choice but to make peace with the leader of the raiders, Godefrid. This did not, however, prevent some of Godefrid's followers from continuing to raid in the vicinity. A detail from the mid-9th-century *Annals of St Wandrille*, compiled at a monastery of that name in Normandy, is of particular interest here, as it reports that in their negotiations with Charles the Vikings acquired permission to stay on an island in the Seine opposite Jeufosse.[39]

A decade later, more detailed entries in the *Annals of St Bertin* reveal how Charles the Bald responded to the arrival of a Viking force led by a certain Weland.[40] They describe several of the tactics hitherto employed by Frankish kings being used in combination, including building bridges, paying tribute to the raiders, forming alliances with them, and converting the Vikings to Christianity. The *Annals* also highlight the rivalries between Viking forces. In 861 Weland and his followers returned from raiding in England and, after burning Thérouanne on the River Scheldt, they sailed up the Seine and besieged another group of Vikings based on the island of Oissel. Charles supported Weland by raising a levy of 5,000 pounds of silver and a large amount of livestock and corn, to prevent his lands from being looted. Another group of raiders arrived to join forces with Weland and those on the island were eventually 'forced by starvation, filth and general misery to pay the besiegers 6,000 pounds made up of gold and silver and to make an alliance with them'. After this, the *Annals* report that the raiders split up 'according to their brotherhoods' and went their separate ways.[41]

This was not, however, to be the last that Charles saw of Weland. In the following year Charles arrived in Senlis, *c.* 45 km (28 miles) north-east of Paris, where he had been expecting his forces to assemble on either side of three main rivers to stop the raiders, only to find that a group was already on its way to Meaux. Charles and his forces were unable to catch up with them 'because the bridges had been destroyed and the ships [ferries] taken over by the Northmen', and so he 'rebuilt the bridge across to the island by Trilbardou, thereby cutting the Northmen's access to the way down the river'; the island was probably Isles-lès-Villenoy in the River Marne. Charles also 'assigned squadrons to guard both banks of the Marne' and at this point the raiders must have realized the difficulty of their situation as they provided hostages and returned their Frankish captives. Weland himself then came to Charles and swore his loyalty and converted to Christianity along with his wife and sons.

Meanwhile Charles issued a law that forbade the sale of armour, weapons and horses to the Vikings; this was another indication that they had been assisted by the locals.[42] He also ordered his leading men and 'many workmen and carts' to assemble at Pîtres, where the rivers Eure and Andelle flow into the Seine, and constructed fortifications, by which 'he closed it off to ships sailing up or down the river. This was done because of the Northmen.' Repair of bridges, and then taking control of both banks of major rivers, became an oft-repeated tactic, such as in 865 when Charles ordered that the bridges over the Oise at Auvers and the Marne at Charenton should be repaired. A royal command issued by Charles in 877 ordered the repair of fortified bridges on both the Seine and the Loire, which had seen a great deal of Viking activity in the 860s and early 870s. It has been argued that a bridge was built at Les Ponts-de-Cé near Angers, where a Viking force had been based for some time before being besieged by Charles in 873 and capitulating to him. There has been much speculation about the form that Charles's bridgework took, given a lack of archaeological evidence, but it seems that some sort of blockade was placed across the rivers and perhaps also that the bridgeheads were fortified, perhaps with banks and ditches.[43]

It is also striking that the Frankish sources contain repeated references to the Vikings basing themselves on islands in rivers. For example, the *Annals of St Bertin* record Viking raiders on islands at Oissel in the Seine in 858 and 861, the Camargue on the Rhône in 859, at Betuwe (Batavia) on the Rhine in the Netherlands in 859–60, near the monastery of St Denis on L'Île-Saint-Denis on the Seine near Paris in 866, and on an unnamed island in the Loire in 871.[44] The use of islands for their winter camps is another strategy that was also adopted by the Viking armies in England, as we will see in Chapter 4. Occasionally we hear of what they did on these islands. After raiding in western Aquitaine in 843 a Viking force 'landed on a certain island, brought their households over from the mainland and decided to winter there in something like a permanent settlement'.[45] A late 9th-century account by Abbot Adrevaldus of Fleury Abbey of a Viking army on an island in the Loire records that they 'held crowds of prisoners in chains and … rested themselves after their toil so that they might be ready for warfare. From that place they undertook unexpected raids, sometimes in ships, sometimes on horseback, and they destroyed all the province.'[46] The 9th-century *Annals of Xanten*, composed initially at Lorsch and then in Cologne in Germany, record a raid up the Rhine in 863, when the church of St Victor at Xanten was burnt down and the Vikings stayed on an island in the river where they 'built a defence and lived there for a while'.[47] After Charles the Bald had besieged the Vikings based at Angers in 873 he struck a deal with them that demonstrates that islands were not just useful for their defensive capabilities:

They requested to be allowed to stay until February on an island in the Loire, and to hold a market there; and, in February, they agreed, those of them who had by then been baptized and wished thenceforth to hold truly to the Christian religion would come and submit to Charles, those still pagan but willing to become Christian would be baptized under conditions to be arranged by Charles, but the rest would depart from his realm, never more, as stated above, to return to it with evil intent.[48]

The fact that the Vikings sought permission to hold a market in their island winter camp reinforces how easily their raiding could turn to trading, and how the establishment of a trading zone was done with local royal assent. It also provides a written context for recent archaeological discoveries in England, as we shall see in Chapter 4.

Living on an island could also have its disadvantages, however, and crowded, watery and squalid camps without proper sanitation might also have been a source of serious epidemics. The *Annals of St Bertin* record that in 865 'Northmen had got into the monastery of St Denis, where they stayed for about twenty days, carrying off booty from the monastery to their ships each day.'[49] St Denis was the most important monastery in France; it was where the Merovingian kings were buried and would have accumulated great wealth. If the annalist is to be believed, however, divine retribution followed and the Vikings did not get away with this huge treasure as those 'who had sacked St Denis became ill with various ailments. Some went mad, some were covered in sores, some discharged their guts with a watery flow through their arses: and so they died.'[50]

In contrast to the detailed account that we can assemble from the written sources, there is little archaeological evidence for the impact of Viking raids on the Continent, not least because metal-detecting was long illegal in the Netherlands and Belgium and still is in France. One of the most important discoveries comes from Frisia. As we have seen, Frisia was subject to multiple Viking raids in the early 9th century, and in 841 Louis the Pious had granted the island of Walcheren to Harald Klak, while Dorestad also seems to have been in Viking hands in the time of Louis. The town was certainly granted to Roric in 850 by Lothar, and Roric appears in various chronicles on multiple occasions in Frisia, serving successive Carolingian kings, eventually accepting baptism, and periodically trying to use his base in Frisia to seize power again in Denmark.[51]

Much of Frisia seems to have remained under Viking overlordship until 882 when Godfred, a relative of Roric, was killed.

Archaeological evidence for this Viking activity in Frisia emerged in 1996, when a metal-detectorist found a hoard of silver at Westerklief, in the Netherlands, on what was once the island of Wieringen [pl. 3]. Today the former island is an area of high ground surrounded by marsh, which in the 9th century occupied a strategic position on the shipping routes to Dorestad and other important trading towns. The hoard comprised six penannular arm-rings of Carolingian manufacture, one twisted arm-ring and one twisted neck-ring, both of Scandinavian type. Such silver arm-rings were distinctive symbols of Viking status and wealth. Later Icelandic poems speak of Viking lords as 'ring-givers' (*hringdrífr*), enthroned on their high seats in their great halls, dispensing gifts of silver rings to their loyal followers. As well as being highly visible signs of status they also provided a practical and secure means of transporting personal wealth, by wearing it. The hoard also included a Carolingian metal fitting (or strap-end) for a leather belt, 3 brooches featuring reused coins (of which two were dirhams), 17 ingots and 78 Carolingian pennies, contained within a pottery vessel that had been made in Badorf, near Cologne. Badorf was a well-known centre of wheel-made pottery production in the 8th and 9th centuries. Badorf ware is cream-coloured but in the 9th century red paint was added as decoration. It was traded widely outside Germany, and is also found in the Netherlands and England, where it may have been introduced as part of a taste for fine German wine. While the majority of the items in the Westerklief hoard are of Carolingian manufacture, the presence of the Scandinavian jewellery and the silver ingots reveals that the hoard had been in Viking hands. The dates of the coins suggest it was buried no earlier than 850. Grass had been stuffed into the pottery vessel, but while there was a lot of grass pollen there were no seeds, suggesting that the hoard was deposited in the spring when the grass was in flower but had not yet seeded.[52]

Three years later, a second hoard was found *c.* 100 m (330 ft) away in the same field, and in 2001, another part of the second hoard was discovered. Westerklief II comprises one complete ingot, 24 pieces of hacksilver, 39 Carolingian coins, an imitation gold solidus of Louis the Pious that had been mounted in a brooch, and 95 dirhams, many of which had been nicked, cut or bent. Nicking or pecking is a common feature on silver coins in Viking hoards, where a suspicious trader has taken a knife or other sharp implement to test the silver content of a coin; this suggests that the coin was being acquired for its silver content, rather than its monetary face value. It was also hidden in a Badorf ware pot, and, allowing time for the dirhams to have made their way to Frisia, the hoard probably dates to the 880s.[53] Both silver hoards were probably hidden by Vikings who were using Wieringen as a temporary base, but never returned to retrieve their loot. Wieringen, like the other island camps chosen by Vikings in Frankish territory, would have provided a strategic location from which to control the navigation route from central Frisia across Lake Almere to Dorestad, and a well-protected base for their wider raiding activities.

Stray finds recovered by metal-detectorists are beginning to reveal other traces of the Viking impact in the Netherlands. While there is yet to be a comprehensive survey of all such finds, a paper published in 2013 by Nelleke IJssennagger lists a handful of isolated finds, including gold and silver arm-rings and ingots.[54] There are also a number of Carolingian coin hoards from Frisia, and Simon Coupland has shown a close correlation between the dates of these hoards and recorded Viking raids in the region, suggesting that the inhabitants hid their wealth in the face of these threats. When these hoards are mapped, they reinforce the link with known Viking raids. A hoard from the 830s from Wijk-bij-Duurstede, for example, coincides with a period of intensive raids on Dorestad. Hoards along the coast at Holtland, Oosterend, Stade and Winsum reflect the uncertainty among coastal communities in the face of frequent Viking raids, reflected in orders by Louis the Pious in both 835 and 837 to reorganize the Frankish coastal defences in Frisia. The *Annals of Xanten* record under 846 that 'As usual the Northmen raided Oostergo and Westergo', and many of the hoards from the 840s are on the route that the raiders are likely to have taken to reach these places.

All but one of these hoards probably date to 845–46, when the Vikings 'took control of virtually the whole province' of Frisia and demanded tribute.[55] Despite Roric now being in control of Frisia, Viking raids continued, which may have led to the burial of four hoards in the 850s. The decline in hoarding after the mid-860s may reflect a reduced threat from Viking raiders, coinciding with a renewed focus of attention on England. However, by then the Rhine had also silted up, and the emporium of Dorestad was in decline, so there may simply have been fewer coins in circulation in Frisia at this time – an important reminder that not every misfortune to befall western Europe in the 9th century should be laid at the door of the Vikings. But it is now to England that we turn, in the next chapter, where archaeology has far more to tell us about Viking armies of the 9th century.

PART II

The Viking Great Army

3
A Pivotal Decade

In AD 865 a Viking army landed in East Anglia. It is likely to have comprised several thousand warriors, arriving in a fleet of over 100 longships, and was larger than any army that had previously threatened the Anglo-Saxon kingdoms. It was made up of experienced warriors who had spent many years travelling along the coastlines of western Europe, raiding deep into its major river systems. They were familiar with the wealth to be had from churches and royal and aristocratic estate centres; they knew where such places were typically located in the landscape; and they also knew at what times of the year large gatherings of people and resources were to be found there. Many separate raiding parties came together in East Anglia that year, some coming straight from Scandinavia, others from northern France, the Low Countries, the northern reaches of the British Isles and Ireland; they did not entirely trust each other, and did not expect to stay together for long. But encouraged by repeated successes, and reinforced periodically by new arrivals, they travelled together for years, a peripatetic community of men, women and children; warriors, merchants and craftworkers.

Over the following years the Army fought numerous battles in all four Anglo-Saxon kingdoms, made (and broke) peace treaties, and deposed or killed at least four Anglo-Saxon kings, replacing them with their own appointees from the local elite. Unlike previous Viking armies that had raided only in the summer months, the Great Army was a constant presence over this period, over-wintering at various locations in northern and eastern England. Many of its members subsequently settled there. Its leaders soon adopted Anglo-Saxon styles of kingship, converted to Christianity, collaborated with local kings and churchmen, fostered industrial activities and began to adapt to – and transform – the societies among which they had settled. This paved the way for generations of Scandinavian settlement, and the two decades from 865 are crucial to understanding the longer-term consequences of Scandinavian conquest and settlement in England. In this chapter we set the scene by introducing the contemporary written sources, and the archaeological evidence that has traditionally underpinned knowledge of the Army.

Until recently, knowledge of the movements and camps of the Viking Great Army has largely been limited to brief entries in the *Anglo-Saxon Chronicle* and Asser's *Life of King Alfred*. They provide important information about the battles the Army fought, the peace treaties it forged and the places where it spent each winter. These sources also provide limited information about the organization of the Army, and the means by which it supported itself during its campaigns. Here we will establish a chronology of its activities and seek to identify the characteristics of its behaviour.

In doing so, it is important to be alert to the focus of our sources on kingship, royal authority and Wessex. The original manuscript of the *Anglo-Saxon Chronicle* was compiled from earlier annals by scribes in Winchester *c.* 892, and copies distributed from the court of King Alfred to churches across England from where individual versions were periodically updated. It provides an annual account of the major political events from 865, but provides far more detail about events in Wessex than in northern England.[1]

Most of what we know about Asser comes from comments that he makes in his *Life of King Alfred*; he had been ordained at the monastery of St David's in Wales (Dyfed), and may perhaps have been its bishop. He was summoned to the court of King Alfred around 885, where he helped the king with his translations of Latin texts into Old English and was rewarded by being made bishop of Sherborne. Around 893 he wrote a Latin biography of the king, which was influenced by 9th-century continental royal biographies and biblical accounts of Old Testament kings, and also incorporated sections of the *Anglo-Saxon Chronicle* translated into Latin. From his text emerges a model Christian king who is powerful, learned, wise and a successful military strategist.[2] Asser fleshes out some of the terser entries in the *Chronicle* about the Great Army, particularly when it enters Wessex or when Alfred engages it in battle.

In 865 the *Anglo-Saxon Chronicle* records that 'a great heathen army [*micel hæþen here*] came into England and took up winter quarters in East Anglia; and there they were supplied with horses, and the East Angles made peace with them',[3] and so begins a decade that transformed England. The origins of this 'heathen army' are not specified by the *Chronicle*, and although Asser claims that it had come from the Danube, he may have been confusing *Dacia*, where the Danube was located, with *Dania*, or Denmark.[4] However, it is likely that the Great Army combined disparate forces gathered together from a wide area, and included groups that had recently been raiding the trading emporia and religious houses of the Frankish kingdoms, as well as those who had been cattle-rustling and slave-trading in Ireland.

Later Icelandic sagas claim that the Great Army was led by the sons of Ragnar Loðbrók, to take revenge on King Ælla of Northumbria for killing their father by casting him into a pit of venomous snakes. The far more reliable contemporary sources list its 'kings' as Healfdene, Guthrum, Ivar, Oscetel, Bagsecg and Anwend, to which 10th-century sources add Ubba.[5] According to the 13th-century saga *The Tale of Ragnar Loðbrók*, Healfdene (or Halfdan in Old Norse) and Ivar were brothers or half-brothers, which is also how they are described by the *Anglo-Saxon Chronicle*. Healfdene may also be the same

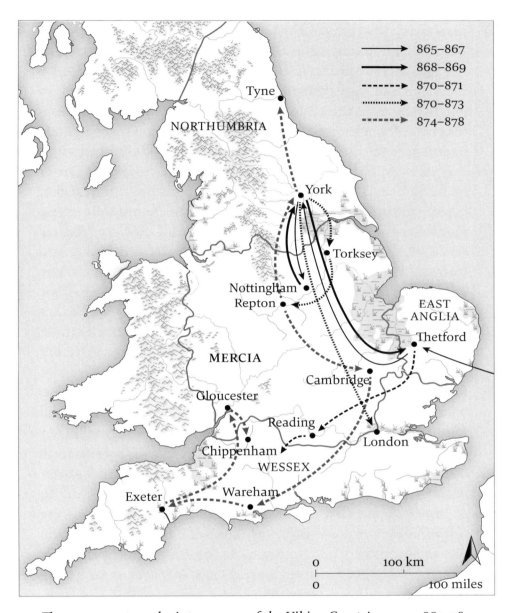

The movements and winter camps of the Viking Great Army, AD 865–78.

person as a character with the nickname Hvitserk ('Whiteshirt') in the sagas. According to legend Ivar was the youngest son of Ragnar and his third wife Aslaug. In Old Norse he was known by the nickname Ívarr Beinlausi which has been translated as Ivar 'the Boneless' or 'the Legless'. The *Tale of Ragnar's Sons* suggests that Ivar's 'bonelessness' was merely figurative, referring to male impotence. According to the *Tale of Ragnar Loðbrók*, however, it was a congenital bone condition resulting from his mother's curse on his father. Aslaug had said that Ragnar must wait three nights before consummating their marriage after his return following a long separation, while he was in England raiding. However, Ragnar was overcome with lust and ignored her words and, as a result, Ivar was born with weak bones. In the *Anglo-Saxon Chronicle*, Ivar is named in 878, after his death, when 'the same winter the brother of Ivar and Healfdene' arrived in Devon; a 12th-century source says this brother is Ubba.[6] It is difficult to be certain about who these individuals were, where they were from and how they were related to each other, but we can be confident that the sources reflect the fact that there were multiple leaders of the Great Army and that it operated over wide areas. Viking armies had been raiding on the Continent and in Ireland for decades and some of the leaders of the Army may well have come fresh from escapades there; indeed, some of the members of the Great Army may even have been born in those regions, growing up on the move.[7]

In 866, in the first of many recorded movements across the Anglo-Saxon kingdoms, the Army travelled north to York, crossing the Humber estuary into Northumbria. We are told by the *Chronicle* that there was 'great civil strife going on in that people', with King Osberht having been deposed in favour of King Ælla.[8] The Army seems to have been drawn to a political situation it could exploit, and had perhaps even been invited by one side to intervene. The Army easily broke into York and in the disastrous Northumbrian counter-attack both Osberht and Ælla were killed, after which the survivors made peace with the raiders. This is a pattern that we find most years over the following decade, albeit that what this 'peace' may have entailed is rarely explained. There is another tradition about these events, in a history of the community of St Cuthbert on the island of Lindisfarne, which was written at Chester-le-Street (Co. Durham), in the mid-11th century. This account places some of the blame for what happened on Ælla, who is said to have seized some of the monastery's lands in the mid-860s, which 'ignited the wrath of God and of the holy confessor [St Cuthbert] against him'.[9] Divine punishment came in the form of Ubba 'duke of the Frisians', who 'entered his kingdom with a great army of Danes and approached the city of York on Palm Sunday'.[10] It was in the ensuing battle that the Northumbrian kings are said to have lost their lives. The reference to Ubba's association with Frisia may reflect the region from which he had come to England to join the Great Army.

Roger of Wendover, a monk of St Albans Abbey writing in the early 13th century, provides further detail about what happened in York in 866, in an account widely regarded as being based on earlier sources, now lost. Roger tells us that following the death of Osberht and Ælla, a man called Egbert became king and that he reigned for six years 'in subjection to the Danes'.[11] Here for the first time we see the Army adopting the practice of appointing a 'puppet king' to rule on its behalf, echoing a strategy used by Frankish rulers when they appointed Viking leaders to control regions such as Frisia on their behalf (see Chapter 2). We know little more of Egbert, but he was clearly a local man, given his Anglo-Saxon name. The fact that he managed to rule for so long confirms that he already had good local connections and this may have been part of the attraction in appointing him king.

In the following year, the kingdom of Mercia was targeted and the Army took up winter quarters in Nottingham on the River Trent. Asser tells us that Nottingham 'is called in the British tongue, *Tiggocobauc*, but in Latin, the "House of Caves"', and there is, indeed, a network of caves beneath the town.[12] Here the Army came up against the combined forces of two kingdoms, as Burgred of Mercia had asked Æthelred I of Wessex and his younger brother Alfred for help. At Nottingham the Army was besieged but a major battle was averted because, according to Asser, 'defended by the protection of the fortress, [the Army] refused to give battle, and the Christians could not break the wall' and so, once again, peace was made.[13] Whether the Army built a fortress or found one to reuse is not made clear and, while there has been much speculation about this question, there is currently no archaeological evidence to resolve it.[14] In the spring of 868 the Army left Nottingham and the following winter was again spent in York. We have no further details about what ensued, but here we see the Army retreating to a base where it already had allies and presumably also measures in place to provision it.

In 869 the Army moved back to East Anglia, following the precedent of the previous year in returning to familiar territory, and it spent the winter at Thetford in Norfolk. Brief accounts in both the *Anglo-Saxon Chronicle* and Asser's *Life of King Alfred* tell us that in the ensuing battle King Edmund of East Anglia was killed; while neither source states it explicitly, it is possible that he died on the battlefield.[15] These sources do not name the leaders of the Army who were responsible for Edmund's death, but later 10th-century accounts identify them as Ivar and Ubba. The political situation in East Anglia after the death of Edmund is unclear. Coins minted in the names of two otherwise unknown kings, Æthelred and Oswald, are similar in form to those of Edmund and minted by one of his moneyers, and they suggest that he was succeeded by two kings of local origins. They may also have been Great Army appointees, in a move that would be consistent with the Army's previous tactics in York.[16]

The death of Edmund had an enduring influence, however, and the king was soon transformed into a martyr and saint. A more detailed version of his death was written in the late 10th century by Abbo, a monk from Fleury in France, who spent time at the monastery of Ramsey (Huntingdonshire), where he learned of Edmund's fate. His account claims that the king had refused to take up arms against the Great Army as he did not wish to shed blood, but consequently died in a particularly gruesome manner: tied to a tree, tortured and then beheaded.[17] This and other later accounts informed depictions of Edmund's death in an early 12th-century illuminated manuscript produced at Bury St Edmunds containing various texts about the saint's life [pl. 4, 5]. It would be easy to assume that the later accounts had grown in the retelling and were informed by expectations of how a candidate for saint-hood should die. The story of Edmund being heard calling out, leading local men to find his severed head beneath a thorn tree and guarded by a wolf, is clearly fanciful. However, some elements of these later accounts were based on local oral testimonies that went back to 869. These were recounted several decades later at the court of King Athelstan (924–39) by an elderly man who had been Edmund's arms bearer, and were heard by a young Dunstan, future archbishop of Canterbury. Many years later Dunstan passed on what he had heard and it was picked up and reported by Abbo of Fleury. What emerges from this is evidence that the local community was quick to develop a cult around Edmund, and that by the end of the 9th century he was already regarded locally as a saint, and depicted as such on coins minted by Scandinavian rulers.[18]

The Army spent the winter of 870–71 at Reading in Berkshire, in the kingdom of Wessex. The *Anglo-Saxon Chronicle* and Asser, both with their focus on Wessex, not surprisingly provide us with the most detailed accounts of the behaviour of the Great Army as it overwintered. While some of the Army began to build a rampart between the Thames and the Kennet to the south of the royal estate there, 'two of their earls [*jarls*], with a great part of the force, rode out for plunder'.[19] Here for the first time we see how the Army operated once it had a base, but this attempt to acquire provisions locally ended in disaster as the force ran into the army of Ealdorman Æthelwulf at Englefield in Berkshire and one of the Viking earls was killed. Reinforcements arrived led by Æthelred I and Alfred, who made their way to the fortress and the Vikings 'like wolves … burst out of all the gates'.[20] In the ensuing battle Æthelwulf was killed and the Vikings won the day, because 'the Christians eventually turned their backs', according to Asser, although there was 'great slaughter' on both sides.[21]

Just four days later at Ashdown, with the West Saxons already 'aroused by the grief and shame' of their defeat at Reading, another battle saw the Vikings suffer notable losses.[22] The location of Ashdown is not known, but may be Kingstanding Hill in the Berkshire Downs, close to the prehistoric Icknield Way. The *Chronicle* informs us that the Vikings were in two divisions, one led by the kings Bagsecg and Healfdene, and the other by the earls.[23] Bagsecg was killed along with five of the earls: Sidroc the Old, Sidroc the Younger, Osbearn, Fræna and Harold. It is notable that Asser emphasizes that Alfred was first to the battlefield, while his brother the king was delayed by 'lingering still longer in prayer', and it was Alfred who took on the Army led by the earls. Here we can see how Alfred was already being promoted as the saviour of the English against the Vikings. He is described as 'acting courageously, like a wild boar, supported by divine counsel and strengthened by divine help'.[24] Over the course of the year, however, there were multiple battles against the Vikings, who generally had the upper hand each time, although they ended the year with the loss of at least another four earls. Amidst all of this, Æthelred I died and was succeeded as king of Wessex by Alfred, then only around 22 years old. Even if Asser's account of the new king's bravery and skill were exaggerated, we can be confident that Alfred will have been under no illusions about the threat posed by the Great Army, not least because, according to the *Anglo-Saxon Chronicle*, 'a great summer army' had come from overseas to reinforce it.[25]

In 871 the Army moved back to Mercian territory and took up winter quarters in London, where peace was made. In the following year the Army returned to Northumbria, and while the

Anglo-Saxon Chronicle and Asser are silent as to the reasons for this, later sources reveal that there had been a revolt against King Egbert, the Army's appointee.[26] Egbert had fled south to the court of Burgred of Mercia, accompanied by the archbishop of York, Wulfhere. However, the Army seems to have failed to reinstall Egbert, if that was indeed its intention, and in any case he appears to have died at some point that year. He was replaced as king by Ricsige, about whom we know nothing other than his name, and that Roger of Wendover fancifully claims that he died of a broken heart when the Great Army settled in Northumbria several years later![27] From York the Army retreated to the district of Lindsey, in Mercia. Here it spent the winter at Torksey, on the River Trent, where it made peace with the Mercians. This is a typically brief entry in the *Anglo-Saxon Chronicle*, not amplified by other written sources, but – as we will see in Chapter 4 – recent archaeological discoveries have transformed our knowledge of the events of this winter.

In the following year, 873, the Army moved on to Repton, some 115 km (70 miles) further inland along the Trent. Here we are presented with a relatively detailed account by the *Chronicle*:

> In this year the army went from Lindsey to Repton and took up winter quarters there, and drove King Burgred across the sea, after he had held the kingdom twenty-two years. And they conquered all that land.... And the same year they gave the kingdom of the Mercians to be held by Ceolwulf, a foolish king's *thegn*; and he swore oaths to them and gave hostages, that it should be ready for them on whatever day they wished to have it, and he would be ready, himself and all who would follow him, at the enemy's service.[28]

This turn of events presents us with another insight into the appointment of a puppet king. That Ceolwulf II was little more than a 'foolish king's *thegn*', appointed, according to Asser, 'by a wretched arrangement', is not to be taken at face value, as he ruled for several years and seems to have been well established with the local aristocracy.[29] He was also acceptable enough to Alfred for the pair later to embark on a joint reform of their coinage, as we will see in Chapter 9. This was despite the fact that Burgred, the king he replaced, was married to Alfred's sister, Æthelswith, who fled with her husband to Rome. It seems likely that Ceolwulf II was a member of a branch of the Mercian royal family who were rivals to Burgred's line, perhaps descended from a Ceolwulf who had reigned in the 820s.[30] In the light of the events at Repton we might look back at the Army's overwintering in Nottingham (867–68) and Torksey (872–73) afresh. Was the existence of a potential rival for his throne the reason why Burgred had been so quick to call on the assistance of Wessex in 868 when the Army first arrived in his kingdom, and was it increasing familiarity with Mercian politics that led the Army to contemplate the exile of Burgred?

We will discuss the archaeological evidence that provides further details about the Army's stay at Repton later, but the written sources reveal that this was the year when the Great Army began to fragment. Healfdene went north with part of the Army and in 874–75 he overwintered on the Tyne and 'often ravaged among the Picts and the Strathclyde Britons'. We do not know where his winter camp was located, but the 11th-century *History of St Cuthbert* records that Healfdene's army 'entered the Tyne and sailed as far as *Wircesforda*'. This name does not survive among local place-names, but it was clearly at a fording point over the river, which is consistent with other locations at which the Army overwintered.[31] It is easy to see what the appeal of the region was: the dense cluster of monasteries along the lower reaches of the Tyne, at Tynemouth, Gateshead, *Monkchester* (probably Newcastle-upon-Tyne), *Urfa* (probably the former Roman fort at Arbeia), Jarrow and *Donamutha*, close to Jarrow where the River Don enters the Tyne. These sites were attractive to the Army as potentially fruitful sites to raid for winter provisions. We might deduce, however, that if the Army had spent the winter at or near one of these well-known ecclesiastical sites, or at any of the former Roman sites such as Corbridge, the chronicler would have known its name, and so it seems reasonable to deduce that the winter camp was at one of the fording points in-between.

The remainder of the Army under its kings Guthrum, Anwend and Oscetel headed south-east and back to East Anglia, spending the winter at Cambridge, before continuing to fight with Alfred across Wessex. We will pick up Healfdene's story in Chapters 7 and 8, and that of Alfred and Guthrum in Chapter 9.

Until very recently there has been little archaeological evidence with which to interrogate this historical account of the movements of the Viking Great Army, and much of it has been prone to speculative interpretation, particularly given the challenges of dating individual finds. For example, the story that the Army ransacked the monastery at Whitby in North Yorkshire in 867 is based entirely on a 12th-century text preserved in the *Whitby Cartulary* and – although David Wilson proposed that an open stone mould excavated there was used for making ingots from church silver plate after a Viking raid – any such attack might fit better with the first Viking raids on Northumbrian coastal monasteries of the late 8th century.[32] The size and impact of Viking armies has also been much debated, especially following Peter Sawyer's attempts almost 60 years ago to challenge previous assumptions about the large scale of the Viking onslaught. Sawyer transformed the study of the Vikings, although much of his own case was equally based on unfounded assumptions and the marshalling of ambiguous evidence. For example, he argued that translating the term *here* as 'army' was misleading; it was used in the early 7th-century laws of King Ine to mean any group numbering more than 35 men: 'If a *here* could be three dozen men, it would be as well not to call it an "army"'.[33] He maintained that the *Anglo-Saxon Chronicle* exaggerated the numbers of ships involved in Viking raids, and argued that

Gannocks Castle, Bedfordshire, was once thought to be a Viking camp, but is probably much later.

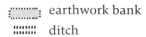 earthwork bank

 ditch

0   60 m

0   200 ft

the difficulty of keeping a large army in the field precluded Viking armies comprising more than a few hundred men.[34]

Sawyer also attempted to mobilize archaeological evidence. However, he relied on antiquarian speculation about possible Viking encampments in his argument for the small size of the armies, and since the sites concerned were undated, they did not readily support his case without some circularity of argument. In the 1920s, for example, Sir Cyril Fox had dismissed the notion that the earthwork known as Gannocks Castle was the site of the Viking fortress of 917 recorded at Tempsford in Bedfordshire, because at *c.* 120 × 84 feet (*c.* 37 × 26 m) it would have accommodated only around 270 men.[35] Sawyer argued that there was 'no reason to think that the *here* mentioned by the *Chronicle* was much larger than this'.[36] In contrast, in 1903 Isaac Chalkley Gould had identified an earthwork some 500 yards (457 m) long as the fortress built by a Viking army in 893 at Shoebury in Essex, and Sawyer explained the larger size by describing it as a place 'intended to shelter the women, ships and property of the raiders during campaigns and … the men and horses as well'.[37] In sum, whatever the size of a putative Viking army camp identified on archaeological grounds, Sawyer could make it fit a preconceived argument that Viking armies were small.

Sawyer challenged old orthodoxies, but his arguments did not go unchallenged. Writing in 1979, historian Nicholas Brooks demonstrated the flaw in Sawyer's insistence that the *Anglo-Saxon Chronicle* is an unreliable witness to the numbers of ships that were involved in Viking raids. He showed that the *Chronicle* is, in fact, notably restrained in its assessment of the scale of most of the raids. Furthermore, the estimates of the numbers of ships – sometimes 300 or more – are corroborated by completely unrelated Frankish, Irish and Spanish Muslim sources: 'the *Chronicle*'s figures for Viking fleets are neither random nor wild; they avoid the obvious exaggerations of less well-placed or more colourful continental sources, and they mostly fit a consistent pattern of Viking activity that is credible and circumstantial'.[38] Brooks also argued that the reason the Great Army was more successful than contemporary Viking armies raiding on the Continent was because it was much larger than them. The sheer size of the Army was the reason for its 'shattering effect' on Anglo-Saxon kingdoms and the Church.[39] While there was still no reliable archaeological evidence concerning the encampments of Viking armies, Brooks drew attention to the fact that, according to the *Anglo-Saxon Chronicle,* the Great Army typically based itself at royal and administrative centres of the Anglo-Saxon kingdoms. He suggested that these bases were chosen 'precisely because they already had defences', some of them substantial Roman fortifications, such as York and London.[40] He concluded that the size of the places the army chose as their winter bases 'would be inexplicable unless the "large" Danish armies were numbered in thousands rather than hundreds'.[41] As we will show in this book, Brooks was right in his deductions, but not for the reasons he offered.

At the time when Brooks was writing, little was known archaeologically about the Great Army's winter camps. Furnished burials at Reading and Sonning in Berkshire, excavated in the 1860s and 1966 respectively, had been associated with the overwintering of the Army in 870–71, as had a group of coins found in 1839 in a stone coffin to the south of St Mary's church, Reading. The eleven known coins comprise seven of Burgred of Mercia, one of Edmund of East Anglia, two of Æthelberht of Wessex (r. 860–65) and one of Æthelred I of Wessex. They represent only a proportion of those deposited, as the coins were found stuck together and many broke when they were separated, but their likely date of deposition is consistent with the Great Army's use of the royal *vill* at Reading as their winter camp.[42] Grenville Astill has proposed that the most likely site for the Viking camp would have been on a gravel ridge *c.* 0.5 km (0.3 miles) east of the minster church of St Mary's, over-looking the confluence of the Thames and the River Kennet. This prominent position was later chosen as the site of an abbey built for Henry I in the early 12th century, and Astill suggests that the

Reading, Berkshire. The Viking winter camp of AD 870–71 may have been on the peninsula of land which became the site of the medieval abbey, with the Anglo-Saxon town to the west.

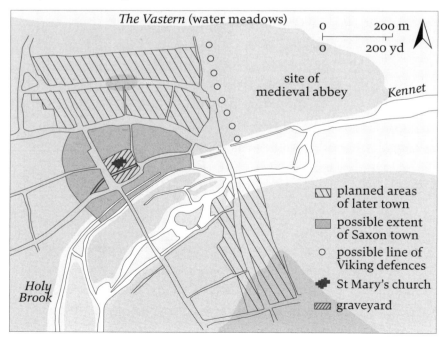

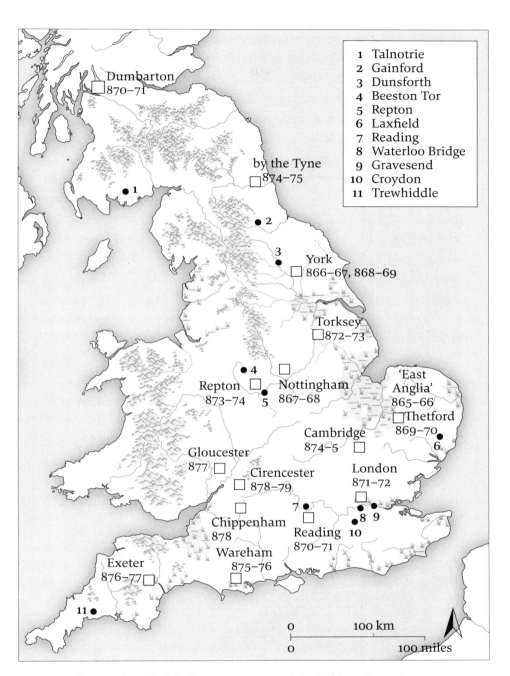

1 Talnotrie
2 Gainford
3 Dunsforth
4 Beeston Tor
5 Repton
6 Laxfield
7 Reading
8 Waterloo Bridge
9 Gravesend
10 Croydon
11 Trewhiddle

Dumbarton 870–71

by the Tyne 874–75

York 866–67, 868–69

Torksey 872–73

Repton 873–74

Nottingham 867–68

'East Anglia' 865–66

Thetford 869–70

Cambridge 874–5

Gloucester 877

Cirencester 878–79

London 871–72

Chippenham 878

Reading 870–71

Wareham 875–76

Exeter 876–77

0   100 km
0   100 miles

Hoards associated with the movements of the Viking Great Army.

western wall of the monastic precinct may have followed the line of the camp's defences. The northern end of this wall terminated at water meadows by the Thames known as the *Vastern*, an Old English word meaning 'stronghold'.[43] A raised location overlooking a major waterway, adjacent to a place named with reference to its defensive capabilities, is a combination of characteristics we will see in other sites associated with the Great Army.

There have been attempts, most notably by Nicholas Brooks and James Graham-Campbell, to track the movements of the Army through various hoards deposited during the period 865–79.[44] These include both Viking hoards of coins and hacksilver, which were presumably deposited by members of the Army while they passed through a district, and Anglo-Saxon coin hoards, hidden to safeguard them from the Army. It is worth revisiting this evidence, even though much derives from antiquarian investigations of the 19th century.

In June 1862 a hoard of coins, ingots and hacksilver was found at a location reported only as 'White Horse' on the northern edge of the old parish of Croydon in Surrey. The Revd Henry Christmas provided a note on the discovery to the editor of the *Numismatic Chronicle*, reporting that the hoard had been found at a depth of about two feet by navvies constructing a new railway line between Victoria Station and Balham. It appeared to have been in a 'canvas' bag placed in what was described as a 'stone coffin without a lid'.[45]

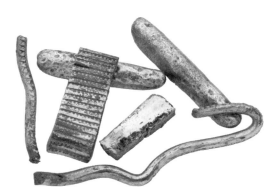

Silver ingots and hacksilver from the Croydon hoard, discovered in 1862.

As in the case of Reading, could the stone coffin have been intended as a memorable hiding place, unlikely to be disturbed, from which treasure could later be recovered, or were the coins deliberately buried as grave offerings, to accompany the dead to Valhalla? No human remains were recorded, however, and James Graham-Campbell suggests that it would have been unusual for the hoard to have been deposited in a Viking grave and that it is more likely that it was concealed in a churchyard.[46] The Croydon hoard, as it has become known, comprised at least four silver ingots and a corroded mass of some 250 coins, many of which were quickly dispersed into private hands, although the presence of Alfredian coins allowed the hoard to be dated to between 872 and 875.[47]

By 1866 the bulk of the hoard had been acquired by Sir John Evans, antiquarian, geologist and a partner in a paper manufacturing business, who provided a follow-up note for the *Numismatic Chronicle*, adding that as well as the ingots there were three fragments of silver bracelets.[48] After his death Evans's archaeological collection was presented to the Ashmolean Museum in Oxford in 1909, although by 1953 Liverpool City Museum had also acquired an ingot and a piece of hacksilver from the Croydon hoard. In 1959 Christopher Blunt and Michael Dolley were able to list 185 coins as possibly being from Croydon, including 94 from Mercia (all of Burgred), 24 from East Anglia, and 56 from Wessex, plus a handful of continental coins and dirhams.[49] The mixture of coins, ingots and hackmetal reveals that this was a collection that had been in Viking hands. The most likely occasion when a Viking silver hoard might have been buried at Croydon has to be the winter of 871–72 when the Great Army was based in London.

Burgred made peace with the Army by collecting 'an immense tribute' of silver from Mercian lords, so it is entirely plausible that an individual member of the Army should have been able to acquire large numbers of East Anglian, West Saxon and Mercian coins to add to whatever hacksilver and Carolingian and Islamic coins he had brought with him from the Continent.[50] On the other hand,

Silver pendant cross from the Gravesend hoard, discovered in 1838.

the absence of nicking on the three complete ingots compared to extensive nicking on the other pieces of hacksilver has led Graham-Campbell to suggest that they were the latest pieces to be added to the hoard.[51] The numismatic evidence implies that the hoard was deposited towards the end of the overwintering, in summer or autumn 872, presumably as the Army was about to move on. Brooks and Graham-Campbell suggest that at that time the estate of Croydon probably belonged to Ælfred, an ealdorman of Surrey. This is the same Ælfred who, with his wife, Werburg, donated a magnificent 8th-century illuminated gospel book, the *Codex Aureus*, to Christ Church, Canterbury [pl. 6]. In an Old English inscription added to the *Codex* recording this donation, Ælfred stated that he and Werburg had bought the book from the 'army of heathens' with pure gold, presumably ransoming it back after it had been stolen in a previous Viking raid. There are too many uncertainties to connect the Croydon hoard with this transaction, but it may not be coincidence that Ælfred appears to have had prior dealings with a Viking army and that the hoard was hidden within the boundaries of his estate. Brooks and Graham-Campbell concluded that the presence of Vikings on this important estate indicates that the

Army was exploiting the existing Anglo-Saxon estate organization as a convenient and effective way of raising food and money.[52]

A number of other coin hoards found along the River Thames are probably also associated with the overwintering of 871–72. In the autumn of 1838, a parcel of Saxon coins was dug up in Pelham Road, Gravesend, along with an Anglo-Saxon cross-shaped pendant, decorated with a dome-shaped marbled glass roundel in the centre. In reporting the discovery to the Royal Numismatic Society, Henry Borrell, who acquired the hoard, noted:

> There is generally concealment or deception on these occasions, as the discoverers fear that some lord of the manor or owner of the soil may lay claim to the treasure and deprive them of their prize; and, consequently, many pieces so found are privately disposed of in separate parcels, and the opportunity lost of an examination of the whole deposit, which would frequently lead to the establishment of doubtful and disputed points. Upon the present occasion, I have reason to believe that the whole of the discovery has come into my hands, and I will proceed to describe it...[53]

In addition to the pendant, the Gravesend hoard comprised 428 Mercian pennies (all but one of Burgred), 61 of Wessex, 49 of East Anglia (including 44 of King Edmund), and a single Carolingian coin of Louis the Pious. Given that the hoard has only a single coin of King Alfred it is thought to be a little earlier than the Croydon hoard, possibly buried in the autumn of 871 when the Army first entered London.[54]

Further up the Thames, two hoards discovered in the late 19th century near Waterloo Bridge and Westminster Bridge may also date to the Great Army's year in London, from 871–72. When workmen were excavating the foundations of the new Waterloo Bridge in 1882 they found a hoard of 96 Burgred pennies, with just one West Saxon coin of Æthelred I, and perhaps another of Alfred's lunette type.[55] The Westminster Bridge hoard, discovered *c*. 1895, was sold off before it could be properly recorded but is known to have contained Burgred coins.[56] It is believed to have been found under the bridge, which was first constructed in 1750 near a known crossing point of the Thames. Both may have been hidden by the Anglo-Saxon inhabitants of London, rather than by the invaders. Finally, in 1724 'several Saxon coins', including at least one of Burgred, were found in Barking close to the Roman road to Colchester, and reported to the Society of Antiquaries. The fact that they were found in a stone coffin may also indicate that they belong to this group of 871–72 hoards.[57] Of course, the number of possible hoards discovered in the London area may partly be due to the fact that the amount of subsequent development has made their discovery more likely.

Other hoards have been attributed to the Army's campaigns in the Midlands and northern England. The limestone cave of Beeston Tor in the Staffordshire Peak District comprises several large chambers in which archaeological finds from multiple eras have been discovered, including undated human bones, interpreted as those of fugitives. The cave system was visited by the Revd George Wilson in 1908 and a small excavation produced two coins of Burgred and what was described as an 'early British brooch'. The main hoard was found in September 1924, in a chamber located about 75 m (250 ft)

Silver Anglo-Saxon disc brooch from the Beeston Tor hoard, Staffordshire, discovered in a cave system in the Peak District in 1924.

from the cave entrance.[58] The hoard seems to have been found loose, all within a single square metre, but it may originally have been in a bag or purse, since traces of skin and leather were noticed. It seems to have comprised a total of 49 coins, including 20 of Alfred, 20 of Burgred, 1 of Archbishop Ceolnoth of Canterbury and 8 of earlier West Saxon kings. There were also one silver and two bronze rings, a bronze binding and two silver brooches decorated with niello (a black inlay), which were acquired by the British Museum. The larger of the brooches was still attached to some fabric with gold thread although the pin fell away on discovery; the second brooch was found with the pin broken but complete. The hoard is unlikely to have been hidden later than 875 and the most likely date of deposition is thought to be the winter of 873–74, when the Great Army was in Repton, 42 km (26 miles) to the south-east, although this may have been an Anglo-Saxon hoard hidden to protect it from the Army, rather than a Viking hoard cached by Army members themselves.[59]

Further hoards may be related to Healfdene's return to Northumbria in the autumn of 874. In 1861 a small hoard was found at Lower Dunsforth in North Yorkshire between the new schoolroom and the church when the old church was replaced by the present one. The contemporary account says that some thirty pennies were found but fifteen were offered for sale by Spink in 1924, comprising six of Burgred, two of Æthelred I of Wessex, and seven of Alfred.[60] Dunsforth, 'the ford by the hill', was at a river crossing, and the next point at which the Ouse could be crossed north of Aldwark (now known to be the site of an apparently undocumented Viking camp, of which more later). Some 70 km (45 miles) further north, a small hoard was discovered in 1864 in the churchyard at Gainford (Co. Durham), at a ford over the River Tees. It contained a single coin of Burgred and three of Alfred, and seems to date to the early 870s.[61] Gainford was the centre of a large estate that belonged to the monastic community of St Cuthbert, with an important church at which one of their abbots had been buried in the early 9th century.

The Talnotrie hoard, discovered in 1912 in Kirkcudbrightshire, Scotland. The cake of wax (top centre) suggests that the hoard was buried by a metal worker.

It was therefore another likely target for Viking raiders.[62] Neither the Dunsforth nor Gainford hoards contained diagnostic hacksilver, but it is the presence of silver coins of the southern kingdoms that suggests they were deposited by members of the Great Army.[63]

A hoard recovered from beneath a peat deposit in Talnotrie, Kirkcudbrightshire, in 1912 includes six stycas, four Burgred silver pennies, a cut Carolingian coin of Louis the Pious, and two dirham fragments, Anglo-Saxon and Celtic metalwork, a lead weight inset with a copper-alloy disc, and a cake of wax, suggesting that this hoard had been buried by a metalworker. Although Talnotrie is now in south-western Scotland, in the 9th century it was within the Northumbrian kingdom. The Burgred coins have been taken to suggest a date of 870–71, which would associate the hoard with the campaigns of Ivar and his kinsman Olaf among the Strathclyde Britons, when he captured the stronghold of Dumbarton Rock, but it could equally be associated with Healfdene's ravaging among the Picts and Strathclyde Britons in 874–75.[64]

Meanwhile, a small hoard from Laxfield in Suffolk has been dated to *c.* 875 on numismatic grounds, but the evidence is insufficient to tie it to the overwintering of Guthrum's half of the Army in East Anglia in 874–75 and their camp in Cambridge.[65] Finally, the famous Trewhiddle hoard was found by tin-workers in a heap of loose stones in mine workings near St Austell in Cornwall in 1774.[66] It appears to have been a collection of church treasure, hidden from a Viking raiding party but never recovered. However, the hoard is difficult to date and although it was once thought to have been deposited *c.* 875, it has now been re-dated to *c.* 868. The Trewhiddle hoard can therefore no longer be associated with the presence of the Great Army in Exeter in 876–77.[67]

There is still a marked peak in hoard deposition and non-recovery during the period of the Great Army's activity. Twenty-six known hoards from Anglo-Saxon England have been coin-dated to the 870s, whereas from the two decades either side, spanning the period 850–900, there are only three recorded hoards per decade.[68] This figure excludes hoards containing only Northumbrian stycas from the 850s and 860s, but these coins may have remained in circulation for several decades after the minting of new forms apparently ceased when the Great Army seized York, so they may well be later. A hoard of 22 stycas recovered in London during excavations in 1996 in advance of the redevelopment of the Royal Opera House in Covent Garden may fall into this category. It was given a date of deposition around 851 on the basis of the latest coins but the date profile of the whole group is no different from that of the stycas found at Torksey. With the hoard was a small fragment of copper-alloy sheet with punched triangles similar to those found on Scandinavian silver arm-rings. The hoard was buried in the rampart associated with a defensive ditch, which was probably dug in response to Viking attacks and the occupation of *Lundenwic* by the Great Army in 871.[69]

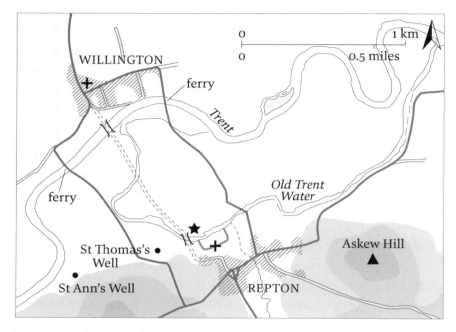

Repton, Derbyshire, showing the modern course of the Trent and the Old Trent Water, and the location of the ferries before the modern causeway was built. The star marks the approximate position of the discovery of human bones and a sword in 1839, to the north of the D-shaped enclosure and St Wystan's church. The hatching indicates built-up areas in 1829.

Until the last decade, the only winter camp to have been subjected to archaeological excavation was that of 873–74 at Repton, and this happened by accident. Today Repton is a small south Derbyshire village, best known for its Anglo-Saxon church and the private Repton School attended by Roald Dahl, among others. The church sits at a strategic point in the landscape, close to a crossing point on the River Trent. It is located on a promontory that looks out over the floodplain of the Trent to the north, from where it is approached across a causeway from Willington. The Trent now flows on the far side of the floodplain from Repton but originally flowed to the south side, below a low cliff, now above the Old Trent Water, a remnant of the former river course. The promontory is defined to the north by the Old Trent Water and to the east by the valley of the Repton Brook, a tributary of the Trent which it joins north-east of the village.

It was on this bluff that a monastery was founded at some time before the end of the 7th century. It was a monastic double house, ruled by an abbess of noble, possibly royal, rank. The monastery was closely associated with the Mercian kings and the crypt of St Wystan's church probably served as a royal mausoleum. King Æthelbald of Mercia (r. 716–57), allegedly murdered by his own bodyguards, was buried at Repton. In 849 the body of Wigstan (Wystan), a later claimant to the Mercian kingship, was brought here for burial following his murder in a dynastic struggle. Wigstan was buried in the mausoleum of his grandfather King Wiglaf (r. 827–40). Miracles took place at the tomb and Wigstan became a saint; his mausoleum, with its twisted columns reminiscent of St Peter's church in Rome, became a place of pilgrimage. The monastery was a rich house, with evidence for stone sculpture of exceptional quality, multi-coloured window glass, silver coins and imported wheel-turned pottery. Its walls were plastered with stucco and the church may have been lead-roofed.

We know all of this because from 1974 to 1988 archaeologists Birthe Kjølbye-Biddle and her husband Martin Biddle excavated at St Wystan's church, in collaboration with Anglo-Saxon architectural church historian Harold Taylor. They were interested in the history of the church and its burial crypt, and had not expected to find traces of the Viking Great Army. Although the Repton excavations have never been fully published there is enough in interim reports to create a coherent account of what was found.

In excavating east of the crypt, the Biddles encountered a small number of Viking graves (to which we shall return in Chapter 6), but also the butt end of a large V-shaped ditch, over 4 m (13 ft) deep, immediately south-east of the Anglo-Saxon crypt and chancel. The ditch had been backfilled from the north side, probably by pushing in an internal bank. There were only three finds of 9th- or

10th-century date from the ditch: two sherds of pottery, both from the bottom fill, and a copper-alloy dress pin with a faceted head decorated with ring-and-dot ornament. The course of the ditch east of the church was located by a resistivity survey in which electrical resistance meters are used to detect and map sub-surface archaeological features. The survey revealed the ditch curving to the north beneath the cloister of Repton School. It was harder to locate its course in the current graveyard west of the church, so a different geophysical survey technique, using a magnetometer, was employed here. This approach maps buried features from magnetic differences between them and the surrounding ground. It revealed a feature running from the west end of the church to the cliff above the Old Trent Water. Excavation here revealed four successive ditches; the earliest of these was V-shaped with a flat, narrow bottom, although later recuts may have been associated with a castle of the earl of Chester, constructed in the early to mid-12th century. No dating evidence was recovered and it appears to have been backfilled with clean earth shortly after its original construction.[70]

Extrapolating from these three sections of ditch, the Biddles proposed that on their arrival at Repton in 873 the Viking Great Army constructed a D-shaped enclosure, with its straight edge along the cliff edge above the Trent, and incorporating the church as a gatehouse into the interior of their enclosure. In this they were undoubtedly influenced by the discovery of ditched proto-towns in Scandinavia. Indeed, in their 1992 paper the Biddles note that: 'This type of earthwork, consisting of a D-shaped enclosure on the bank of a river or other expanse of water, is well evidenced in the Viking period in Scandinavia, on both a small scale as in the beginnings of Aarhus, or later on a vast scale as in the defences of Hedeby.'[71] This is despite the fact that the southern Scandinavian proto-towns are generally located within rounded C-shaped enclosures set against the coastal shoreline. The boundary ditches of these Scandinavian proto-towns are generally no more than 0.5 m (1.5 ft) in depth and are thought to mark controlled trading zones, rather than providing any defensive function. Therefore, the Repton enclosure has both a different shape and a far deeper ditch than the early Scandinavian towns.

The area enclosed was also relatively small compared with the Scandinavian towns; the Biddles originally published it as having an area of 1.46 ha (3.6 acres), although recalculation has shown it to be no more than 0.4 ha (1 acre).[72] This did nothing to challenge the view that Viking armies can only have numbered in the hundreds, with one historian commenting that 'the physical dimensions of the Viking encampment at Repton do not encourage one to think in terms of a "great army"'.[73] The interpretation of the Repton enclosure as the winter camp of the Viking Great Army has therefore met with some scepticism. At Repton, apparently, only an army comprising a handful of ships' companies could stay out the winter which, to adopt Guy Halsall's phrase, 'would reduce the *Micel Here* to almost "Magnificent Seven" proportions'![74]

In conclusion, the places at which the Great Army spent each winter between 865 and the mid-870s, when permanent settlement commenced, are critical to our understanding of the scale of the Army, its composition and the range of activities in which it engaged. Although the *Anglo-Saxon Chronicle* records the overwintering sites, this contemporary source is only partially useful for locating and exploring Viking encampments; in some cases it is unhelpfully vague ('East Anglia'), and even where a town is named, as in the case of Nottingham and London, modern development may have rendered the sites archaeologically inaccessible.[75] In the case of Repton, other than the churchyard, the core of the village is now largely occupied by the buildings of Repton School and its grounds; it therefore cannot be extensively excavated or metal-detected. Nonetheless, for many years the excavations at Repton provided the prototype for a Viking winter camp, of a small D-shaped enclosure.[76] As we shall see in the next chapter, this interpretation can now be shown to be flawed. The newly discovered winter camp at Torksey tells a very different story.

4
The Winter of AD 872–73 and the Camp at Torksey

Around the bend in the river the Viking camp spread out along the eastern shore of the Trent [pl. 7, 8]. Longships of various sizes were lined up on the riverbank, 50–100 vessels in total. Most had been dragged up onto the floodplain, clear of the water. Their sails were furled and in most cases the masts had been lowered. A few men were working on some of them, replacing rotten planks, with incessant hammering as iron rivets were banged into place. Behind the ships, the land climbed to the drier ground above, where the Great Army's tents and eagle banners had been pitched. The tents ran all the way back from the cliff edge – from where anyone approaching by land or river could be seen long before they arrived – and continued downslope to the marshy ground beyond, forming what was effectively a semi-circular island, which could be reached on foot only by a few dry routes across the marsh. The tents stretched almost as far as the eye could see, but there were also open spaces separating the different forces that made up the Army.

Roads and trackways had developed within the camp, churned up by horses, and rutted by the wheels of wagons, bringing supplies from the hinterland. Along the roads there was a hustle and bustle of activity, and an array of smells and sounds. Here were the booths of traders and craftworkers. Along one street were the blacksmiths, forging new rivets for the ships, but for a few coins they were also willing to sharpen a knife or sword. It was noisy here with the sound of metal grinding against stone, and the air was smoky as they pumped their bellows, making the flames dance above their forges. Further along was the silversmith. His anvil was much more delicate but there were broken crucibles and ingot moulds on the ground. When the market was open, he would lay out glittering arm-rings on his workbench, alongside his hammer and punches, and his weighing balance and set of lead weights. In the meeting place on the highest ground, in the centre of the camp, slaves were traded on market days and large quantities of gold and silver changed hands. In another part of the camp were the bread ovens, where loaves were made from grain ransacked from the granaries of the local lord. There were also animal pens holding stolen cattle, sheep and pigs. Several thousand people lived in the camp and it was a struggle to keep them all fed.

The tents themselves were mainly simple affairs: timber A-frames, covered with canvas. Outside there was not much protection from the winter winds which seemed to blow all the way from the North Sea, but the tents were lined with furs and blankets, and each tent housed at least a half-dozen warriors, their swords hanging from the awning, and shields and spears stacked outside. They might as well make themselves comfortable, as they were planning to stay throughout the winter months. The tents were grouped according to ship's companies and in the open space in the centre of each cluster there were trestle tables and open hearths, lined with clay and edged with stones. Iron tripods stood over most of the hearths, suspending cauldrons of steaming broth. As night fell, the camp's inhabitants would huddle around the fires, drinking, gambling, telling stories of heroic battles or arguing over the outcome of a board game. Sometimes tempers flared and lead gaming pieces and silver dirhams were scattered across the ground, where in the dark they were trampled into the mud. Voices were raised in anger, in many tongues. Many spoke in various dialects of Old Norse but there was also the Old English swearing of local hostages, as well as the voices of Irishmen and Franks who had joined the Army during previous campaigns. There were women too – some were wives who had travelled with their husbands from Scandinavia; others were slaves who had been captured or purchased in England and Ireland. Children ran laughing after the hens between the tents, and the cries of infants could be heard throughout the long winter nights, echoing across Turc's Island.

The *Anglo-Saxon Chronicle* entry for 872 records that 'In this year the army went into Northumbria, and it took up winter quarters at Torksey in Lindsey; and then the Mercians made peace with the army.'[1] However, while the Great Army's camp was long assumed to have been in the vicinity of the present-day village of Torksey on the River Trent, its actual location was a mystery – until two metal-detecting brothers from South Yorkshire, Dave and Pete Stanley, discovered it by chance, one afternoon in the autumn of 1989.

On that afternoon, Dave and Pete were driving north along the A156, which runs parallel to the Trent on its eastern side until it reaches the inland port at Gainsborough. They had heard rumours of Viking finds from Torksey and wanted to visit a local farmer to ask for permission to detect on his land south of the village, where they thought the finds must have come from. Dave and Pete worked in the building trade, but had grown up on a farm so knew how to talk farmers into letting them metal-detect on their land, which they had done as a hobby since the 1970s. The farmer they wanted to visit wasn't in, however, so they had given up for the day. Heading north of Torksey village towards Marton, they spotted that one of the fields between the road and the river was being ploughed. They stopped and spoke to the tractor driver; he turned out to be the landowner, so they asked him if they could go on the field with their detectors for a couple of hours. The ground was very sandy but the ploughing had left it full of air pockets so conditions were far from ideal, and for several hours they found almost nothing. Dusk was falling so they decided to go home, but just as they were leaving Pete got a signal. It was a tiny copper-alloy coin. Pete thought it was Roman but then Dave identified it as a Northumbrian styca, quite a rare find for rural Lincolnshire. Their interest was heightened. They came back to the site repeatedly and over the next 25 years recovered an amazing quantity of Anglo-Saxon and Viking finds [pl. 9–11], including many more stycas – so many that they christened one field 'styca alley'.

Dave and Pete reported their finds to Rachel Atherton at Derby Museum. Rachel was a Finds Liaison Officer (FLO) for the Portable Antiquities Scheme (PAS), a national voluntary recording scheme for archaeological finds made by members of the public. A network of some 36 FLOs, generally based in local museums and county council offices, identify finds (predominantly made by metal-detectorists) and record them on a searchable online database, which now catalogues nearly 1.5 million objects.[2] The Stanleys' finds were out of the ordinary, however, as they included silver Anglo-Saxon pennies, and also tiny fragments of Islamic dirhams [pl. 11]. Rachel put them in touch with Mark Blackburn, Keeper of Coins and Medals at the Fitzwilliam Museum in Cambridge. Mark was a Viking coin expert and he recognized the importance of the finds coming from Torksey, arranging to purchase many of them for the museum's collection. In a paper published in 2002, Mark highlighted the concentration of 9th-century coins, which implied 'a period of exceptional activity at Torksey', and he linked the finds, which then included eleven dirhams, as well as hackmetal, ingots and copper-alloy weights, with the Viking overwintering of 872–73, although the precise location from which the material was coming was unknown to him.[3]

Mark had collaborated with Julian on a previous project using PAS data and encouraged us to investigate the site archaeologically. Meanwhile Dawn had excavated in Lincolnshire for many years and was interested in the origins of the Saxon town at Torksey

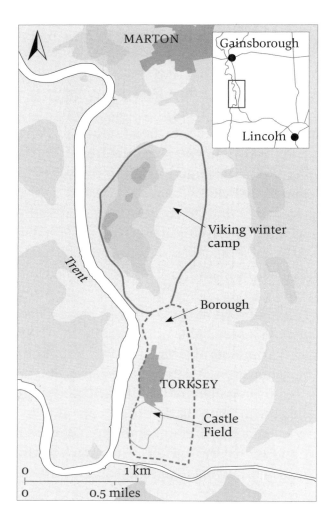

Location plan showing the approximate outlines of the Viking winter camp and the Anglo-Saxon town at Torksey.

and its pottery industry. She and Julian had worked together on a Viking book project ten years earlier and one wet and windy evening in late 2009 they decided to collaborate again to investigate Torksey, and set about bringing together an interdisciplinary team. Tragically Mark Blackburn died of cancer in September 2011, aged 58, the same year as our work at Torksey began. However, his legacy was taken up by his PhD student, Andrew Woods, now a senior curator at the Yorkshire Museum, and a key member of our team, and Andrew put us in touch with the Stanley brothers.

The distribution of finds from our metal-detector survey of the winter camp at Torksey.

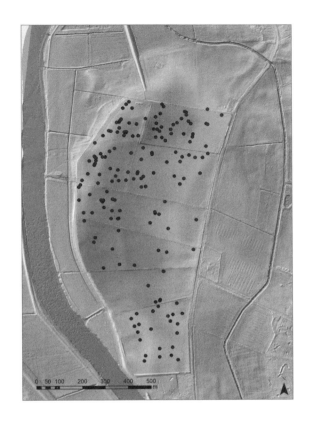

Several thousand pieces of early medieval metalwork and coins have now been recovered from six fields to the north of the modern village of Torksey, *c.* 14 km (8.5 miles) north-west of Lincoln. To set this exceptional metal-detected assemblage in context, we have carried out an archaeological investigation, employing a variety of techniques including geophysical survey, fieldwalking, environmental analysis and small-scale excavation. The two landowners have been hugely supportive and have allowed us access to the site to conduct a wide range of fieldwork. We have also equipped the detectorists with mobile GPS, so that they can record the exact position of all their finds. Taken together this work has demonstrated that these fields were indeed the site of the Viking winter camp of 872–73 and that it was enormous: *c.* 55 ha (136 acres), the size of some 75 football pitches.[4]

When the Great Army fleet sailed up the Trent in the autumn of 872 the choice of location for their camp was not simply chance. The site lies at a strategically important junction in the regional transport network. It is just 2 km (1.25 miles) south of a major crossing point over the river, from which the prehistoric trackway and Roman road now known as Till Bridge Lane ran south-east to join Ermine Street just north of Lincoln. On the other side of the Trent Till Bridge Lane proceeds north-west to former Roman sites at Bawtry and Doncaster, then swings north through Castleford to Tadcaster and finally north-east to York. For travel by water, the Trent would have provided access from Torksey to the Humber Estuary and thence to York or the North Sea, or upstream into the Midlands.[5] This location not only facilitated movement of the Army by road or river between Mercia and Northumbria, but also allowed control over other travellers passing through the area. It is also possible that waterborne access into Lindsey was controlled from Torksey, which was on its western boundary. Torskey is also adjacent to the Foss Dyke, a canal of probable Roman construction, which connects the Trent to Lincoln. Although we cannot be certain that it was navigable in the 9th century, in the following century the transportation to Lincoln of pottery produced at Torksey suggests that the canal was open by at least the 10th century.[6]

The route of the modern River Trent does not necessarily correspond with its early medieval course. It is likely that climatic deterioration from the 4th to 10th centuries led to an unstable river system, prone to flooding, with semi-permanent wetlands across the wider valley floor, interspersed with areas of raised ground formed by sand and gravel islands. To understand what Torksey was like in 872 when the Great Army arrived, we needed to understand this landscape. Dawn recruited a PhD student, Samantha Stein – now a scientific advisor for Historic England – to undertake a programme of coring. Her work showed that the present landscape is completely unlike that of the late 9th century. To the east of the winter camp there had been an old channel of the Trent up until the Bronze Age, when radiocarbon dating indicated that silting cut it off from the main river, and peat deposits began to form.[7] Without an active channel, and with water levels averaging 1–2 m (3–6.5 ft) higher than they are today, the low ground east of the camp would have remained a wetland, allowing peat to accumulate into the early medieval period. Sediment mapping to the north and south of the site revealed not peat but silt, suggesting that these areas were periodically inundated by the Trent, as naturally occurring seasonal tidal ports with gently sloping sand banks leading up to the higher ground of the winter camp. These sand banks provided a perfect place to beach a fleet of longships, with the dry land above them suitable for camping. The area to the north of the site would have flooded regularly with the tidal influx of the Trent, as it continues to do to the present day when the Trent is in flood. Indeed, the place-name for the nearby village of Marton comes from the Old English *mere-tun*, meaning 'pool farm', probably derived from its position on the Trent floodplain.[8] Modern land management, including the digging of drainage channels and the installation of a pump house at Marton in the 19th century, has had a significant impact on the landscape, so geoarchaeological analysis was essential in determining the landscape setting of the winter camp.[9]

In the winter of 872–73, the site of the Viking camp was effectively on an island, bounded to the west by the Trent and surrounded by wet and marshy ground. A prominent bluff, 5–10 m (15–30 ft) high, overlooked the floodplain, gradually becoming less pronounced towards its northern end, sloping gently down to the east and north-east. Although the highest point is only *c.* 10 m (30 ft) higher than the modern village, this is a significant difference in the context of the surrounding landscape. The vantage point offered by the elevated location, combined with access to the Trent, must have made it particularly attractive to the Great Army. Indeed, the clue was always there in the Old English place-name which incorporates a personal name, probably *Turoc* or *Turc*, with *eg* (meaning an island, or dry ground in a wet area).[10] This was Turoc's or Turc's Island.

Looking east across the River Trent to the prominent bluff that was the location of the winter camp at Torksey.

In the winter of 872–73, the site of the Viking camp at Torksey was effectively an island, bounded to the west by the River Trent and surrounded by wet and marshy ground. Sediment mapping south [1] and north [4] of the site revealed river silts, suggesting that these areas remained open to the Trent; low ground east of the camp was a peaty wetland [2]; and sandy dunes provided high points in the landscape [3].

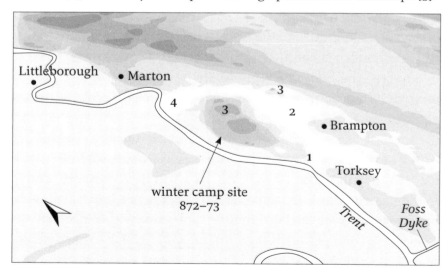

Our next step was to use geophysics to see if we could identify any structures or defensive features. Our geophysicist, Hannah Brown, took time off from working for Wessex Archaeology to undertake a magnetometer survey comprising two transects 60 m (65 yds) wide, which traversed the site north–south and west–east, but she found no evidence of a defensive ditch. As we compared her findings with Samantha's, we realized that the Viking camp would have had little need of a ditch with a river on one side, a marsh on all other sides, and a big army inside it. Hannah found the most striking archaeological anomalies in the centre of the transect, where her plot showed a number of rectangular enclosures towards the northern end of the ridge of high ground that forms the 'island' on which the winter camp was based. But these enclosures were not Viking, and excavation confirmed that this area was a Romano-British settlement, incorporating ditched fields, drove-ways and pits, some containing metalworking waste (but only Roman finds). Indeed, the Viking Great Army was invisible in our extensive geophysics survey. Where were they?

The answer, again, came from Samantha's coring programme, which found considerable build-ups of windblown sand blanketing most of the camp to a depth of up to 3–4 m (10–13 ft). Tree clearance, accelerated by the establishment of the Roman farmstead, had created an unstable sand dune landscape. Even today farmers are reluctant to plough their fields until they are ready to plant the next crop, in case a strong wind spreads their ploughsoil across the A156. The deposits of windblown sand have obscured detection of archaeology which, under better conditions, should have been visible in the magnetometer survey. Such deep sand deposits may, however, have ensured the survival of Viking layers intact beneath the reach of the plough. Indeed, one of our test excavations, intended to assess a line of anomalies identified in the magnetometer survey, revealed that silty sand extended to a depth of 2 m (6.5 ft) below the modern ground surface, with a gaming piece, fishing weight and buckle found at a depth of more than 0.5 m (1.6 ft).

We have so far failed to identify any features such as ditches or buildings in Torksey that we can definitely link with the winter camp – and we should probably question what, over a thousand years later, would remain of a temporary settlement of tents anyway. Nonetheless, the windblown sand contains one of the richest assemblages of early medieval finds discovered in the British Isles. This became well known, and in the early years the Stanley brothers were not the only detectorists who were allowed to search these fields. We estimate that over the last 20 years some 70 metal-detectorists have been working the site of the winter camp. The majority of their finds are still in private collections, although some have been sold online. Many have, however, been logged by the PAS and, given the wide area from which the detectorists have been drawn to Torksey, objects have been reported to a number of FLOs, including those in Sheffield, Derby, Lincoln, Scunthorpe and York. Over the last ten years we have worked with Andrew Woods to continue Mark Blackburn's task of cataloguing and studying all the finds.

It is the metalwork, and specifically the coinage, which allows the assemblage to be dated so precisely and confirms Torksey as the site of the Viking winter camp of 872–73. Over 400 early medieval coins have been recovered, including 40 English silver pennies, with a notable concentration from the 860s and early 870s. This is striking given that on more 'normal' Anglo-Saxon sites coin finds of the early 9th century are generally more prolific than those of the middle and later parts of the century.[11] The English silver coins have an end date in the early 870s, and they are likely to have been lost close to their date of production, as there is no evidence for pecking or nicking, a phenomenon that, in England, seems to have emerged later.

Remarkably, over 200 Northumbrian copper-alloy stycas have been found at Torksey. These coins did not circulate widely outside of Northumbria, and are generally only recovered in Lincolnshire as single finds.[12] Most of them were struck in the 840s, particularly

1 *PREVIOUS PAGE* Viking longship, the *Sea Stallion from Glendalough*, reconstructed by the Roskilde Ship Museum, Denmark. The reconstruction was based on a 30 m warship known as *Skuldelev 2* which had been built in the Dublin area in the mid-11th century. It was one of five vessels deliberately sunk in an attempt to block the Roskilde fjord from an attacking force.

2 *BELOW* Artist's reconstruction of the early trading centre at Ribe, Denmark, in the early 8th century. Excavations have revealed a network of regular plots, separated by shallow ditches. The plots were laid out when the first merchants arrived, and have been taken as direct evidence for royal patronage and organization.

3 9th-century Viking hoard, from Westerklief on what was the island of Wieringen in the Netherlands, including silver arm- and neck-rings, 3 brooches made from coins, 17 silver ingots and 78 Carolingian pennies. The hoard had been buried in a pottery vessel made in Badorf, near Cologne, Germany.

4 The landing of the Viking Great Army in East Anglia in AD 865, in an illustration inspired by Abbo of Fleury's *Passio Sancti Edmundi* for a manuscript containing texts about St Edmund, king of East Anglia, made *c.* 1130 in Bury St Edmunds (New York, Morgan Library, MS M. 736, fol. 9v).

5 The martyrdom of St Edmund, as illustrated *c.* 1130 in MS M. 736, fol. 14r. The scene shows the Anglo-Saxon king tied to a tree and shot with arrows by members of the Viking Great Army. He looks up at the hand of God reaching towards him in a gesture of blessing, signifying that he is about to become a saint.

6 The 8th-century Stockholm *Codex Aureus* (Stockholm, National Library of Sweden, MS A. 135), also known as the *Codex Aureus* of Canterbury. Marginal notes were added by Ealdorman Ælfred in the 9th century, indicating that it had been bought by him and his wife Werburg from the 'army of heathens', and donated to Christ Church, Canterbury.

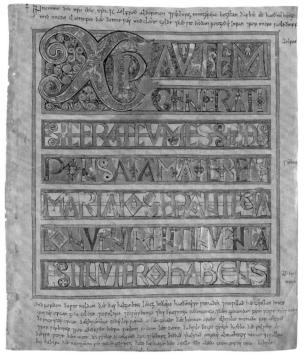

7, **8** Artist's reconstructions of the Viking Great Army winter camp at Torksey, Lincolnshire, 872–73. The aerial view of the camp is from the north-west, with the floodplain of the River Trent to the lower left of the scene, below the embankment.

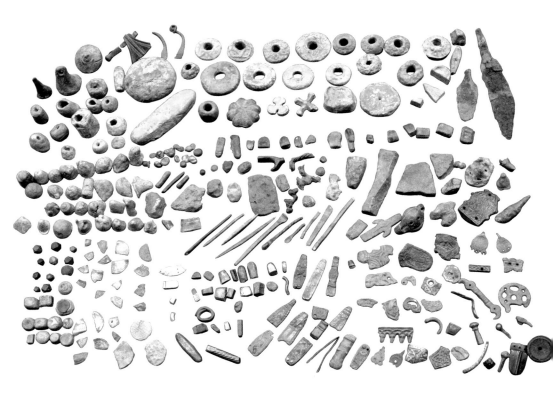

9, 10, 11 *ABOVE* Selection of metal-detected finds from the Viking Great Army winter camp at Torksey. *BELOW LEFT* Broken and cut pieces of scrap copper-alloy metalwork. *BELOW RIGHT* Fragments of Islamic dirhams and a piece of silver arm-ring.

during the reign of Æthelred II of Northumbria (r. 840–44, 844–48). There are also eleven late stycas of Osberht (killed in York in 867), dating towards the final days of the kingdom of Northumbria. The concentration of stycas at Torksey suggests that these coins had remained in circulation, and had been brought there directly from Northumbria, from where the Great Army had retired to Torksey.[13]

One of the most striking discoveries from Torksey are the 144 silver dirhams, the largest concentration on any site in the British Isles. These coins had been cut into smaller fractions, indicating that they had been kept for their silver content as bullion, rather than for their monetary face value.[14] Dirhams were minted across the Middle East and Central Asia, in what is now Iran and Iraq, and even as far away as Samarkand in Uzbekistan. They must have been brought to England all the way from the silk and slave markets of Asia and Arabia, although they had probably travelled via Scandinavia, as concentrations of dirhams have been found at Scandinavian trading centres such as Birka and Kaupang.[15] Large numbers of dirhams were flowing into the Baltic in the 860s and 870s, and their date range is similar to those from Torksey, although the sudden break in the late 860s at Torksey is not reflected at the Scandinavian trading sites, which continued to receive dirhams into the mid-10th century.[16] A similar span of dates to that at Torksey, comprising both relatively recent and considerably older coins, occurs when dirhams are found in hoards in England.[17] Significantly, the latest dirhams from Torksey have a *terminus post quem* in the late 860s, postdating the arrival of the Great Army in England. This demonstrates that there was continuing contact with Scandinavia during the years of campaigning, either from reinforcements, or merchants joining the army. Allowing for the time it would have taken for the dirhams to reach England, they appear to indicate a depositional date remarkably similar to that of the English silver coins in the early 870s. It is astonishing how rapidly these tiny pieces of silver travelled along the Viking trade routes, at least *c.* 3,000 km (*c.* 1,900 miles) in some five years. In summary, it is clear that the

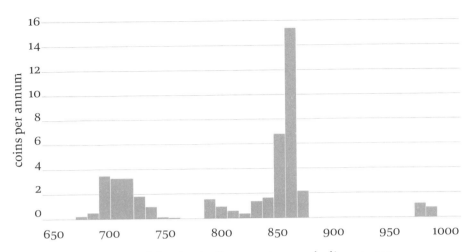

The age structure of the Anglo-Saxon coins, excluding stycas, found at Torksey.

Two Northumbrian copper-alloy stycas found at Torksey (obverse and reverse views of each).

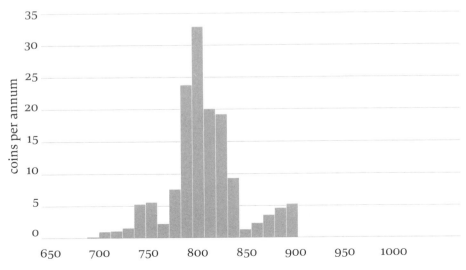

The age structure of the dirhams found at Torksey.

early medieval coins can only have been brought to the site by the Great Army, given the combination of silver coins of the 860s and early 870s, dirhams used as bullion and the exceptional concentration of stycas outside of Northumbria.

A handful of 7th- and 8th-century Anglo-Saxon finds and a few late 10th-century dress accessories have been recovered from the same fields, but in insufficient amounts to suggest significant earlier or later settlement, if any. Fourteen late 7th- to early 8th-century sceattas (silver pennies) have been found, but this is a far smaller assemblage than is generally associated with Anglo-Saxon trading sites. It is clear, then, that the exceptional assemblage of finds from Torksey largely represents a single year of activity, which may be linked exactly to the overwintering of 872–73 recorded in the *Anglo-Saxon Chronicle*.

At first sight the amount of metalwork recovered from the camp seems remarkably large to have come from only a single overwintering, yet it is clear that in certain circumstances single events can lead to massive accumulations of material. The detritus left by more recent armies, or even by modern music festival campsites, reminds us of how easy it is to mislay items in muddy and trampled fields. The fact that even gold and silver objects were not recovered at the time indicates the sheer quantities of portable wealth that must have been accumulated by the Army. The assemblage is invaluable in showing what a Viking army did while it was overwintering, including trade and exchange, coin production, and metal processing, as well as its leisure activities.

We should not be surprised that the Great Army was trading while camped at Torksey. As we saw in Chapter 2, continental texts provide examples of Viking armies doing the same in Frankia. It is apparent, however, that there were several types of exchange operating alongside one another in the camp. Bullion clearly played an important role in exchanges by weight, even for relatively small transactions. Although dirhams begin life in the Arab world as complete coins, by the time they reach a field in Lincolnshire they are largely fragmented. Sixty pieces of hacksilver have been recovered, including whole and fragmentary silver ingots, which were probably also being used in trading, along with fragmentary Anglo-Saxon, Irish and Scandinavian decorative silver jewellery.[18]

Fifteen pieces of hackgold, which are very unusual finds, have been recovered at Torksey. Several pieces had been chisel-cut from gold ingots; one twisted piece may have been cut from an arm- or neck-ring. This is an important insight into Viking activity, because, unlike hacksilver and silver ingots, gold in any form rarely occurs in Viking Age hoards in Britain. However, the remarkable concentration of gold finds from Torksey suggests the melting down of church treasures and trading in gold. It also appears to have been worth going to some effort to try to pass off base metal as gold, as fake hackgold has also been found, in the form of gold-plated copper alloy, including a fragment of an ingot and two sections cut from square rods. Clearly some members of the Army were not above trying to swindle their trading partners. Three Frisian imitations of gold coins, or solidi, of Louis the Pious may also have been bullion, although one is a poor forgery, again with gold plate disguising a copper-alloy core.

Copper-alloy artefacts were also being melted down and turned into ingots. There are seventeen copper-alloy ingots from Torksey, one of which has the same sort of hammering often visible on silver ingots. These ingots may have resulted from the melting down of scrap jewellery, and we have recovered over 200 fragmentary copper-alloy artefacts, many deliberately cut, suggesting they were to be melted down. There is also something unusual about the range of such finds. Most Anglo-Saxon sites that have been metal-detected yield a roughly equal proportion of dress pins and strap-ends. Both are types of costume jewellery: the former are generally seen as adornments or fastenings for clothing such as cloaks; the latter were attached to the ends of belts or straps. At Torksey, however, there are relatively few pins, suggesting that the strap-ends, with their higher metallic weight, were being deliberately collected, probably

Selection of weights from Torksey, including examples of
cubo-octahedral, truncated spheroid and lead-inset types.

to be melted into ingots. While it is possible that the copper-alloy
ingots found at Torksey were being used in metalworking, there
is some evidence for the economic use of copper alloy in bullion-
based exchange, and copper-alloy ingots are increasingly being
found across eastern England.[19] Copper-alloy ingots have been found
more broadly across the Viking world in several hoards, such as
one from Spillings on Gotland in Sweden which has an earliest
possible date of 874.[20]

Fragments of lead, silver and gold indicate an extensive range
of metal processing and metalworking in the camp. Metalworkers
travelling with the Army were melting down and processing the
loot that had been acquired during the previous year, turning it
into bullion or new objects. Three strips of lead on which decorative
punches had been tested indicate the production of Scandinavian
silver jewellery, such as arm-rings. A fragment of a lead die could
have been used to impress decoration onto gold foil which was to
be applied to other objects.[21] Another piece of lead was a casting
for a strap-end.

A bullion economy required the weighing of the metal, and over
350 weights have been recorded. Nearly 100 of these are distinctive copper-alloy cubo-octahedral weights, shaped like cubes with
clipped corners. Each surface has a number of tiny rings with a dot
in the centre, and they look remarkably like polyhedral dice, but

the number of dots is assumed to indicate the weight. Our analysis has not identified any consistent weight standards, although the composite nature of the Army may account for this diversity, as many partial sets of weights must be represented. The design of these weights may have been copied from those used by Arab traders, and similar examples appear in considerable numbers on Scandinavian sites from the 860s and 870s. There is also some evidence, from Birka and the Swedish island of Gotland, that these weights were being manufactured there.[22] Nearly 250 lead weights have been recovered. The majority are plain cubes, domes or ovals but 37 are inset with pieces of copper-alloy metalwork, largely fragments of jewellery or strap-ends of English or Irish origin. These would have made it easier for their owners to identify them, and these inset weights appear to be an innovation in the operation of the metal-weight economy in the winter camps. Their production also provides another example of manufacturing during the earliest phases of Scandinavian settlement.

The sheer scale of the precious and base metalwork from Torksey does not, in and of itself, demonstrate the nature or extent of economic transactions undertaken there, which are likely to have been diverse. The distribution of precious metals was undoubtedly one way that Viking leaders maintained their status and secured the loyalty of their followers. While the imported dirhams show extensive fragmentation, this is not true of the Anglo-Saxon coins, which must reflect their use within a monetary economy, not simply as bullion. The use of bullion alongside a managed currency has been dubbed a 'dual economy'. It had previously been assumed that this did not come into place until coins began to be minted for Scandinavian rulers from the 880s/890s until the 920s, but it now appears that it existed from the very outset of Viking settlement in England.[23] The picture that emerges from Torksey, however, suggests not a 'dual economy' proper, but multiple metal economies operating simultaneously, with gold, silver and copper alloy all used in both coined and bullion form.

It also appears that the Great Army began minting coins itself during its campaigns. A strip of lead from Torksey bearing the impression of the die for a gold coin, a solidus of Louis the Pious, supports the theory that gold imitation solidi were being minted by Vikings in the region, since a number of these forgeries have been found in eastern England.[24] They seem intended to have been used as coins, not pendants, since there is no evidence of suspension loops. A lead impression of a lunette coin of Burgred of Mercia from Torksey also suggests minting; it bears what numismatists describe as a blundered inscription, as do almost a quarter of the stycas. In a blundered inscription the lettering imitates the style used on the standard coins, but the letters themselves are nonsensical, as if copied by someone who is illiterate, suggesting that these were Viking imitations. If the Vikings were trying to copy stycas it reinforces the idea that the stycas brought to Torksey by members of the Great Army were being used by them in monetary exchange, not simply as a source of base metal. A plated copper-alloy lunette was also evidently a forgery, and one of the dirhams appears to have a green patina, again suggesting a contemporary forgery. Once they had seized control of the Anglo-Saxon kingdoms, Viking rulers such as Guthrum began to mint coins. However, the lead impressions of dies and blundered stycas from Torksey suggest that the minting of coinage had emerged earlier, during the overwintering phase, even before the Viking leaders had adopted

Evidence of coin and metal production at Torksey. *LEFT* Lead bearing the impression of lunette type A coin of Burgred of Mercia. *CENTRE* Lead trial piece for triangular punches. *RIGHT* Lead striking from dies of a lunette type A coin.

the administrative apparatus of Anglo-Saxon kingship. To a Viking army used to dealing in bullion, coins were not necessary for economic transactions, but their minting of imitations suggests that they understood the political value of coinage, and the locals may have been more willing to accept familiar-looking coins. The Army may have been minting coinage for a variety of reasons: to use it locally for buying supplies, to display the political aspirations of Army leaders and to establish their authority within the Anglo-Saxon kingdoms, and also as a way for rival Viking leaders to assert their individual authority.

It is unlikely that the Great Army acquired the wealth that is reflected in the finds from Torksey solely through raiding and plunder. Tribute-taking may have been an element of the peace treaties that the Great Army is repeatedly recorded as making with local Anglo-Saxon leaders during overwintering. Furthermore, leases of land from ecclesiastics are known to have occurred in the late 9th century as a means of raising tribute to pay Viking armies.[25] Slave trading may have been another means of acquiring wealth, and may ultimately be the origins of the dirhams from the Middle East. Irish and continental sources record the capture and sale of slaves by Viking armies in Ireland and Frankia, and while this is not directly documented in contemporary sources in England, it must have occurred; indeed, a peace treaty between Alfred and Guthrum from the 880s contains a clause in which the rulers agreed not to harbour the runaway slaves from the other's realm.[26] Slaves may also have been used in the Great Army camp for labour or to provide sexual services. The ransoming of hostages may have been another method by which the Army accumulated wealth, and hostages were also politically useful: following the arrival of the Great Army at Repton, the new ruler of Mercia, Ceolwulf, gave hostages and swore oaths that he would be ready 'at the enemy's service' whenever required. The details of the peace agreement between the Army and the Mercians at Torksey are not provided in the *Anglo-Saxon Chronicle*, but it may have included similar arrangements.

Clench nail from Torksey:
evidence of ship repair.

In the early stages of our project we had more gold than iron objects from Torksey. Metal-detectorists often set their machines to discriminate against ferrous metals, to avoid spending most of their time picking up bits of farm machinery and other rubbish. To prevent this selective distortion of the picture at Torksey, we persuaded the metal-detectorists to start picking up iron objects, no matter how mundane, and since then we have begun to see evidence for a range of other activities in the camp. Weaponry are obvious finds, including sword hilts, guards and pommels, battle-axes, spear-heads and arrowheads. We have large numbers of iron nails, which are ubiquitous finds on most archaeological sites, but several distinctive clench nails have been recorded. It is very likely that ships were drawn up onto the floodplain below the camp for repair over the winter. A hoard of iron woodworking tools, including four axe-heads, an axe hammer, an adze and a two-edged blade shows what they were using, although the tools are of Anglo-Saxon type, and reveal the use of local equipment, if not labour. A separate discovery of an iron bark-stripper indicates the preparation of felled trees as replacement planks for a longship. It may even have been used in the first stage in the production of tar, essential for waterproofing ships; in Scandinavia tar would have been made from pine, but here they may have used birch, which is common in areas of well-draining sandy environments such as Torksey.[27] The felling of trees is also supported by our environmental evidence for landscape clearance, which was probably the decisive factor in the creation of a large sand dune, up to 4.5 m (15 ft) in depth, to the east of the site in the years after the overwintering. We also have many hooks, and several pieces of chain, of a type used for suspending

Selection of lead spindle whorls from Torksey.

a cauldron of stew or soup above a campfire. The ironwork hoard contained fifteen fragments representing several iron cauldrons, and two tripod stands. Spindle whorls, needles, punches and awls suggest textile-working, presumably including the repair of sails, tents and clothing.

Some of the most interesting finds are also the most mundane. We have now recorded over 300 conical pieces of lead, no more than 2–3 cm (1 inch) in height. They were crudely manufactured; some had been cast, but others appear to have been cut from fragments of lead sheet, pressed into shape. The majority are hollowed; some have little spikes on the top, like crowns. The Vikings were avid board-game players and a favourite game seems to have been one of strategy, referred to in Norse sagas as *hnefatafl*. Clearly the pieces of lead at Torksey were gaming pieces. Although the rules are now lost it seems that *hnefatafl* was played on a chequered board of 13 × 13 or 11 × 11 squares. The defender had a smaller number of pieces, which he used to defend his king, or *hnefi* (presumably the crowned gaming piece), while the attacker attempted to surround and capture the king with his larger army. Maybe the Vikings preferred the odds to be uneven. The sheer number and variety of lead gaming pieces from Torksey shows that many warriors must have had their own gaming sets, but that these were also disposable items, made for the occasion. Indeed, given that none have been reported from sites known to have been visited by the Army prior to Torksey, might they first have been made here? Lead stripped from the Roman villa, or acquired from local churches, could have provided a ready source of easily worked material from which to manufacture cruder versions of the glass, antler or bone gaming pieces known from high-status burials in Scandinavia.[28] The association of gaming pieces in these burials with weapons, horses and sometimes ships reveals that gaming was regarded as a characteristic pastime of elite men who were skilled in strategy as well as in warfare. It has been suggested that they reflect a belief that success in battle was not merely a product of military might but also of intelligence and an ability to predict the actions of your opponents. We can envisage long winter evenings spent

Selection of lead gaming pieces from Torksey.

sitting around the camp-fire, reliving past battles, plotting tactics for forthcoming encounters, and gambling looted treasure on the outcome of board games.

The winter camp at Torksey was occupied not only by warriors, but also by merchants and craftworkers. It is also very likely that both women and children were present, and not only as slaves. While no oval brooches typical of female Scandinavian dress have been recovered, and the other items of jewellery and dress accessories found cannot be confidently assigned to a specific gender, the textile-working equipment from Torksey may reflect a female presence in the camp. Elsewhere, textile-working spindle whorls, needles and needle cases, linen smoothers and shears are overwhelmingly found in female graves.

While there are no references to women and children in accounts of the Great Army in the *Anglo-Saxon Chronicle*, women and children are certainly recorded as accompanying Viking armies in contemporary continental sources. Regino of Prüm, writing in the early 10th century, recounts the arrival of a Viking army at the deserted town of Angers in the Loire valley, where the raiders based themselves in 873 'with their wives and children'; the late 9th-century Latin poem *Bella Parisiacae Urbis* mentions the presence of women alongside the Viking army that besieged Paris in 885 and 887.[29] Entries in the *Anglo-Saxon Chronicle* that refer to an army raiding in the 890s also reveal their presence. In 893 the Viking fortress at Benfleet, Essex, was captured by an English force, which 'seized everything inside it, both property and women and also children', while in 895 the army 'placed their women in safety in East Anglia'.[30] Given how long the Great Army was moving around England, many children were doubtless born and raised on the move. As we will see later, offspring of members of the Army proved very useful during the process of settlement and acculturation in England.

The presence of Anglo-Saxon slaves and hostages, and perhaps even allies, acquired by the Viking Great Army during their campaigns, may explain some of the Anglo-Saxon dress accessories and jewellery recovered from Torksey. These artefacts were almost exclusively Anglo-Saxon in origin, and include 136 copper-alloy strap-ends, the majority decorated in the distinctive late 9th-century Trewhiddle style, which takes its name from the hoard discussed in Chapter 3. There were also many garment hooks, also known as hooked tags, which are assumed to have been used by the English for fastening clothing, possibly leggings. However, it is also possible that Anglo-Saxon material culture was being acquired and used by Scandinavians even before they began to settle permanently in England. Indeed, a disc brooch of the flat Anglo-Saxon form decorated in the Scandinavian Borre style may suggest the presence of local metalworkers producing dress accessories to meet the tastes of the raiders. Furthermore, the presence in the camp of metalwork from Ireland and Frankia may reveal something of the diverse places to which members of the Great Army had previously travelled, and the people, cultures and economic systems they had encountered.

Members of the Great Army also died during the overwintering, whether from battle wounds or natural causes, and we have recovered fragmentary human remains from two areas within the camp, perhaps reflecting separate burial grounds for different elements within this large force. Both were on higher ground, but our excavation revealed that modern ploughing had removed all traces of the graves, although two samples were radiocarbon-dated to the late 9th century.[31] Unfortunately, the remains were so fragmentary that in her analysis of them the project osteologist, Lizzy Craig-Atkins, could confidently identify a minimum number of only two adults, both probably male, aged 18–25 and 25–35 years respectively. A skull fragment showed evidence of two separate blows from a sharp implement, suggesting a violent and probably fatal encounter.

The evidence from Torksey has considerable implications for our understanding of the size of the Viking Great Army. Although not all of the 55 ha (136 acre) site is likely to have been as densely occupied as a later town, the scale of the camp is striking given that the estimated sizes for the four major urban places known in Scandinavia are considerably smaller, even at their maximum extent in the 10th century: Birka *c.* 6 ha; Kaupang, *c.* 5.4 ha; Ribe, *c.* 12 ha; and Hedeby, *c.* 24 ha.[32] Given the large size of the camp it is clear that the Great Army and its followers comprised thousands of people. Neil Price notes that Roman army manuals suggest a maximum occupancy of marching camps of 740 men per hectare. This would allow a force of up to 40,700 to be camped at Torksey, but both Price and Gareth Williams observe that Viking camps are unlikely to have been as densely occupied as Roman camps and Williams suggests that 10 per cent of that figure is more realistic, giving a force of *c.* 4,000.[33] We can never know exact numbers camped at Torksey, but if a fleet comprised 50–100 longships, and each ship had a crew of 30–50 warriors, then an army within the range of 1,500–5,000 is not implausible, and could easily have been accommodated on the island at Torksey. The references in the *Anglo-Saxon Chronicle* to fleets of several hundred ships may not have been exaggerations after all.

A settlement on this scale, even a temporary one, would have required a high degree of organization. The camp may have had separate zones for the distinct groups that made up the Army. The Viking raiders on the River Seine in the early 860s (see Chapter 3) divided up into their 'brotherhoods' when they left, providing a rare insight into the composition of armies which we can assume was also relevant when they set up a camp. In doing so there would also have been a need to separate industrial, food processing and trading activities, and to have distinct areas for living and for burial. Streets must have developed within the camp, and it would have been important to know where to go to get a sword repaired or sharpened, and where to get a loaf of bread or some ale. The Trent would have provided water for drinking and washing, but this would also have required the regulation of the areas used as latrines, to avoid the risk of spreading dysentery or cholera. At sea, the Viking longship was the important unit of organization. It was vital that every member of the crew knew his place. These men may well have grown up together as, according to later Scandinavian sources, the ships' crews were recruited from the same local areas and therefore maintained allegiance to their local leader in the Scandinavian homeland.[34] It is likely that the same close-knit unit fought together in battle, too, and when the Army camped it would have made sense to organize things along the same lines, with each ship's company responsible for its own provisioning. The leaders of the Great Army were not just fearsome warriors but they, and their ships' captains, also evidently had to act as early town planners.

It would have been a major challenge to provision an Army of several thousand people during the winter, and potential access to the food renders (or tax in kind) that were collected by major estate centres in England, including churches, may have been another key factor in choosing where to overwinter. Food and other resources may have been offered by local residents as part of the frequent peace settlements made when the Army overwintered, as is recorded in Frankia in the 860s.[35] Anglo-Saxon law codes reveal that food renders for the king were expected from large estates. For example, the late 7th-century code of Ine of Wessex, which was appended to Alfred's law code in the late 9th century, specifies that an estate of 10 hides owed the king a food rent comprising 10 vats of honey, 300 loaves, 12 ambers (each of which would have comprised 32 gallons) of Welsh ale, 30 ambers of clear ale, two full-grown cows or 10 wethers, 10 geese, 20 hens, 10 cheeses, 1 amber of butter, 5 salmon, 20 pounds of fodder and 100 eels.[36] There are several major churches (where similarly large stores of food might have been gathered) in the vicinity of Torksey, which may be another reason why it was chosen as a base for the Army. Stow, just 4 km (2.5 miles) to the north-east, was an episcopal possession in the 11th century and possibly an endowment of the bishopric of Lindsey from the 950s, and while we have no earlier evidence its status is consistent with that of other major churches founded in the 8th or

9th centuries.[37] Across the Trent from Torksey at South Leverton in Nottinghamshire is a church with more secure early origins where fragments of late 8th- or early 9th-century sculpture have recently been recovered; a piece of a gold ingot has been discovered nearby reflecting a visit by the Army.[38] We can assume that these wealthy minster churches were not only sources of church plate but also collecting points for grain, as well as salted fish and meat, which were stored overwinter to feed the monks.

Even with churches and estates in the vicinity to raid for food, feeding many thousand people for several months in the camp would have been a major undertaking. Animals could be rounded up from nearby farms and slaughtered for meat, but others were probably reared within the camp, including pigs and hens, which would have provided welcome dietary supplements of fresh meat and eggs. The Trent itself was an additional food source, as demonstrated by the metal-detected discovery of lead fishing weights. The hinterland of the camp likewise provided other essential natural resources, including peat and wood as fuel for the campfires, although the best timber would have been reserved for the repair of the longships. South and east of the camp are natural sources of clay that could have been used for the manufacture of moulds and hearths for metal casting and smithying. These resources may have been acquired by a combination of foraging, of the type that Asser says occurred during the overwintering at Reading, and purchase, which some of the coinage and bullion may have facilitated. Clearly the Army must have reached some form of accommodation with the local population, albeit an enforced arrangement. No doubt the sudden arrival of a settlement the size of a small town must have had a major impact on the surrounding community.[39]

In summary, our work at Torksey has revealed not only the location of the Viking winter camp, but something of its character as well. The sheer quantity and value of the metalwork assemblage forces a radical reappraisal of the amount of wealth that was amassed by the Viking Great Army. Plunder was being processed on a massive scale. There was intensive trade and exchange, both within the camp and with those outside it, in goods and probably also in slaves. The evidence from Torksey suggests a hybrid economy with monetary as well as bullion transactions, and the minting of coins, reflecting the multiple economic systems that co-existed during the Viking Age. Torksey also forces us to reassess our interpretation of the size of the winter camps, and of the Great Army that occupied them. The unusually high concentration of people in the winter camps, as revealed by our work at Torksey, may have given many of the members of the Viking armies their first experience of urban living. Other urban features in the winter camps included a range of industries: the processing of precious metals; smithying and other metalworking; and textile-working. Although pottery manufacture was not undertaken in the camp, the Torksey ware industry appeared soon after the Army departed and, as we shall reveal in Chapter 9, may have developed as a direct result of its overwintering.

Where does the discovery at Torksey leave the only previously excavated Great Army camp at Repton, which served as the prototype for Viking encampments for a generation? The range and richness of the finds recovered from Torksey certainly shows what was missing at Repton, perhaps hidden under the later village where it could not be discovered by metal-detecting. Furthermore, the scale of the camp at Torksey (55 ha compared to only 0.4 ha within the D-shaped enclosure at Repton), and the lack of any enclosure or fortifications, must cast doubt upon the interpretation of Repton as the typical Viking winter camp, at least as representing the full extent of a Great Army camp site housing thousands of warriors, craftworkers, raiders, women and children.

Although we await full publication of the Biddles' 1974–88 excavations, it is worth rehearsing what the evidence for the ditch at Repton entailed, particularly as its sharp V-shaped profile and

4 m depth make it unlike anything found anywhere else in the 9th-century Viking world, and more in keeping with later medieval castle defences. Indeed, the interim publication of Repton in the proceedings of the 1997 Viking Congress illustrates a complex sequence of earthworks beneath the present-day church and school, with the Viking enclosure succeeded by a second enclosure representing the bailey of the earl of Chester's castle of the early to mid-12th century, itself replaced by an Augustinian monastery of the late 12th to mid-13th century.

Furthermore, an unpublished interim report of 1987 makes it clear that the course of the D-shaped enclosure ditch was largely extrapolated from resistivity surveys in the churchyard and Repton School cloister; the ditch itself could only have been observed in excavation trenches in three places.[40] In the first of these, where the western arm of the putative Viking ditch would have reached the cliff at the edge of the floodplain, it was assumed that it had been recut by the later outer bailey ditch, thereby removing any evidence for the Viking layers. Similarly, in a trench dug in the school cloister all traces of it had been removed by the junction of inner and outer bailey ditches, which pottery indicated were 12th-century features. That leaves just one deep trench, where the Viking ditch runs up against the chancel of St Wystan's church, and where its stratigraphic relationship with a series of graves becomes crucial to its dating and where the excavation archive needs further study. Finally, in this interim report, what had initially been interpreted as a Viking *naust* or harbour within the camp was now seen to be the inner bailey ditch; an iron clench nail was recovered from the fill, although this should probably now be seen as having been disturbed from earlier layers and redeposited in a later feature. A reconstruction drawing shows the castle outer bailey following the line of the D-shaped enclosure. The report concludes that: 'We thus have the classic situation of a Norman castle with a church "at the castle gate" included within its defences'.[41] There are countless examples of churches being placed within a castle bailey, and often against the defensive circuit, including an early 12th-century example from Weaverthorpe in North Yorkshire where the church projected across the castle ditch, leading Richard Morris to suggest that this may have been intended to facilitate dual access to the church, with the lord from within, and the villagers from outside the enclosure.[42]

It is clear that, at best, the Repton D-shaped enclosure could only have been a small defended area within a much larger camp; at worst, it has been misinterpreted entirely. Despite the lack of metal-detecting there are signs of Viking activity over a wider area including a sword found in 1839 'in the midst of a large quantity of human bones' while workmen were digging a culvert beneath the new road to Willington, north of Repton. In 2018 Cat Jarman excavated in the vicarage garden, adjacent to a trench dug by the Biddles. Here, in an area which would have been to the west of the D-shaped enclosure, she found evidence for metalworking, and finds consistent with those from Torksey, including an iron arrowhead, the tip of an iron axe-head, two clench nails and four lead gaming pieces.[43] Already it was becoming clear that the camp must have extended beyond the enclosure.

However, in 2019 fresh evidence came to light suggesting that the main winter camp of 873–74 was not within the modern village of Repton at all, but 3 km (2 miles) to the east, centred on an area known as Foremark. Here a metal-detectorist, Rob Davies, had recovered large numbers of Viking finds over at least ten years, but had never reported them to the Portable Antiquities Scheme. On a Channel 4 television programme he admitted to Cat Jarman that he and his partner had found gaming pieces, dirhams, Anglo-Saxon strap-ends and brooches, cubo-octahedral weights and a Thor's hammer pendant.[44] Small-scale excavations in 2019 recovered a further lead gaming piece and an iron ploughshare matching those found in Torksey, near what may have been a building which had evidence of burning, radiocarbon-dated to the late 9th or early 10th centuries.

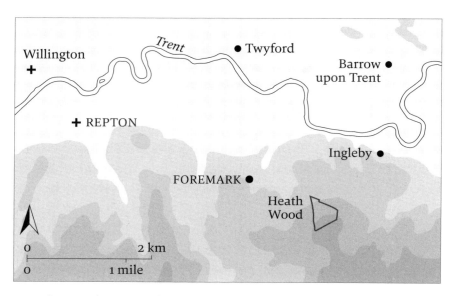

Map showing location of the Viking winter camp sites at Repton and Foremark, and the Viking cremation cemetery at Heath Wood, Derbyshire.

Foremark is on low-lying land, probably bordering the Trent's original course, and it is about 1 km (0.5 miles) to the north-west of the Viking cremation cemetery on the higher ground at Heath Wood (see Chapter 6), while the major Mercian centre at Repton, from which the camp may have taken its name, was on higher ground to the west. It seems likely, therefore, that the main Viking force camped beside the Trent at Foremark, while a small force at Repton was engaged in looting and guarding the captured monastery. As was the case with Torksey, the clue, all along, was in the name: Foremark – or, to give its Scandinavian origins, *forn* ('old') *-verk* ('defensive fortification').

5
Beyond the Winter Camps

The winter camps provide the most distinctive archaeological traces of the Viking Great Army, and extend considerably the insights provided by the *Anglo-Saxon Chronicle* and Asser. However, in 2016, after publishing our findings about Torksey, we began to wonder whether it was possible to trace the impact of the Army beyond the winter camps. Its members must have visited places not mentioned in historical sources, as they travelled great distances across the kingdoms of Anglo-Saxon England, and would have needed to secure supply lines and strategic points in the landscape. It also seemed likely that they did not remain holed-up in their camps all winter; this much is clear from the written accounts of events when they overwintered at Reading in 870–71 (Chapter 3). Given the size of force now apparent from the camp at Torksey, it seemed to us that it would have been essential for both foraging and trading parties to venture into the hinterlands of the camps to gather provisions, including food and fuel. Other groups may have ventured out to reconnoitre for hostile forces, sources of loot and slaves and, as we shall see (Chapter 7), places to settle in the longer term.

As 2017 approached, we began to turn our thoughts to the Viking Congress, the quadrennial gathering of experts on Viking Age studies, which was due to take place in Copenhagen that summer. Dawn decided to tackle the issue of the wider impact of the Great Army, by looking for traces of settlement dislocation and abandonment in the later 9th century and investigating whether any assemblages similar to those from Torksey could be found beyond the known winter camps. Since there are relatively small numbers of relevant excavated sites, her principal source of evidence came from the Portable Antiquities Scheme (PAS) database. Given that the information in this database is the product of a range of non-random factors which lead to objects being lost in the first place, and then recovered and reported, it is inevitably subject to a number of limitations and biases.[1] These include the lack of evidence from modern urban areas (which is an issue with many of the other known winter camp sites recorded in the *Anglo-Saxon Chronicle*, such as Nottingham, Thetford, Reading and London), as well as the relative paucity of detected finds in north-east England, including in the former Northumbrian sub-kingdom of Bernicia.[2] Another difficulty in using PAS data is that some categories of finds have hitherto been unrecognized by both detectorists and Finds Liaison Officers: for instance, the lead gaming pieces, which are often unassigned to a specific period on the database. Other artefact types, such as weaponry, including iron axes, spears and swords, were no doubt common possessions among members of the Great Army, and have been found at Repton and Torksey, but they are underrepresented on the PAS because metal-detectorists generally ignore the iron finds.

While there are, then, some notable limitations in using PAS data, the areas of eastern Yorkshire and Lincolnshire that were later subject to longer-term Scandinavian settlement are largely ploughed agricultural land today and are therefore well-served by the PAS. In these regions we were able to identify many additional sites that appear to have been visited by members, or former members, of the Great Army. In this chapter, information derived from the PAS uses the location names by which the find-spots are known on the database. Distribution maps and detailed grid references are not provided since these are held as confidential information by the PAS.[3]

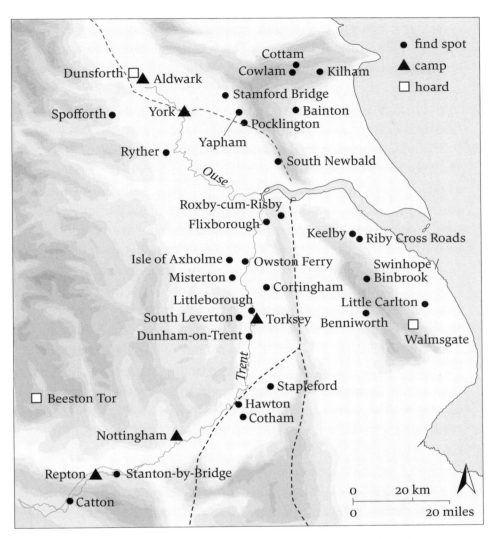

Places visited by the Viking Great Army and its offshoots in eastern England. The dotted line shows the Roman roads Ermine Street and Fosse Way.

For the Viking Congress, Dawn set about examining the PAS records for Lincolnshire, where she had excavated several early medieval sites and previously written about its estate structures and ecclesiastical organization.[4] She began her quest with the evidence from the Lincolnshire Wolds, a spine of rolling chalk uplands between Lincoln and the coast, rising to 170 m (560 ft) above sea level and surrounded by fens and coastal marshland. Here in 1985 the only coin hoard datable to the late 9th century had been found at Walmsgate, close to Barton Street, which is the major north–south route through the Wolds and probably of prehistoric origins. This hoard comprises nine West Saxon and Mercian coins, and has been dated to *c*. 873.[5] There is nothing Scandinavian about this hoard, as the coins are typical of finds from the region and it does not include any hackmetal or imported coins. Nonetheless, Dawn believed that the date of deposition could not be coincidence and that it was highly likely that these coins had been hidden from the Army for safekeeping. She therefore set out to trace whether there was any other evidence for the Army passing through this area in the early 870s, and how we might begin to seek its wider impact in the Wolds. Two sites jumped out immediately as revealing evidence for settlement disruption in the late 9th century: Little Carlton and Riby Cross Roads.

Little Carlton is located just to the east of the southern end of the Wolds, in the coastal marshes.[6] It has produced more than 700 late 7th- to late 9th-century metal artefacts, including 8 styli used for writing on wax tablets, at least 20 copper-brazed iron bells of a type found at ecclesiastical sites where they were used for calling the faithful to prayer, over 60 coins, and an inscribed lead plaque, which may have been a coffin fitting, bearing the Old English name *Cudburg*. The site has also yielded a very large assemblage of 8th- and 9th-century Ipswich ware pottery, the most technologically sophisticated pottery in production in England at that time; it is found across eastern England and was used to transport wine and other traded goods. Imported continental pottery from Badorf has also been found at Little Carlton. This high-status, possibly ecclesi-astical, site has, however, produced very few traces of any activity after the late 9th century and the latest coin found there is one of Burgred from the early 870s. There is little of the wheel-thrown pottery characteristic of the 10th century, and only a handful of metal artefacts that may date to that period.[7] By the time we next hear anything of Little Carlton – in *Domesday Book*, William the Conqueror's great survey of his newly won lands from 1086 – it is a small settlement of no great significance. It is difficult to escape the conclusion that the fate of Little Carlton in the late 9th century was shaped by the activities of the Great Army in the region and that its descent into obscurity began then.

At the north end of the Wolds on Barton Street is Riby Cross Roads, where excavation of a pipeline in the early 1990s revealed a settlement occupied from the 7th to mid-9th centuries, after which point both pottery and metalwork petered out.[8] Looking back at the excavation report Dawn could see no finds that provided any evidence for the Great Army, but the PAS database revealed that since the excavations were published, metal-detecting had recovered artefacts that had similarities with items from Torksey, including three lead gaming pieces. There were also three fragmentary 9th-century strap-ends, a piece of a brooch or mount that had been deliberately cut, another mount that must have been brought from Ireland, and a solitary Northumbrian styca, out of place south of the Humber. The PAS database also revealed a site that seems to have been abandoned at the same time, *c.* 1 km to the north 'near Keelby', where metal-detecting has recovered over 100 Anglo-Saxon artefacts, but very little that could be securely dated to the late 9th or 10th century. The evidence was tentative, but a pattern was beginning to emerge.

Dawn then consulted the PAS database more widely for the Lincolnshire Wolds and additional assemblages of finds that were reminiscent of material recovered from Torksey began to emerge. The most significant concentration came from the parishes of Swinhope

Selection of finds from Swinhope and Binbrook, Lincolnshire.

and Binbrook. Over 120 mid-7th to mid-9th century metal artefacts have been found in these neighbouring parishes, among which are a handful that can be associated with the Great Army, including 12 lead weights, one of which seems to have been of the inset variety, 4 lead gaming pieces, 1 dirham fragment, 3 stycas, and 1 piece of hacksilver. An imitative coin struck from lead may have been a trial piece for a die, and is similar in form and function to the lead trial piece for a Louis the Pious solidus and the lead impression of a lunette coin of Burgred of Mercia from Torksey (Chapter 4).[9] There are also later finds from Swinhope displaying Scandinavian influence, including jewellery, bridle fittings and dress accessories.[10] These suggest that the Scandinavians returned to settle in the area in the 10th century, which may also account for an unusual burial of an adult female and a juvenile in a Neolithic long barrow. There were no grave goods and the radiocarbon date range was very broad, enabling the burials to be dated no more precisely than to the 9th–11th centuries, yet there is a striking similarity between this funerary practice and better-known examples of 10th-century Scandinavian reuse of prehistoric burial mounds such as Hesket in the Forest in Cumbria and Claughton Hall in Lancashire.[11]

This new work by Dawn makes it possible to identify additional places visited by the Great Army using archaeological evidence, helped by the distinctive nature of the activities undertaken at the camps. The early medieval artefacts recovered from Torksey are not a typical settlement assemblage. They reflect instead the specialist nature of activities carried out while the Army and its followers overwintered. These activities include trading, using both bullion and coins, and possibly minting the latter; metal processing and manufacture, including melting down looted objects and trans-forming them into ingots; repair of ships and weapons; as well as gambling and gaming. The characteristic finds left by the same range of activities can also be seen in another metal-detected assemblage from a second recently discovered camp at Aldwark, near York. Although this camp is not explicitly referred to in the *Anglo-Saxon Chronicle*, it has been associated with Healfdene's recorded return to Northumbria in 874 and his journey to the Tyne (see Chapter 7).[12]

The specific nature of the activities at Torksey and Aldwark, and the limited 'background noise' from the remains of earlier or later early medieval activity at these sites, means that it is possible to define a Great Army 'signature' that comprises six main elements:[13]

1 Hackmetal, including complete and fragmentary silver and gold ingots, and dirhams (generally cut into small pieces).

2 Lead and copper-alloy weights, which also indicate the operation of a bullion economy.

Selection of weights from various sites visited by offshoots of the Viking Great Army.

Selection of gaming pieces from various sites visited by offshoots of the Viking Great Army.

3 Stycas, although common at 9th-century sites in Northumbria, are a distinctive part of the Great Army signature when found outside their normal monetary circulation area. Those deposited at Torksey were probably acquired while the Army was in Northumbria, but were then used for small-scale transactions. Over a quarter are 'blundered' – i.e., they have illegible or nonsensical inscriptions, which may even suggest attempts by the Army to mint them.[14]

4 Anglo-Saxon silver pennies, outside their primary area of circulation, or where pierced or cut, such as coins of Mercia and Wessex at Aldwark.[15]

5 Anglo-Saxon and Irish dress accessories and mounts, deliberately pierced or cut for reuse (e.g., as decorative insets in lead weights). The fact that there are many Anglo-Saxon strap-ends but very few dress pins at Aldwark and Torksey reinforces that these are not typical 9th-century settlement assemblages, in which pins and strap-ends tend to be found in roughly equal numbers.[16]

6 Lead gaming pieces, comprising hollow or solid domed cones, sometimes with raised protuberances or knobs, and often crudely made. They are known in large numbers from Torksey, but have subsequently also been identified at Repton and Aldwark. Given that none have been reported from sites known to have been visited by the Army prior to Torksey, the gaming pieces provide a highly important earliest possible date of 872–73 and are a key element of the Great Army signature. The fact that they are crudely manufactured objects, easily made and readily discarded, enhances their value as dating indicators since they were not treasured, and they do not occur in 10th-century Anglo-Scandinavian deposits, such as those at Coppergate in York.

It is possible to apply this signature to areas of the country known to have been visited by the Army in order to identify its archaeological traces. This allows us to find other sites that the Army and its offshoots may have visited. In all the examples discussed below the locations were initially identified from elements of the Great Army signature traced on the PAS database. Although the number of finds may be small in comparison to the winter camps, these sites have not undergone the sustained level of metal-detecting to which Aldwark and Torksey have been subjected. The assemblages reflect a range of settlement histories: some Anglo-Saxon sites yield a few Viking finds and seem to have been abandoned shortly afterwards; some sites were occupied by later generations of Scandinavian settlers; others have only Viking finds, but neighbour Anglo-Saxon sites. It should also be noted that many of the finds have been recovered from a broad area, and may reflect several concentrations of activity, relating to repeated visits by members of the Army to the locality.

Along the Trent Valley, there are numerous such sites with elements of the Great Army signature. These locations may represent places that members of the Army visited regularly while they were based at Torksey or Repton, or places encountered en route as they travelled to and from their winter bases. It is also possible that despite the *Anglo-Saxon Chronicle* only naming a single place as the Army's base, its members may have spread over the immediate area whenever it overwintered. Derbyshire has witnessed far less metal-detecting than counties to the east because of its largely rough upland terrain, which tends to be used for pastoral grazing instead of being ploughed for crops. Nonetheless, there are several concentrations of finds around Catton, *c.* 15 km (9 miles) south-west of Repton on the banks of the Trent. After identifying this site via the PAS database during the research for the Viking Congress paper, we heard that some of the items that had been found there were on temporary display at Derby Museum and Art Gallery. Over the Christmas break we took a trip to see the finds, which included fifteen lead gaming pieces, two weights (one inset with an Anglo-Saxon coin), a silver ingot, a Thor's hammer pendant and a dirham. Shortly afterwards, Dawn mentioned Catton in a talk to the Leicestershire Archaeological and Historical Society; the Leicestershire FLO Wendy Scott was in the audience and she put Dawn in touch with Roger Thomas, the metal-detectorist who had been working in Catton. We paid a visit to Roger and his friends in Witan Archaeology, a local amateur group, a few weeks later, and on a cold and windswept February afternoon they showed us around the fields from which Roger's finds had come. The group had been focussed on investigating the archaeology of Catton Hall, a privately owned stately home that now hosts temporary camps for pop concerts instead of for Viking armies. Roger had found Viking artefacts concentrated in several locations throughout the estate, suggesting Great Army activity across a huge area. Catton is close to the site of several medieval and later crossing points over the Trent, including that of the 19th-century toll bridge at Walton Bridge.

The correspondence between components of a Great Army artefact signature – including hacksilver, weights and gaming pieces – and riverine crossings is widespread, such as at Stanton-by-Bridge, 8 km (5 miles) downriver of Repton, and at Hawton and Cotham, both on the River Devon but also within 3 km (2 miles) of a crossing point over the Trent and close to the Roman Fosse Way. These locations may have been occupied on a temporary basis as strategic outposts of the winter camps to monitor and control movements. We know little else about them, although some appear to have been significant existing centres. One such is Stapleford in Lincolnshire, within *c.* 3 km (2 miles) of the Fosse Way and close to the River Witham, where a silver ingot and 21 lead gaming pieces have been found. Stapleford must also have been a crossing point, to judge from its place-name, which is formed from the Old English word *stapol*, meaning 'post' or 'pillar', and *ford*.[17] 'Stapleford' place-names are found across England, typically located near Anglo-Saxon royal or urban centres. Indeed, on the opposite banks of the Witham to the Lincolnshire Stapleford is Brant Broughton, which has a place-name (*burh*, *tun*, 'farmstead of the fortified place') often associated with Mercian royal centres and minster churches.[18] It has been suggested that the term *stapol* referred to a distinctive feature in the landscape at which speeches were made. This is reflected in the use of this term in the Old English epic poem *Beowulf*, when King Hrothgar steps up to a *stapol* to make a speech in the great mead hall Heorot. John Blair has envisaged a *stapol* as 'carved or painted in the manner of totem poles'.[19] We can, then, see Stapleford as a place adjacent to a river crossing where people gathered to hear important pronouncements. Given how well informed the Great Army was about local politics, perhaps it was drawn to just such a gathering-place.

Traces of Viking activity have been recovered at many places along the Trent, no doubt as it provided the Army with easy riverine access to the Humber estuary. Some can be associated directly with the winter camp at Torksey itself, including several places on the opposite banks of the Trent. Indeed, one of the largest assemblages of stycas outside Northumbria, other than Torksey itself, comes from Littleborough (literally the 'little fortification', referring to the Roman fort of *Segelocum*), 2 km (1 mile) downstream of the winter camp, where Till Bridge Lane crosses the Trent.[20] The date profile of the 25 stycas is almost identical to that of the Torksey assemblage, suggesting contemporaneous activity, maybe even a strategic lookout post guarding the key crossing point. There was also Army activity at the next crossing point upstream of Torksey, near Dunham Bridge. Today it costs 40 pence to drive your car across the toll bridge, which still rests on the piers constructed in the 1830s, but prior to the bridge there was a ferry, so this was probably another ancient crossing point that may have been used in the 9th century. Two lead weights, one of which appears to have been inset with a coin, have been found in Dunham-on-Trent, *c.* 0.8 km (0.5 miles) east of the toll bridge. Dunham may well have been an important royal and ecclesiastical site, as it certainly was at a later date.[21]

Further downstream of Torksey there are more sites with elements of a Great Army signature, marking a major route northward. Close to the point where the Trent joins the Humber estuary, lead weights, gaming pieces, a Borre-style brooch and strap-end, another strap-end of Irish Sea type, a styca and an East Anglian penny have been recovered from the Isle of Axholme. Drainage since the 17th century has obscured its earlier character as an island, but in the 9th century it was bounded by the Rivers Trent, Idle and Don, and the peat bogs of Thorne and Hatfield moors. The former landscape is reflected in the place-name Axholme, which means 'the island' (Old Norse *holmr*) 'of Haxey' (Old Norse personal name *Haki* with Old English *eg* or Old Norse *ey*, meaning island). There is a crossing point from the Isle of Axholme over the Trent at Owston Ferry, and on the opposite side of the river at Laughton two lead gaming pieces and a weight have been recovered. Immediately to the south, in the parishes of Corringham and Blyton, metal-detecting has produced three lead gaming pieces identical to examples from Torksey, at least 20 other lead gaming pieces or weights, a copper-alloy weight, copper-alloy and silver metalworking debris, and two copper-alloy ingot fragments. The clustering of finds within a 2 km (1 mile) radius suggests that there may have been two separate focal points of the Great Army's activity in the vicinity. Little is known of the 9th-century status of any of the settlements in this area, but the church of Corringham may have been an early foundation, as it was certainly of regional significance in the later medieval period, the centre of a deanery, with its income granted to Lincoln cathedral by Henry I.[22]

The only place along the Trent at which it is possible to combine excavated and metal- detected evidence is Flixborough. Excavations between 1989 and 1991 revealed a settlement occupied from the 7th to the 11th centuries, but where there was significant disruption in the later 9th century. At this time continental imports ceased; there was a reduction in the range of craftworking activity; and the high-status lifestyle, involving 'conspicuous consumption of larger cattle and wild "feast" species', became unattainable.[23] The excavation report speculated that this may have been due to estate reorganization; the impact of Viking raiders was not seriously considered, given the small number of Scandinavian finds from the site. However, in the light of the Great Army 'signature', we should examine the Flixborough finds afresh. Indeed, there is evidence for the operation of a bullion economy, including a silver ingot, which metallurgical analysis suggested was melted down from coins, and twelve lead weights.[24] Furthermore, the presence of 27 stycas is unusual south of the Humber. Most of these stycas are irregular issues, attempting to copy the names of Northumbrian kings, using dies that were not for official coinage and made from low-quality materials, and many have blundered inscriptions, suggesting they were forgeries, perhaps even minted by the Great Army.[25]

Although this evidence for the presence of the Great Army at Flixborough is slight, it is reinforced considerably when we look across the parish boundary to Roxby-cum-Risby, which has been a focus of intensive metal-detecting activity in recent years. Signature finds have been recorded over an area of *c.* 400 ha (1,000 acres) including weights, a silver ingot, a lead gaming piece, a 9th-century Irish mount, a Thor's hammer, and a range of metalworking debris. A coin of Alfred found in 2012 is of a type that we know to have been in the hands of the Army in large numbers in the late 870s. It is a rare single find of the cross-and-lozenge type, which dates to after the coinage reform of *c.* 875, and was the first such coin to be reported to the PAS. Since then 180 examples have been found in the Watlington hoard (Chapter 9).[26] There seems to have been a continuing Scandinavian presence in the Roxby area, reflected in Scandinavian place-names, such as both Roxby and Risby, but also an array of artefacts with Scandinavian stylistic influences, including a brooch, rings, bridle fittings and buckles.[27] A flat circular brooch of the type worn by Anglo-Saxons is decorated in the Borre style, suggesting an item manufactured by a local craftworker adapting to new fashions.

A tiny copper-alloy bell is of a type found widely in areas of Scandinavian settlement. Such miniature conical or pyramidal copper-alloy bells, often decorated with ring-and-dot ornament, are distinctive finds, apparently invented in eastern and northern England, and best described as Anglo-Scandinavian bells. They are not found in Scandinavia, but have become widely known in areas of Scandinavian settlement overseas. The bells were an early 10th-century introduction and are not found in the Great Army winter camps. In York they are not present at the 8th- and 9th-century Anglo-Saxon trading site at Fishergate, but are found in the 10th-century levels at Coppergate. Their function is unknown; they may have been dress fittings, although it is tempting to interpret them as bridle mounts.[28] The Army's activity in the Roxby area seems to have paved the way for long-lasting Scandinavian settlement. Yet at Flixborough there are no such 10th-century Scandinavian artefacts, which reveals how diverse the impact of the Army was, even within the space of a little over a kilometre.[29]

North of the Humber, there is further evidence for the presence of elements of the Great Army along the major routeways, and in the vicinity of Anglo-Saxon estate centres. In East Yorkshire the majority of Anglo-Saxon sites identified by metal-detecting were abandoned in the late 9th century, and some have a small proportion of Viking finds that probably reflect brief visits by parts of the Viking Great Army, either as part of raiding or trading activity, and possibly as reconnaissance. These sites include several in the vicinity of the Anglo-Saxon royal estate centre at Driffield.[30] Cottam is one of the best known as it developed from an Anglo-Saxon settlement and marketplace into one of the first Anglo-Scandinavian farmsteads to be recognized in England. It will be discussed in detail in Chapter 7 when we consider the long-term Scandinavian settlement.

View from the churchyard at Spofforth, North Yorkshire, looking across the valley to the site visited by members of the Great Army.

Selection of finds from Spofforth.

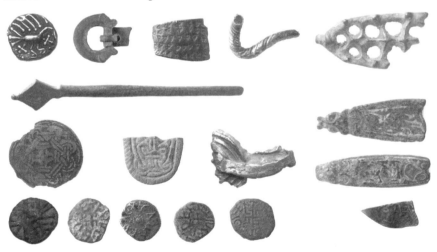

Other sites that appear to have been visited by offshoots of the Army – given finds of lead weights, gaming pieces and pieces of silver ingot – include Cowlam, 1 km (0.5 miles) west of Cottam; Bainton, a recently discovered site 9 km (6 miles) south-west of Driffield; and Kilham. Additional sites follow the line of the Roman road from the Humber crossing up to York, including Yapham, South Newbald, and a site known as 'Near Pocklington'. Stamford Bridge, where part of a chain from a balance and two ingots have been found, is also at a key location where the Roman road crosses the River Derwent. There are also several sites on or near the Wolds that have aspects of the Great Army signature but also have a broader range of domestic artefacts and dress accessories associated with permanent Scandinavian settlement. For example, at a second location close to Stamford Bridge weights and fragments of a dirham and of a solidus coin of Louis the Pious have been found, consistent with the presence of the Army, but this site has also yielded a range of Anglo-Scandinavian jewellery, spindle whorls and two Anglo-Scandinavian bells – all objects associated with permanent settlement. Similarly, members of the Army appear to have returned to settle at Yapham, where domestic items, jewellery and spindle whorls have been found, as well as also silver bullion, weights and gaming pieces. In both the Lincolnshire and Yorkshire Wolds, therefore, there is evidence for the impact of the Great Army, whose visits led to the abandonment of many settlements, but with a smaller number continuing in use with a 10th-century Anglo-Scandinavian presence.

West of York, instances of the Great Army signature are potentially linked with the camp at Aldwark, or the trans-Pennine communications corridor to Dublin. A particularly striking example comes from Spofforth ('the place by the ford'), at a site overlooking the causeway over the floodplain of the River Crimple, on the opposite bank to the medieval and modern village. Metal-detecting here has recovered a 9th-century dirham, hacksilver including part of an arm ring, a Borre-style brooch, an Irish kite-shaped pin and thirteen stycas.

Spofforth was the location of an important later medieval church, while excavation nearby at Village Farm has revealed a cemetery dating to the 8th/9th century, containing high-status burials in wooden chests.[31] Spofforth appears to be another high-status site, with an early church, at a river crossing visited by the Great Army.

While discussing finds on major northern routeways, it is also worth mentioning the Æthelswith ring, which was ploughed up in 1870 near Aberford in West Yorkshire, close to Ermine Street, the modern A1(M) or Great North Road, where it crosses the Cock Beck. It is said that the finder initially attached it to the collar of his dog, but the ring was later purchased by a York jeweller who sold it for £30 to the renowned antiquarian and barrow-digger Canon Greenwell. It eventually entered the British Museum as one of many items bequeathed by the antiquarian and collector Sir Augustus Franks.[32] The ring was manufactured in gold and niello for Queen Æthelswith of Mercia, whose name is incised on the reverse of the bezel. Æthelswith was Alfred's sister but in 853 married Burgred, lived abroad following his exile at the hands of the Great Army in 874 (see Chapter 3), and died at Pavia in Italy in 888, where she was buried.[33] The ring was probably never worn by Æthelswith, and was more likely bestowed as a gift upon one of her followers. It featured a lamb with a halo, between the letters A and D for Agnus Dei ('Lamb of God'), a symbol of peace. The circumstances whereby it ended up in a field in Yorkshire will never be known, but it is tempting to suspect Viking involvement, whether through an act of theft or as a symbolic token of one of the many recorded peace treaties of the period.

The Æthelswith ring, discovered in 1870. The ring shows a lamb with a halo, between the letters A and D for Agnus Dei ('Lamb of God').

Further north, few Viking finds have been recovered in the Tyne region, although this may reflect the built-up and industrialized nature of much of the area and the lower levels of metal-detecting. Nonetheless, a site on the south bank of the River Coquet, enclosed within a peninsula formed by the Thirston Burn, may be associated with Healfdene's activities in the area. This site has produced seven lead gaming pieces; two irregular stycas and a third embedded in a copper-alloy disc, which may have been a weight; a lead weight inset with glass; and a copper-alloy domed stud of Scandinavian type.

The signature of the Great Army is also surprisingly rare in East Anglia, compared to its visible presence in Lincolnshire and Yorkshire, even though we know that the Army arrived in East Anglia and overwintered in 865, and spent winters there on two further occasions. A small group of finds associated with the Army, comprising three gaming pieces and a weight, comes from Little Wilbraham, 11 km (7 miles) east of Cambridge. If we are correct that the gaming pieces post-date Torksey then this cluster dates to Guthrum's return to East Anglia, and his stay at Cambridge in 874–75.[34] Further corroboration for the theory that the lead gaming pieces found at Torksey were invented there during the 872–73 overwintering is provided by the fact that while numerous Viking weights have been found in the Thetford region, where the Army overwintered in 869–70, not a single gaming piece has been recovered thus far, nor have any been recovered from the many excavations undertaken within the late Saxon town. Nonetheless, there is a great deal of Scandinavian material culture of 9th- and 10th-century date in East Anglia, and also some evidence for settlement disruption in the late 9th century.[35] The 8th- and 9th-century elite site at Staunch Meadow in Brandon, Suffolk, for example, appears to have come to an end in the late 9th century, with occupation then moving closer to the site of the later medieval village.[36] Brandon is similar in nature to Flixborough and Little Carlton, with evidence for ecclesiastical activity, and while there is no evidence for any Viking raids there, it is just 5 km (3 miles) from Thetford. At the very least the supply chains on which the Anglo-Saxon inhabitants of the Staunch Meadow site depended would have been disrupted by the Viking activity in the area.

There are also few finds which can be associated with the documented Great Army bases at Reading, Exeter, and Chippenham, although in those regions there has been far less metal-detecting. The exception is a cluster of finds around Wareham in Dorset, the location of a winter camp in 875–76, including two lead weights inset with lunette coins dated to 873–74, probably minted in Mercia, a Carolingian sword-belt mount, an offcut of Irish metalwork and a gold ingot, none of which would be out of place at Torksey. There is also a dirham from Monkton Deverill and a trefoil brooch from Longbridge Deverill, both of which were situated on an ancient routeway leading north from Poole Harbour to Chippenham, where the Vikings camped immediately prior to the Battle of Edington in 878.[37]

Having identified some 30 additional sites that appear to have been visited by members of the Great Army and its offshoots, what conclusions can we draw about how the Army moved about the country, and the places it favoured? There were two main forms of early medieval warfare: small-scale plundering raids and larger-scale campaigns.[38] Success in the former was often achieved through surprise, with small, highly mobile warbands operating like modern special forces; for the latter, set-piece battles were more the norm, and as well as being able to bring a larger force to the battlefield it was important to identify and claim the best ground. Such set-piece battles were largely fought on foot between lines of warriors armed with spears, swords, axes and shields. Warriors arranged in wedge-shaped formations would try to drive a hole through the enemy line where they could engage in hand-to-hand combat. The shield-wall was an essential part of attack and defence. Lines of overlapping shields provided a protective barrier, from behind which the warriors in the second rank could slash and thrust at the enemy with swords and spears, driving them back upon themselves until their line collapsed.[39]

The ability of Viking warbands to move freely within enemy territory was the key to their success. Given the river-side location of many of the winter camps (as well as evidence for the presence of ships, such as clench nails, at Torksey, Repton and Aldwark), and many of the other sites with a Great Army signature, it is safe to assume that much of the Army and its entourage reached these sites by boat. The shallow draught of Viking longships and absence of a deep keel would have allowed them to penetrate far up the English river systems. Similarly, as the timber masts were erected by slotting them into a square hole in the middle of the boat, they could also be taken down and laid temporarily in the centre of a longship, allowing it to pass under bridges. While Viking warriors could travel quickly on horseback using surviving Roman roads, their movements could be shadowed by the fleet carrying supplies and reinforcements.

We know that the Army must also have travelled overland, since it was 'supplied with horses' in East Anglia in 865 and 'rode across Mercia into East Anglia' in 870–71.[40] In their book on Anglo-Saxon civil defence in southern England, John Baker and Stuart Brookes emphasize the distances that the Great Army was able to travel when attacking central places deep within opposition territory. They note the close association between the recorded movements of the Army and the principal navigable waterways and roads, including the prehistoric Icknield Way, and the Roman Watling Street, Ermine Street and Fosse Way. They deduced that the Army must have had accurate information about communications routes, as well as the ability to take effective control of them.[41] Our knowledge of smaller roads and navigable waterways in early medieval England is too limited and patchy to gauge which ones the Army might have used: while in southern England the secondary routeways can sometimes be inferred from charter evidence, this information is unavailable for most of eastern and northern England. Similarly, place-names containing the Old English word *here-paeð* ('army road') are largely confined to Wessex.[42] Baker and Brookes note that our ability to map the extent of waterborne mobility in this period is limited by the lack of reliable written evidence for navigation, and they suggest that models for the importance of river navigation may sometimes be misleading as they depend upon 13th-century and later sources, following medieval improvements to waterways.[43] Nonetheless, the upper reaches of rivers would probably have been reachable in winter, when river levels were higher, and it is notable that in each case the long-distance movements of the Great Army appear to occur immediately before taking up winter camp.[44]

The evidence we have accumulated from the PAS database reveals the importance of river crossings to the Great Army, especially for journeys involving transfers between boat and land. It is striking how many of the places we have identified either have 'ford' in their place-names, or were the known locations of river ferries. They would have been strategic locations for the control of movement through the landscape, and were also places of political negotiation, possibly with symbolic significance. In Viking Age Scandinavia, rivers and other watercourses were perceived as liminal features separating political territories as well as the worlds of the living and the dead. Watery locations were also dangerous places where gods and monsters dwelt. The construction of bridges across marshy ground was later undertaken as part of the process of Christianizing or 'taming' the landscape, to be recorded on runestones.[45]

The sites discussed in this chapter are in precisely those regions where the *Anglo-Saxon Chronicle* records that the Great Army was active, but the metal-detecting evidence is subtle and it reveals a number of patterns. The assemblages may reflect a range of activities, including looting, foraging and trading, and they illuminate a number of ways in which settlements developed. Some Anglo-Saxon sites were visited and subsequently abandoned; others were transformed into new settlements. The new data derived from metal-detecting also highlights the favoured targets of forays from the camps, the locations of subsidiary outposts, and the communications routes used by the Army. In particular, activity was focussed in the vicinity of former Anglo-Saxon estate centres, royal residences and major churches. This is not surprising, as such places would have represented ready sources of additional loot, food and hostages. We already know that the sites of the major winter camps were chosen for their strategic locations. Torksey, Repton and Aldwark were each positioned at the junction of major river and road networks. They are still important crossing points today and it seems more than coincidence that modern toll bridges survive close to Aldwark, and Torksey (at Dunham Bridge). Indeed, Aldwark is the closest crossing point to York of the Ouse and its tributaries. The coin hoard from Lower Dunsforth, discovered in 1861, and dated to no earlier than *c.* 873, was found only 2 km (1.25 miles) up-river from Aldwark, and can now be linked to that camp. Many of the smaller sites identified by the Great Army signature are notably also at or adjacent to known crossing points. There is no reason to assume that the presence of the Army was confined to the camps named in the *Anglo-Saxon Chronicle*. These crossing points may not have been permanently occupied, but they would have channelled movement and provided the Army with the opportunity to transfer from road to river and vice versa, but would also have allowed them to observe and control the movement of any other forces through the landscape.

These sites are also clustered along the major river networks (of the Trent, the Ouse, and the Wharfe), or along ancient road systems. In the Yorkshire Wolds they are found on the major Iron Age trackways that continued to be used during the Anglo-Saxon period; in the Lincolnshire Wolds many lie adjacent to the prehistoric Barton Street. Others are adjacent to the Fosse Way (the A46) as it runs south-west of Lincoln to Leicester, or on the course of Ermine Street (the modern A15 and A1) as it heads north from Lincoln to the Humber crossing, and then continues north-west to York, the

Tyne and beyond. We know that this route was one the Army used: in the entry for 867 the *Anglo-Saxon Chronicle* records that the Army went from East Anglia to Northumbria 'across the Humber estuary to the city of York' and the PAS data helps us to trace this route.[46] Clearly it was the combination of the relict Roman road system and the major river routes that allowed the Great Army to travel across the Anglo-Saxon kingdoms so rapidly in the 870s.

Can the signature of the Great Army be found beyond the British Isles? The Viking Age settlement at Füsing, now in northern Germany, is situated on the northern shores of the Schlei fjord, within sight of the trading site at Hedeby, and with a direct connection to the Danevirke fortification (see Chapter 1). The site was discovered in 2003 through a metal-detector survey, and from 2010 to 2014 it was excavated by a team from Aarhus University in Denmark. This revealed that the settlement had flourished from around 700 to the end of the 10th century. The presence of quality finds and several longhouses indicates a high-status residence and excavators think that Füsing was the centre of a manorial estate. It may therefore have had a military role related to the Danevirke and may even have been the home of a royal representative connected to the emporium at Hedeby. Certainly the large numbers of arrowheads and axes found there suggest a military function. In 2013 the site director, Andres Dobat, heard us talk about Torksey at the Viking Congress in Lerwick, Shetland, and he recognized that a small group of four inconspicuous hollow lead domes found by metal-detectorists at Füsing were identical to some of the hundreds of gaming pieces that had been discovered at Torksey. They had been found in the plough-soil associated with a sunken hut, dated to the second half of the 9th century. Objects like this had never before been identified in Denmark despite 30 years of metal-detecting, although three similar objects have now been identified from Hedeby itself. At each site two types were present: plain examples, and those with raised ridges, forming a cross. Given the lack of other examples from Scandinavia it seems likely that the objects originated from England, possibly even from Torksey. Other finds of British origin in Scandinavian assemblages certainly indicate that not all warriors who participated in the raids in England settled there, and that many returned home. Maybe the Füsing gaming pieces belonged to one such warrior, who had fought with the Great Army in England, perhaps even camping in 872–73 by the River Trent at Torksey, but who had then boarded a ship returning to Hedeby. There he had joined a group of battle-hardened troops guarding a highly strategic point on the Schlei fjord, protecting the southern borders of the early Danish kingdom.[47]

The Füsing gaming pieces also raise the possibility of tracing the movements of former members of the Army as they continued raiding in northern Europe or headed to the trading centres of Scandinavia, northern Frankia and the Baltic to make use of their newly acquired wealth. Northumbrian stycas have been found in several Scandinavian, Frisian and Slavic trading centres, including Hedeby, Birka, Dorestad, Mainz, Menzlin (Germany) and Staraya Ladoga (Russia). In the light of our work, this provides more compelling evidence for the activities of former members of the Great Army in the 870s and later than it does for continental trading connections with Northumbria in the 840s or 850s, the period when the coins were minted. Solitary Northumbrian copper-alloy coins can have had little monetary value in the Baltic and Scandinavia, so they are best seen as trophies or souvenirs. The two examples from Birka are from graves, one of which also contains a ring-headed pin of Irish type, providing further evidence of connections with areas of Viking raiding. Two stycas have been found at Janów Pomorski on the Baltic coast in Poland, near the town of Elbląg. The site has been identified as the 9th-century trading place of Truso, described at the court of Alfred c. 880 by a visitor called Wulfstan who had travelled around the Baltic and North Sea trading sites (Chapter 1). Excavations at Janów Pomorski have retrieved not only

Slavic material culture, but also numerous finds of Scandinavian origin including weapons, jewellery, Valkyrie figures, and extensive evidence for production of amber, metal, bone and horn artefacts. Evidence for trade emerges from over 1,000 coins, mainly dirhams, as well as more than 1,200 weights, including cubo-octahedral types that were common in Scandinavia in the 860s and 870s, but also lead weights, some inset with cut-up copper-alloy artefacts following the practice adopted by the Great Army. Some thirteen non-Islamic coins have been found, from Frisia, Frankia, Denmark and England, including a coin of Æthelwulf of Wessex (r. 839–58), almost all of which have been pierced to enable them to be suspended, showing that they were no longer of monetary use.[48] While these seem to date to no later than the 850s, when the form of the coins and the presence of the later weights is considered, there are grounds for suggesting that the stycas, and perhaps some of the other coins, reflect the arrival of a former member of the Great Army, looking to trade.

Raiding in northern France and Flanders, including several documented raids along the River Rhine in 881–82, may also have involved former members of the Great Army. These raids have previously been associated with an army that had briefly been in England over the winter of 878–79. The *Anglo-Saxon Chronicle* records that this newly arrived Viking army assembled in 878 and based itself at Fulham, and Asser tells us that the newcomers made contact with the Great Army. The following year this army left for Ghent (Belgium), and spent several years raiding in Flanders and the Low Countries. In June 2019, Dawn was invited to give a keynote lecture about the Great Army at the annual Middeleeuwen Symposium at Zutphen, in the eastern Netherlands, and made a discovery that suggested that this Fulham army had taken members of the Great Army with it back to the Continent.

In 882 the *Annals of Fulda* recorded that 'The Northmen burned the port called in the Frisian tongue Deventer ... with great loss of life', and archaeological evidence of large areas of burning and destroyed buildings found beneath the later town rampart has been associated with this recorded raid on the eastern Netherlands.[49] At Zutphen, some 18 km (11 miles) to the south of Deventer, archaeological evidence for another Viking raid at this time had been identified when a new town hall was built in 1997.[50] Excavation by the municipal archaeologists revealed evidence of destroyed buildings comprising two houses and five sunken huts, sealed beneath a burnt layer containing late 9th-century pottery. Within the buildings were large amounts of tuff stone, typically used in church construction in the Carolingian period and acquired from derelict Roman buildings; this suggests that the church of Zutphen may have been attacked and subsequently demolished. The skeletons of a *c.* 12-year-old child and a woman aged 30–40 were found lying on the floors of two of the sunken huts, and had clearly been

The skeleton of a woman aged 30–40 was found lying on the floor of a sunken hut during excavations in 1997 in Zutphen, Netherlands. She had been violently attacked while lying on the ground and had sword wounds on her leg and knee. Her death has been associated with Viking raids in the region in AD 882.

there when the building was destroyed by fire and collapsed. The female showed traces of having been violently attacked while lying on the ground as her knee had been cut away and there were sword wounds on her leg. One of her feet lay in the corner of the hut, and the remains of the child were scattered in the other hut; it appears that after they had been killed their bodies had been disturbed, probably by scavenging animals. Among the other debris in these buildings were many lower limbs and skulls of cattle, suggesting that the meat-bearing portions had been taken away, perhaps by Viking raiders acquiring food supplies. However, during a visit to the town museum to see the excavation finds, a styca of Æthelred II (c. 841–44) caught Dawn's eye. It had been discovered among the charred grain on the floor of one of the huts, next to the skull of the child. This coin is of a type well represented in the late styca hoards from Northumbria and at sites associated with the Great Army.

Confirmation of the link with the Great Army was to emerge later that day. After hearing Dawn's lecture the municipal archae-ologist Michel Groothedde spoke to her about the lead gaming pieces from Torksey which he had seen in her presentation. He realized that he had seen similar items among finds on the oppo-site bank of the River Ijssel from Zutphen, but had not appreciated what they were. Metal-detecting here had also uncovered a Borre-style mount, an Anglo-Saxon strap-end, Irish cross-shaped brooch, and a Carolingian mount and Trewhiddle style strap-end which had both been deliberately cut.[51] Taken together this is compelling evidence for the activities of former members of the Great Army finding new places to plunder after they had departed England, and takes us well beyond the winter camps. Intriguingly, these finds were recovered from an island of c. 5 ha (12 acres) in the floodplain of the Ijssel, in a location not dissimilar to that of Torksey, albeit rather smaller.

There is also tantalizing evidence that some former members of the Army eventually returned to Scandinavia, and died at home. A burial in south-east Norway at Vig, Fjære, contains two stycas set in lead weights. This is a practice that has all the hallmarks of Viking activity in England in the 860s and 870s where they first developed the habit of decorating their lead weights with bits of copper alloy that they had acquired. Intriguingly, in both cases the reverse side of the coin is face-up, featuring not only the name of the moneyer rather than that of the king but also, perhaps most significantly, a cross. The decorative insets may have served to personalize the weights and to convey something of the places their owner had travelled, and their encounters with different ways and beliefs. The burial was placed under a mound *c.* 20 m (65 ft) diameter, and as well as the inset weight it contained a third plain lead weight, a sword and axe. There were also items used in smithying, including an iron anvil, a hammer and pliers, a mould for casting ingots, and a piece of soapstone with a hole in it which would have been used in the forge to direct the current of air from the bellows onto the fire.[52] These items would have been used in the transformation of precious metals into ingots. The individual buried at Vig was being commemorated as a warrior, a silversmith, and a trader – the skillset typical of veterans of the Great Army.

6

The Army's Dead

The Viking Army that landed in East Anglia in AD 865 was described in the *Anglo-Saxon Chronicle* as 'heathen' (Old English *hæþen)*, and in contemporary sources 'heathen men' was the most common term used to refer to what we now call Vikings.[1] To the Anglo-Saxon chroniclers, in a society led by Christian kings and powerful bishops, it was the paganism of the invading army and their lack of respect for clerics, churches and monasteries that stood out. But the Scandinavians had a different concept of religion, one perhaps better described as a belief system, a way of looking at the world, with a pantheon of gods who were not to be worshipped uncritically. According to Norse mythology, everything ended at Ragnarök, when all humans and gods were killed and burnt. Within this worldview the outcome of human actions was predetermined; individuals could not change their fate, and what was important was the manner in which they went to meet it.[2]

In Viking Age Scandinavia there was tremendous regional variation in burial rites. The most common practice was to bury the dead fully clothed with personal adornments, together with a selection of tools and utensils of everyday life, whether the rite chosen was cremation or inhumation. The intention appears to have been to equip the dead for the next world, which was imagined as being much like this one. The majority of graves were poorly furnished, but slain warriors should be buried with their weaponry, and the wealthy might be accompanied to Valhalla by sacrificial animals and slaves. Burials with boats and wagons represented the journey into the next life, and if a whole boat was not available a stone setting in the outline of a ship might do.

Such furnished burials were rare in England in the 9th century.[3] As we shall see (Chapter 9), many warriors of the Great Army were obliged to follow their leaders in being baptized. Later waves of settlers adopted burial in Christian churchyards, although at first the graves of many of the new lords were marked with stone crosses of a Christian form, but decorated with Norse symbolism and mythical heroes such as Sigurd the Dragon Slayer.[4] Nonetheless, it is the decade of the 870s, during which the pagan Great Army was fighting the Christian Anglo-Saxons, which gives us some of the most remarkable Viking burials ever found in England. These burials come from just three locations, all associated with the overwintering at Repton in 873–74: a small number of inhumation graves placed immediately adjacent to the Mercian mausoleum; a large charnel deposit interred in the remains of a second mausoleum c. 80 m (260 ft) to the west; and a cremation cemetery on the promontory at Heath Wood, 4 km (2.5 miles) to the south-east. Although the

Repton: hypothetical plan of the enclosure, previously thought to represent the Viking winter camp of AD 873–74, and location of Viking burials.

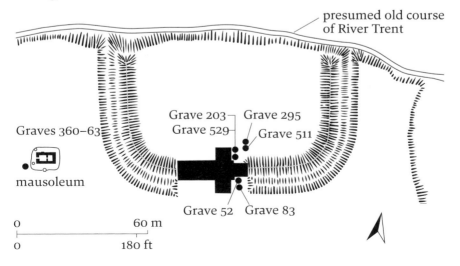

Repton burials were excavated 1974–88 they await full publication, and interim accounts have focussed on the dates, identities and causes of death of those in the inhumations and charnel deposit.[5] In our re-interpretation we explore the complex symbolism of the Repton burial rituals in the light of Scandinavian mythology.

In the winter of AD 873–74 a member of the Great Army met a gruesome death at Repton, perhaps during an attack on the Mercian royal shrine itself. He was around 35–45 years old and a big man, almost 1.8 m (6 feet) tall, but in the battle he suffered a massive blow to the skull and, as he reeled from that, the point of a sword found the weak spot in his helmet – the eye slit – gouging out his left eye and penetrating the back of the eye socket, entering his brain. While he lay on the ground, a second sword blow sliced into his upper thigh, between his legs, cutting into the bone at the top of his leg and probably slicing away his genitals.

After the battle, the comrades of the slain Viking warrior buried him adjacent to the Mercian mausoleum, where St Wigstan (see Chapter 3) had been interred some 25 years earlier. They chose a plot of land beneath the eaves of the church, adjacent to the shrine, but an area that had not previously seen any burials. The warrior (Grave 511) was buried on his back with his head to the west, his hands together on his pelvis. He wore a necklace of two glass beads, a Thor's hammer amulet and a leaded bronze gilt fastening. There was a belt around his waist and two knives; one of a folding type, like a modern Swiss Army penknife, had probably been suspended from the belt. The other warriors had placed his sword back in its fleece-lined wooden scabbard, and laid it by his left side, where it had doubtless hung in life. Alongside it they placed an iron key, although there was no trace of the treasure chest it might once have opened; in Old Norse mythology keys were symbolic of power over the household and fertility, but also gave access to the after-life.[6] They also carefully placed the tusk of a wild boar between his upper thighs, to replace what he had lost in battle, as another symbol of fertility, associated with the god Freyr, and substitute penis. He had died a warrior's death, and was destined for the pleasures of Valhalla. More mysteriously, a jackdaw's wing had been placed lower down between his legs. It seems likely to have had a symbolic meaning now lost to us, perhaps related to the fact that jackdaws are intelligent birds that can form close attachments with humans and make good pets, and in some cultures are regarded as foretellers of death.[7] The symbolism of flight represented by the wing may have seemed particularly apt for an individual about to depart on a journey to the afterlife, and can be paralleled in Viking Age sacrificial contexts at Trelleborg in Denmark where bird wings, including one from a jackdaw, have been found alongside human remains deposited in wells.[8]

A second, younger man, aged 17–20 years old, had been cut down by a savage sword blow that sliced into his skull, and was buried on the warrior's left side, accompanied only by a knife (Grave 295). The grave was slightly later, but the interval could have been anything between just a few weeks or a few years. His injuries indicated that he had also died in battle and he was originally interpreted as the warrior's weapon-bearer.[9] However, in 2018 DNA analysis of the bones showed that they were first-degree relatives on the paternal side. They could have been half-brothers but, given the age difference, are more likely to have been father and son. Cat Jarman has recently proposed that the pair might be Olaf, a Viking king active in Ireland and Britain from 853 onwards, and his son Eysteinn.[10] However, Olaf is reported by the *Annals of Ulster* to have been killed in Scotland by King Constantine in 874, and Eysteinn was apparently killed the following year at an unknown location in Ireland by someone named Albann, thought to be the Great Army leader Healfdene (see Chapter 3).[11] There were certainly tensions among the Viking leaders, but even if this identification is correct, it is a remarkably long distance for the corpses of both Olaf and Eysteinn to have been transported. What we can say, based on the dietary

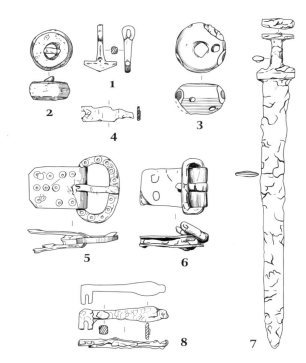

Repton: Grave 511. The grave goods (not to scale) included a silver-alloy Thor's hammer [1]; glass beads [2, 3], [2] with the loop of the Thor's hammer protruding through the hole; a copper-alloy fastener [4]; a copper-alloy belt- or sword-strap buckle [5]; a copper-alloy buckle from a sword sheath [6]; an iron sword [7]; and an iron key [8].

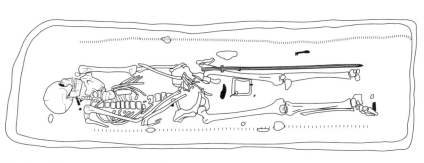

Repton: Grave 511.

0   1 m
0   3 ft

stable isotope analysis, is that both men grew up in the same area of southern Scandinavia, possibly Denmark, but that in later life they had both replaced a largely marine diet with a more land-based one.[12] They had travelled together as Viking warriors in life, and would also go together into the next world.[13] A substantial post was erected at the foot of the graves, marking their location, and presumably bearing carvings or a banner indicating the status of two men whose deaths clearly had been a great loss to the Army. Finally, the burial party smashed up one of the Anglo-Saxon crosses that had stood in the monastic graveyard, incorporating at least four fragments of it in a stone cairn, 1.8 m (6 ft) square, which they built over the two graves.[14]

At least two more warriors were buried adjacent to the crypt. One is represented by a spearhead found to the north of Graves 295/511, while an axe found in 1923 may have come from a burial (Grave 52) immediately south of the crypt. In addition, Grave 529 was the burial of a man aged 25–35, wearing a gold earring in his right ear, and placed within a wooden coffin to the north of the crypt.[15] He was accompanied by five silver coins, datable to the mid-870s, placed beside his head and shoulder; areas of dark staining suggest that the coins may have been placed in the coffin in a leather or textile bag. They comprised two coins of Burgred from late in his reign, *c.* 871–74, and three coins of Alfred, one of which could date

Repton: Grave 295 (above) and Grave 511 (below), with a stone setting for a marker post placed between them.

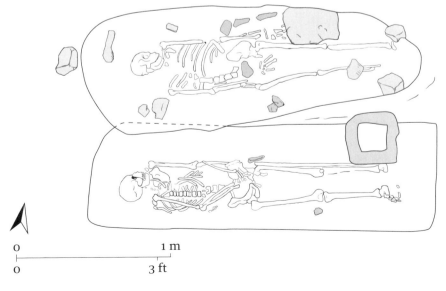

0
1 m

0
3 ft

to a few years after the overwintering in Repton in 873–74. One of the Burgred pennies had been struck by the moneyer Ealdulf from an obverse die similar to that used to make another coin minted by Ealdulf in the 1924 Beeston Tor hoard. As we have already seen in Chapter 3, there are antiquarian records of groups of coins found in stone coffins at other locations linked with Great Army camps, including Reading and Croydon. Similarly, at Hook Norton in Oxfordshire thirteen coins with a deposition date of *c.* 873 were 'found under the bones of a human body'.[16] In the case of the Repton burial, at least, it seems likely that the coins were placed in the coffin as grave offerings, rather than for safe-keeping and later recovery.

South of the crypt, there was also at least one more double grave, of two men interred in wooden coffins in a pit. Grave 83 was of a man aged around 50, with a copper-alloy ring on the third finger of his left hand. His companion, buried to his left, was a younger man, around 20 years old. The parallels with the double burial to the north of the church are striking. The latest furnished burial to be excavated (Grave 203) was of a woman, aged about 45, who had been buried with an iron knife, its handle bound with silver wire, and a strike-a-light. Given the absence of lavish grave goods these burials may not seem particularly Viking. However, any furnished grave is very rare in late Anglo-Saxon England, so these individuals must have been associated with the 873–74 overwintering or its immediate aftermath. Nonetheless, it is interesting that these individuals, including the slain warrior in Grave 511, though presumably not Christian by birth, were buried in an extension to a Christian graveyard adjacent to a royal mausoleum. They may have been hedging their bets, adopting aspects of Christian burial practice just as Viking settlers initially assimilated the Christian god into their wider pantheon. Alternatively, the raiders recognized that churches were powerful symbols of authority for English rulers and sought to associate themselves with these highly visible monuments in the landscape.

A different approach was adopted for the second group of Viking burials at Repton. Some 80 m (250 ft) west of the Anglo-Saxon church there had been another Mercian mausoleum. By the time Martin Biddle and Birthe Kjølbye-Biddle began excavating around the church in Repton the mausoleum was simply a mound in the vicarage garden. However, in 1980 the vicar, fed up with the inconvenience caused by the mound when he wanted to mow his lawn, gave the Biddles permission to excavate it. In fact, the mound had already been re-opened *c.* 1686 by a labourer called Thomas Walker who reported to Derbyshire antiquarian Dr Simon Degge that when 'cutting Hillocks' he had uncovered a square enclosure containing a stone coffin. After removing the cover, with some difficulty, Walker had found a 'humane body nine foot long', surrounded by 100 skeletons with their feet pointing to the coffin. It was examined again in 1787 by landowner George Gilbert who found the bones had been 'thrown in a heap together'[17] and in 1914 by antiquary J. C. Cox, who concluded that any remains had been long destroyed.[18]

However, the Biddles' re-excavation revealed that this had been a two-roomed stone building of 7th- or 8th-century date. It was aligned east–west, and was entered down a sloping ramp leading to a narrow doorway in the centre of the west wall. An internal doorway directly opposite led into the eastern compartment, in which members of the Mercian royal house would have been laid in stone sarcophagi. This may have included King Æthelbald, to whom a commemorative stone cross depicting a mounted warrior was erected in the late 8th or early 9th century, making it the earliest-known large-scale depiction of an English king.[19] Excavation revealed that this mausoleum was already in decay when the Vikings arrived in 873 with stucco peeling off the walls and lying on the floor. Analysis of the animal bones indicated that a barn owl had made its home in the dilapidated structure, bringing back its catch of small mammals, including voles, shrews and mice caught from the rich hunting grounds of the Trent floodplain. A large number of frog skeletons were also found in the remains.[20]

The excavation also revealed that the western compartment had been used by the Great Army for what the Biddles interpreted as a workshop. The floor was covered with charcoal and animal bones, along with a fragment of delicate metalwork, possibly from a book cover. Iron tongs, metal waste, coloured window glass from the monastery and broken carved stones were also found among the debris on the floor.

Before they left Repton in 874, members of the Great Army turned this decrepit former Mercian shrine into their own mausoleum. The building was cut down to ground level to serve as a burial chamber, and the floor of the eastern chamber was covered with a thick layer of Mercia mudstone. This material had been brought from at least a kilometre away, reflecting just how far the Army's control over the local landscape extended. A body was placed in a stone coffin in the centre of the chamber, and thousands of bones were then placed around it. Timber planks were laid over the burial chamber, and a low cairn of irregular stones heaped over it, followed by an earth mound, its edges defined by stone kerbing, creating a substantial structure, some 11 × 13 m (36 × 43 ft).

On re-excavating the burial mound, the Biddles found no trace of Thomas Walker's 'nine foot' giant, whose head had in any case been given to the master of Repton School in the late 17th century, and the 100 skeletons were no longer intact. In the north-east corner, however, lay a stack of sorted long bones that may have represented the only surviving part of the original burial; the rest of the bones were in a disorganized heap, which post-medieval pottery and clay tobacco-pipe fragments suggest had been disturbed in the 17th century or later, possibly by Walker himself. There was no trace of the stone sarcophagus reported to have been in the chamber. However, a fine coped grave cover of the late 8th or early 9th century was found immediately adjacent to the mound, lying on top of post-medieval pottery, presumably where Walker had dumped it.[21] It may have come from one of the Mercian burials originally in the mausoleum, and been reused by the Great Army

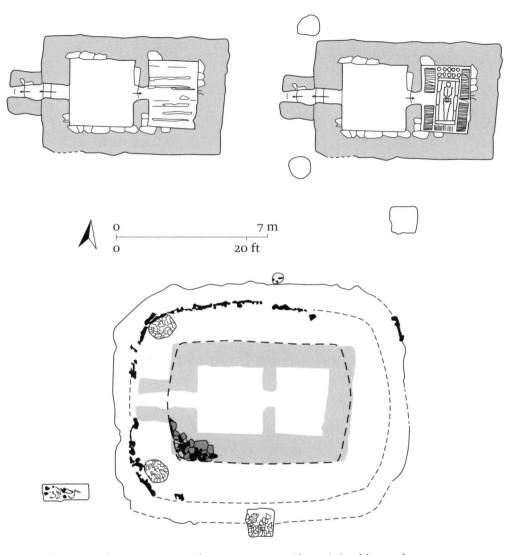

The second Repton mausoleum. *TOP LEFT* The original late 7th- or early 8th-century Anglo-Saxon sunken stone building. *TOP RIGHT* The building cut down and the eastern room used as a Great Army burial chamber *c.* 874, including a reconstruction of how the bone deposit may have been arranged, with the supposed central burial and possible external offering pits. *ABOVE* Wider view of the mound, showing the outline of the stone cairn, mound and kerb above the burial chamber, the offering pits filled with stone and, to the south-west, the burial of three children and a teenager, interpreted as a sacrificial deposit.

to inter one of their own leaders. Although the central burial did not survive, the deposit contained many objects that may originally have been buried with it, including an axe, a fragment of a sword, two large seaxes (small swords or daggers), a series of smaller seaxes and other knives, a chisel, a barrel-padlock key and other iron objects. There were also fragments of 7th- or 8th-century silver and silver gilt with cloisonné work, possibly from a sword hilt, and six pins. A parcel of five silver pennies, also found in the deposit, are an unusual group: they comprise a complete coin of Burgred of Mercia, and another cut in half; an imitative coin struck in the name of Æthelred I of Wessex; and a curious coin that purports to be of Alfred on the obverse but has a die usually used on Burgred coins minted in London on the reverse. These coins were struck no later than c. 872, while a coin of 873–74 also bears the name of Alfred but was struck by a moneyer usually associated with Burgred coins. In sum, these are not coins of the West Saxon kings, but are best seen as Mercian forgeries.[22]

Osteological examination has revealed that the charnel deposit comprised the remains of at least 264 individuals, including 253 adults and 11 juveniles. However, as there were no complete or articulated skeletons, these totals are based on the minimum number of individuals that must be represented by their body parts. Smaller bones were very under-represented, with only 1.4 per cent of the expected number of phalanges (finger and toe bones), for example. This strongly suggests that the assemblage must have been transported from elsewhere. Although skulls and limb bones could have been collected relatively easily, it would have been difficult to gather the smaller bones, assuming the tissue and ligaments had already rotted away. Nor was it a normal population: over 80 per cent were robust males in the age-range 17–45; there were very few children or younger teenagers. The Biddles concluded that these were the remains of Viking warriors, although others observed that Anglo-Saxon monks would also have been healthy males.[23]

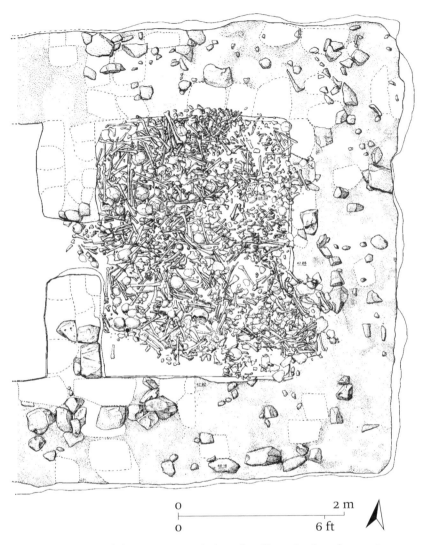

Repton: the charnel deposit, containing the disarticulated remains
of at least 264 people, in the eastern chamber of the mausoleum.
The drawing shows the upper level of bones that had been disturbed
when the mound was opened in the late 17th century by gardener
Thomas Walker.

The central burial – the alleged 9-ft giant – was clearly someone of high status to be given a reused royal sarcophagus. In a paper published in 2001 the Biddles suggested that this may have been Ivar the Boneless of saga tradition.[24] The *Annals of Ulster* record that the Viking leader Ivar died in 873, and it has generally been assumed that he died in Dublin, but the Biddles argue that although he was there in 871 it cannot be assumed that he stayed there. Indeed, the saga tradition says he was buried in England under a barrow placed on a boundary. We will never know if the focus of the burial display was Ivar, but the individual in the sarcophagus must certainly have been an important Viking leader, and we know that Healfdene, Guthrum, Oscetel and Anwend all left Repton alive in 874, while Ubba continued to raid into the latter part of the decade.

A group burial of three children and a teenager had been cut into the south-west corner of the mound, interpreted by the Biddles as a sacrificial deposit marking the completion of the charnel mound. Three were crouched on their sides (Graves 360–62): two were aged 8–11 and were positioned back to back with each other, and the other was aged *c.* 17. They had been laid over an extended burial (Grave 363), a fourth child, aged 8–12. Before the grave had been backfilled a sheep's jaw had been placed at the foot of the grave. While this could have been the leftovers of feasting, animal jaws, including sheep, are frequent in Scandinavian sacrificial deposits. Sheep are scarcely mentioned in Norse mythology, but they have an association with sacrificial offerings, with the Old Norse word for sheep (*sauðr*) deriving from the same root as the Gothic term (*sáuþs*) for 'sacrifice'; similar symbolism featured in Christianity, where the sacrificial lamb was a symbol of Christ.[25] There was a stone base, probably for a marker post in the middle of the south side of the grave, suggesting that the significance of the deposit was meant to be remembered. A group of broken pilaster fragments was found in the stone packing of an offering pit next to the mound, and other sculptural stone fragments were incorporated in the kerb around the mound. Cat Jarman's recent excavation next

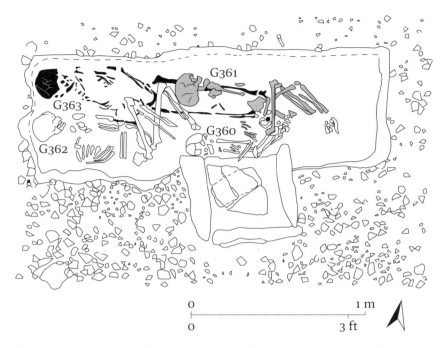

Simultaneous burial of four young people at Repton. Graves 360 and 361 were two children aged 8–11 years placed in the grave crouched back-to-back. They were placed above supine Grave 363, a child aged 8–12 years, and adjacent to Grave 362, the crouched remains of a youth aged *c.* 17.

to the mound has uncovered another cross-head fragment, as well as shattered querns that match those in the kerb surrounding the charnel mound. Radiocarbon dating for the juvenile burials, combined with their stratigraphic position, places them in a relatively narrow date range of AD 872–85, consistent with the 873–74 Repton overwintering.[26] It is not possible to say whether these juveniles had been travelling with the Great Army or were captives. Given their ages, stable isotope analysis may not help to answer this question, because if the three youngest had been with the Army from its arrival, or had been born after it arrived, then their teeth would have been forming while in England. Nonetheless, there were certainly children who travelled with the Great Army; the individual buried in Grave 295 was aged between 17 and 20 years, and if he had been with the Army since it arrived then he would have been travelling with them since the age of 9–12 years.

The mausoleum may have been reused by the Great Army as a convenient mortuary space, although its ritual associations with the Mercian royal family will not have been lost on the Vikings. However, burials in Viking Age Scandinavia frequently reference domestic architecture, through the use of doorways into mounds, and we believe that the mausoleum may have been selected for this reason. The excavation revealed two pits at the base of the mound marking the division between the western and eastern chamber, suggesting that the form of the building within the mound remained relevant to the Vikings who reused it, and it is striking that the burials are restricted to the east compartment beyond the doorway. The western compartment may have been a place where funerary rituals were conducted and offerings made, rather than being a workshop as the Biddles initially suggested. In Norse mythology doorways were understood as providing symbolic portals to the afterlife, and as boundaries between this life and the next. The early 10th-century traveller Ibn Fadlan wrote an Arabic account of a funeral among the Rus, descendants of Scandinavian settlers on the River Volga in Russia.[27] He described a sacrificial slave girl being lifted up in front of a wooden door frame over which she was able to see into the afterlife. In Scandinavia, some burial mounds have doorways built into them, with stone thresholds; others incorporate stone settings, or portals, on which food and other offerings were placed.[28] Two other large pits were excavated at the western end of the mound. These were interpreted by the Biddles as offering pits, but they may have been intended to hold above-ground markers, perhaps even forming part of an entranceway into the mound.

The Biddles suggested that the Repton charnel deposit represented a war cemetery of members of the Viking Great Army gathered from various battlefields, intermingled with the disturbed remains of the Mercian royal family. Radiocarbon dating of the charnel bones initially suggested that the deposit reflected at least two groups of burials, the first of the 7th century, potentially representing occupants of the Anglo-Saxon monastery (the majority of whom would also have been robust males), and the second one belonging to the late 9th century and the time of the overwintering of the Great Army.[29] However, new samples taken by Jarman and corrected for the so-called Marine Reservoir Effect (whereby the bones of individuals with diets high in fish produce earlier radiocarbon dates) are now consistent with the late 9th century. All samples that had appeared to predate the Viking Age were, in fact, those of individuals whose diets were characterized by relatively large amounts of seafood, and so they could indeed have died in the 870s. This does not prove that they were all members of the Great Army, but given the context, it does make it more likely that many of them were. Indeed, stable isotope analysis of 61 individuals by Jarman demonstrates that they were not local to Repton.[30] While not conclusive, it does show that these people grew up in a variety of places, which is consistent with what we know of the Army's composition.

Yet, if these were the remains of over 250 members of the Army, rather than bodies of Anglo-Saxon local residents disturbed from the monastic graveyard and mausoleums, it raises several questions about how their partial remains came to be gathered in a charnel deposit in Repton. None of the bones were articulated, so the corpses must have decomposed long enough for ligaments, muscle and other tissue to have rotted away before the bones were gathered in the mausoleum. It is difficult to imagine a series of events in which these individuals could have died and been buried elsewhere, then disinterred and their bones collected and brought to Repton. Would Viking warriors who died during other overwinterings not have been buried at those camps, as demonstrated by the burials at Torksey? Or if they all died at Repton, how did their skeletons decay so quickly, unless their bodies had been left lying around unburied for scavengers to pick up, and why would they not have been given normal graves like those buried around the

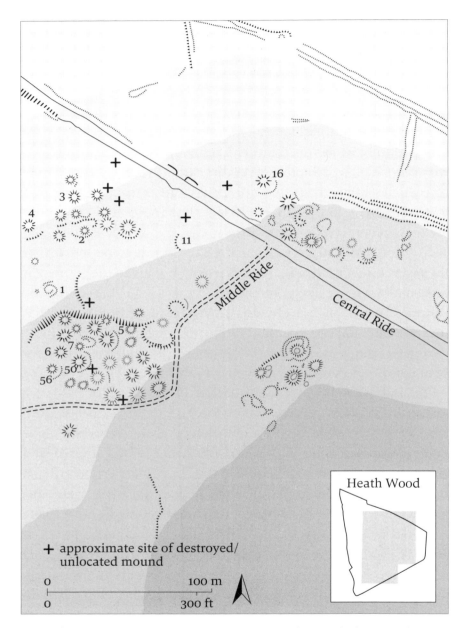

Plan of the Viking cremation cemetery at Heath Wood, showing the location, or approximate location, of 59 burial mounds, and other landscape features. Only those mounds referred to in the text are numbered on the plan.

church? None of these explanations seem very plausible, but until the full skeletal report is published, judgment must be postponed.

✤

There is, however, another cemetery that seems to be linked to the overwintering of the Viking Great Army in 873–74. On a promontory overlooking the floodplain of the Trent, some 4 km (2.5 miles) to the south-east of Repton, is the only Viking cremation cemetery ever discovered in the British Isles [pl. 14–16]. It also has the largest group of Viking burials known from England, interred beneath 59 burial mounds. The site is now in a block of mixed woodland known as Heath Wood, probably established in the late 18th century as part of the landscaping of Foremarke Hall, then home to Sir Robert Burdett, but now Repton Preparatory School. Heath Wood lies en route between Foremarke Hall and the Burdett's summerhouse at Knowle Hill, bisected by a carriageway that connects the two properties, possibly sited so that the barrow cemetery could be viewed from it. But in the late 9th century the hill was open heathland, commanding impressive views northwards and taking in the monastic enclosure and Viking camp in the foreground. In the light of the newly discovered metal-detected Viking finds from Foremark (see Chapter 4), it seems likely that the Heath Wood cemetery was adjacent to the south-eastern extent of the Viking camp, which was framed by the Repton cemetery at its north-western end.

A number of Viking warriors were brought to Heath Wood to embark on their journey to Valhalla. Burial platforms were created by clearing the ground around each mound down to bedrock, and sometimes levering up massive stones to form a ring-ditch. Funerary pyres were then constructed, on which the bodies of the warriors were laid out, accompanied by their weaponry, including swords and spears. In some cases the warrior's faithful hunting dog and horse were led to the pyre, across a narrow causeway that crossed the surrounding circular ditch, and there they were slaughtered, to rejoin their master in the afterlife. Cremated remains of women have also been identified, but we cannot be sure whether these were high-status females, or slaves sacrificed to accompany their masters. The pyres were then lit and the bodies consumed by fire. The pyre would have burnt for hours, and as dark fell the flames would have been visible for miles around, rising up to the sky. Feasting took place, and the remains of joints of beef, mutton and pork were also thrown onto the pyre. Next day, once the remains had cooled, the pyres were raked, and stones and sand were heaped up over the ashes and cremated bone to create a domed mound. The presence of the Great Army will have been indelibly imprinted on the Mercian landscape through this display.

The Viking cemetery at Heath Wood is also known by the name of the adjacent village, Ingleby, recorded as *Engelbi* in *Domesday Book*, and probably a Scandinavian name, as it ends with -*by,* commonly used to denote settlements in Denmark. It must have stood out as the 'English village', denoting an isolated survival of English inhabitants in a predominantly Scandinavian landscape. The name Foremark is also of Scandinavian derivation. In *Domesday Book* it is recorded as *Fornewerke*, or the 'old fortification', the equivalent of the Old English *Aldwark*. Although no trace of fortifications has been found in the vicinity of the Hall or Heath Wood, it reinforces the idea that the enclosure at Repton should be seen as part of the larger landscape of Great Army activity, including the camp at Foremark, and of which the cremation cemetery also formed a part.

Archaeological interest in Heath Wood goes back many years. On 22 May 1855, the notable Derbyshire antiquarian and barrow digger Thomas Bateman opened five mounds, possibly while staying at Foremarke Hall as a guest of the Burdetts. In *Ten Years Digging* he describes how in each case:

> the mound had been raised over calcined human bones, which lay in the same place on the natural surface as they occupied when the funeral pile was smothered out by the casting up of the tumulus. The bones and black ashes of the pyre, reduced by

compression to a layer about an inch thick, generally covered a space about four or five feet diameter in the centre; above were accumulated stones bearing marks of fire, which had been first thrown on the glowing embers, and over these earth was heaped to form the bowl-shaped mound.[31]

Bateman was probably sorely disappointed by his excavations at Heath Wood. He was used to Bronze Age barrows, which would typically contain a funerary urn and often impressive grave goods, but the only finds he recorded here were: 'two very small fragments of iron, found with two separate interments, one only having the definite form of a very slender pin, 1¾ inches long'. Nonetheless, his interpretation of the site was surprisingly prescient as, noting the similarity of the mounds, he concluded that: 'no great variation of date, if any, existed as to their age'. From the presence of iron, he further concluded that the mounds were unlikely to be ancient and that he 'would rather seek to connect them with the eventful period in which tradition affirms the place to have been the scene of a sanguinary conflict between the Saxons and their Danish enemies'. No record of the position of the barrows opened by Bateman survives, although the later earthwork survey identified one barrow (Mound 16) that appeared to have a hole dug in its centre, but which could not be linked to an otherwise documented excavation [pl. 14].[32]

For almost a century Heath Wood then appears to have been forgotten about until it was rediscovered in 1941 by Camden Clarke and William Fraser. Under their leadership, members of the Burton-on-Trent Natural History and Archaeological Society excavated six barrows, digging most weekends throughout the summers of 1941 and 1942, which now strikes us as an unusual wartime leisure activity.[33] Clarke and Fraser generally cut a trench across the centre of each mound but two of the six appeared to have been empty, while a third produced several pieces of metalwork and disturbed charcoal and bone but lacked any identifiable burial. The remaining

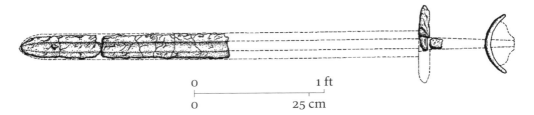

Remains of the sword from Mound 1, Heath Wood.

three all produced *in situ* central 'cremation-hearth' deposits and metalwork. The principal finds included a fragmentary iron sword, together with a number of sword-belt fittings.

Unable to date their discoveries, Clarke and Fraser approached T. D. Kendrick at the British Museum who thought that the burials were Anglo-Saxon, but counselled: 'I am afraid the proper thing to say to inexperienced diggers is to ask them to postpone the work until they can get a trained archaeologist to supervise it, for barrow-digging now is a big undertaking'. It appears that Kendrick also contacted W. F. Grimes of the Inspectorate of Ancient Monuments and Historic Buildings. Grimes had been seconded to the Ministry of Works during the Second World War to undertake rapid excavations ahead of new airfields and other military constructions. He visited the site in May 1942 and confirmed that the burials must be Anglo-Saxon. Kendrick and Grimes offered to help with publication but suggested that Clarke and Fraser contact the notable Anglo-Saxon archaeologist E. T. Leeds at the Ashmolean Museum for assistance with the finds. Leeds immediately questioned the early Anglo-Saxon dating. On full examination of the finds he wrote: 'I am convinced the finds are not Saxon though of the late Saxon period. Bateman after all was not very far from the truth ... I feel that meagre as in some respects they are, your finds illuminate some of the sepulchral darkness of late Saxon times.'

Clarke and Fraser excavated a seventh barrow in Heath Wood in the autumn of 1948, and issued a rather summary report on it the following year. The excavation uncovered a central cremation-hearth deposit and various pieces of metalwork including part of a second sword, again dated by Leeds to the 9th/10th centuries.

Following the publication of Mounds 1–7, in 1951 the Heath Wood cemetery was designated a Scheduled Ancient Monument by the Ministry of Works. In theory this gave it protection, but the mounds remained under threat from forestry operations and in 1955 the Forestry Commission agreed to clear but leave unplanted the four principal barrow concentrations, while the Ministry excavated seven 'outlying' mounds at risk during forestry operations. These seven were excavated in c. 3 weeks by Merrick Posnansky and the results subsequently published, but Posnansky then moved to California and became a social anthropologist. Without him present to remind British archaeologists about the site, only the inclusion of a plan of the cemetery in a popular synthesis by Holger Arbman in 1969, entitled *The Vikings,* rescued it from complete obscurity.[34] One mound proved to be natural and, of the other six, only one contained a cremation hearth and metalwork; the others were apparently empty and described as cenotaph burials. The metalwork was fragmentary, but included at least one piece of apparent silver-wire embroidery compared by textiles expert Elizabeth Crowfoot to examples from the Swedish cemetery at Birka.

While the Viking cemetery remained neglected, and was ignored by the Biddles when they excavated at Repton, the Ministry (by now

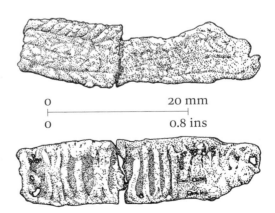

0   20 mm

0   0.8 ins

Silver-wire embroidery (front and back views of same fragment) from Mound 11, Heath Wood.

operating as English Heritage) monitored it and, in 1992, commissioned an earthwork survey undertaken by Marcus Jecock. This confirmed that the 59 barrows cluster into four distinct groups with only a few isolated barrows lying between them. It also highlighted the need for further excavation under modern conditions and from 1998 to 2000 Marcus teamed up with Julian and the University of York to excavate three mounds. One was adjacent to Burdett's 18th-century carriageway, in the group probably investigated by Bateman, and was so badly disturbed by later ploughing as well as by rabbit and root action that no traces of any burial survived. The other two mounds we investigated – Mounds 50 and 56 – were both in the main cluster of burials. In 1998 we found them in a small clearing within the wood, fringed by bracken, trees and rhododendron bushes. The mounds were scarcely visible and Mound 50, the larger of the pair, appeared as a relatively gentle bump in the ground, rising little more than 0.5 m (2 ft) above the surface.

We decided to tackle both mounds using the quadrant method, dividing them up like a cake into quarters and excavating diagonally opposite quarters first, thereby providing two complete sections across the mounds [pl. 15]. As we started to trowel the surface of Mound 50, however, we discovered a smooth black surface. Around the mound it sloped down below centuries of accumulated forest leaf-mulch which, when cleared, revealed a circular ring-ditch, cut into the bedrock. This black surface represented the turf that had originally covered the mound, either as a natural build-up or as a deliberate sealing layer, but which had been eroded away from the upper half of the mound. The barrows were much more substantial than first thought and, as we excavated, Mound 50 emerged like the bulk of an iceberg hidden beneath the ocean surface. In the north-western quadrant, however, the slope of the mound was interrupted by a causeway that had crossed the ditch, presumably so that the burial party could access the centre of the mound.

In the centre of the mound we encountered the first trace of the burial ritual: the remains of a cow jaw, possibly an animal sacrifice or the remains of funeral feasting, or both. Then the cremation hearth appeared: an oval area of burnt sand and charcoal mixed with cremated bone [pl. 16]. After the fire died down the hearth had evidently been swept and larger objects removed. We know that there must have been a sword on the pyre, as we found a fragment of a silver sword-hilt grip, less than 30 mm (1 inch) in length and 8 mm (0.3 inches) wide, decorated in Trewhiddle style [pl. 17]. There must also have been a shield, as there were four pieces of folded iron which had been used as clamps around the shield rim [pl. 18], similar to examples from chamber graves at Birka, although the absence of a shield boss suggests that it, too, had been collected by the funeral party after the pyre cooled. Other objects included a knife, and large numbers of small nails, some quite possibly from a chest or coffin, or from planks which had been used as fuel for the pyre.

Fortunately for us, Viking cremations were less efficient than modern ones and, despite the raking of the pyre, enough bone remained to tell us something about who – and what – was cremated on Mound 50. Most of the burnt remains actually belong to animals – the majority from a horse and a dog, but pig, sheep (or goat), and possibly an ox were also represented. While the beef, mutton and pork were probably further remains of the funeral feast, the dog and horse were whole animals, presumably sacrificed so as to accompany their owner to the next world. There were also at least two individuals cremated on Mound 50. One was an adult, aged 18–45 years old, and possibly a female, while the second was a juvenile, or even a child. This makes it difficult, of course, to identify the owner of the weapons, or the sacrificed animals. Maybe it was a young male warrior who was buried with a female slave or companion, as seems to have been the case in the Rus funeral described by Ibn Fadlan. Perhaps, alternatively, it was the young son of one of the Great Army's leaders who had yet to reach adulthood, and this necessitated an elaborate burial to compensate for the tragic loss. As Dawn has pointed out in her work on children and migration, across the Viking diaspora there are examples of unusual burials of older children. She interprets these burials as an indication that such children were critical to the process of adapting to new environments, representing the hopes of their families for permanent settlement and establishing a lineage in new lands. Accordingly, their loss was keenly felt and reflected in elaborate burial rituals.[35] However, in the light of the possible identification of a female warrior from Birka grave Bj.581, some might argue that the Mound 50 adult burial was a warrior queen, cremated with a younger male slave. Or perhaps, given that the sex attribution is only probable, we discount the bioarchaeology and say this was a male burial on the basis of the weapons alone. Maybe this is simply a case (to borrow from Jacquetta Hawkes's discussion decades ago of how interpretations of Stonehenge seem to change to suit the times), of every age getting the Vikings it wants, or needs.

What we can say with more certainty, following recent stable isotope analysis, is that neither the adult nor the horse from Mound 50 grew up in England. Indeed, they most probably came from Norway or Sweden.[36] This is less significant in the case of the person than it is for the animal. It is no surprise that the Viking Great Army included those of Scandinavian origin, male or female. However, despite the vivid depictions in the Bayeux Tapestry of the Norman Vikings disembarking their horses from their fleet of longships prior to the Battle of Hastings, this is the first archaeological evidence that the Great Army brought their own mounts with them, some 200 years earlier. Although the *Anglo-Saxon Chronicle* tells us that the Great Army was given horses on arrival in East Anglia in 865, clearly this is not the full story; the Vikings had arrived with some of their personal horses, and hounds, and on death they sometimes travelled with them to Valhalla.

Meanwhile, in Heath Wood, in the year 2000, our excavations of Mound 56 – the smaller barrow to the south-west of Mound 50 – were proving problematic. Over two seasons we had excavated two diagonally opposed quadrants all the way down to the natural sand and bedrock, and found absolutely nothing – no trace of a cremation hearth and no grave offerings. We were beginning to suspect that Posnansky, following Clarke and Fraser, had been right: that many of the mounds were empty 'cenotaph' burials. Nonetheless, in our final season we decided to excavate a third quadrant. Even if different parts of the mound had eroded unevenly, we should find traces of a cremation hearth here, if there was one.

There was no hearth, but we did find something else. Towards the north-western edge of the mound, at the level where a cremation hearth might have been expected, there was a thin spread of blackened loam, *c.* 1 × 1.5 m (3 × 5 ft) across, in the middle of which were several fragments of human bone, and a single 9th-century ringed pin, of the type adopted by Scandinavian settlers following the Irish fashion of using a pin to fasten a woollen cloak. Analysis of the cremated bone showed that there was far less of it than one would expect from a whole cremation: less than a fifth of the normal expected weight, in fact, and only enough to say that these were the partial remains of an adult, aged 18–40, of indeterminate sex. There was also a very small fragment of burnt pig bone. Combined with the fact that there was no trace of any burning of the surrounding matrix, this led us to conclude that these were the token remains of an individual who had been cremated elsewhere, but that on clearance of the pyre a sample of burnt bone had been collected, mixed with charcoal, and placed in some form of container – maybe a canvas or leather bag – which was perhaps then fastened with the unburnt cloak pin. The remains were then brought to Heath Wood for a monumental burial in one of the barrow graves.

These rather sparse remains recovered during the near-complete excavation of Mound 56 made us reconsider the so-called empty mounds found by Clarke and Fraser, who had only trenched across

A 9th-century ringed pin, Mound 56, Heath Wood.

the centre of the barrows. Their approach would have completely missed any such token offerings placed towards one edge of these mounds. In summary, therefore, our excavation of two mounds revealed two variants of the Viking cremation rite: one involved *in situ* cremation; the second saw burial of the partial remains of an individual who had been cremated elsewhere. The second rite is reminiscent of the bones found in the reused mausoleum at Repton, also interpreted as reinterment of Viking bodies from elsewhere. If that is the case, then both Repton and Heath Wood can be regarded as war cemeteries for members of the Great Army that remained in use for a limited number of years.

In other respects, however, the Repton and Heath Wood cemeteries are worlds apart in terms of what they say about the ideological approach to burial. The Repton burials reused a Mercian royal mausoleum, adjacent to one of the holiest Christian shrines in England. But those buried at the other end of the winter camp, at Heath Wood, displayed overtly pagan practices with animal sacrifice, cremation with weaponry and mound burial, evoking and even over-stating traditional Scandinavian practices. Why such different approaches? We already saw that the Army that overwintered at Repton was a combination of several disparate bands under multiple leaders, including those that made up the original Great Army, now reinforced by the summer army that according the *Anglo-Saxon Chronicle* joined them at Reading in 871 (Chapter 3).[37] On departing from Repton they split again, with Healfdene's forces heading north while Guthrum went to East Anglia. Maybe the rivalries or arguments that led to the forces dividing were also reflected in differing ideas of what was a suitable burial for a warrior.

Whatever the reason, the Repton/Foremark/Heath Wood complex provides us with the best evidence from England for what happened to the Army's dead. At Torksey modern ploughing appears to have badly disturbed any burials within the camp, although the distribution of human remains again suggests multiple burial locations (see Chapter 4). Otherwise, burials that can be associated with the

Great Army are extremely rare, as with Viking burials in England in general. It is tempting, however, to link two skeletons with Viking weapons found in Nottingham in 1851 with the overwintering of the Great Army there in 867–68. The spearhead is 9th-century and although one of the swords may be later, it would be highly unusual to find 10th-century weapon burials in lowland England.[38]

The Army spent the winter of 869–70 at Thetford, where two burials appear to be of Scandinavian type. One was accompanied by an Anglo-Saxon sword that had been deliberately bent as a possible act of ritual destruction of the weapon, a practice seen in Viking burials elsewhere; the second was accompanied by a spear and a knife. A handful of other burials excavated nearby appear to have been unfurnished but may have been associated with the two furnished ones, echoing the arrangement at Repton.[39] It is notable that Thetford is located close to the only other known furnished graves of Scandinavian type in East Anglia, and these may also derive from the overwintering of the Great Army. Just 6 km (c. 4 miles) to the north-west at Santon Downham, one or more burials were excavated close to the church and the River Ouse. While the record of this 1867 excavation is thin, the surviving grave goods include an Anglo-Saxon sword and a pair of Scandinavian oval brooches, suggesting a double burial of a male and female, although only the remains of a single individual were reported. Around 11 km (7 miles) to the east of Thetford a furnished grave was excavated in 1982–83 in a ditch on the edge of a churchyard at Middle Harling. Unfortunately, some of the bones were left on the London Underground as they were being taken to the British Museum (Natural History) for analysis and the remains of the skull were never recovered – presumably heads rolled! Nonetheless, the surviving skeletal remains suggest that they were male. The grave goods included four knives, a whetstone, a prick spur and a copper-alloy ear-scoop; the individual appears to have been buried clothed and wearing a belt, as there was a copper-alloy buckle above the left pelvis and an iron buckle near the left knee.[40]

Two separate inhumation burials near the Thames at Reading have also been linked with the Great Army, simply based on their association with the overwintering site of 870–71, as the graves are not closely datable.[41] At a meeting of the Society of Antiquaries of London in March 1867, John Akerman, a Berkshire antiquary, exhibited a sword said to have been found in June 1831, 'in the ballast pit at Reading, about a hundred yards from the end of the engine sheds; about two to three feet below the surface of the ground'.[42] This places it within the area known as the *Vastern*, on the northern side of the postulated site of the Viking camp (see p. 72). Akerman reported that according to the finders there was a male burial and the sword was found bent into the ribs of a complete horse skeleton.[43] The sword is unfortunately now lost, but a surviving drawing shows that it had 'gripping-beast' ornament on the hilt. In 1966 another quarryman was working at Sonning, only

Sword with decorated hilt, found in Reading in 1831.

c. 300 m (1,000 ft) north of the present bank of the Thames, opposite Reading. He noticed a sword projecting from the load of gravel in the bucket of his machine. He stopped work to investigate, and in the gravel bank he found the rest of the sword blade, together with human bones, a ringed pin (comparable to that from Heath Wood), an iron knife, six arrowheads and an iron strip with a rivet, of unknown purpose. Later examination of the bones indicated that there were two males present.[44] On balance, it seems likely that both the Reading and Sonning burials occurred during the 870–71 overwintering.

Many pieces of Viking weaponry have been recovered from the River Thames as it passes through London, including swords, axes and spears, but most are not convincing as evidence of burials, and they have been variously interpreted as ritual deposits and battle losses.[45] One, however, warrants further consideration: a sword found in 1948 in excavations for a new boiler-house for the Houses of Parliament. The find-spot of the Westminster sword is close to the south-east side of Thorney Island, a small gravel island on which Westminster Abbey and the Houses of Parliament now sit. The abbey was founded by St Dunstan in the 10th century, but it has been suggested that there was already a minster church here, and there is evidence for 8th- and 9th-century activity.[46] At that stage the island was surrounded by marshy alluvium, through which passed two branches of the River Tyburn, one of which joined the Thames about 50 m (160 ft) south of the position of the sword. Although no burial was located in the excavations, it is recorded that two horse skulls and limb bones were found nearby.[47] The Westminster Bridge hoard of Burgred coins (see Chapter 3) was also hidden on Thorney Island. The modern Westminster Bridge opened in 1862 and replaced an earlier bridge of 1750, which itself may have been near a possible crossing point of the Thames.[48] The location of the island, *c.* 1 km (0.6 miles) upstream from the Anglo-Saxon trading site at *Lundenwic*, makes it a reasonable candidate for the hitherto unidentified Viking winter camp of 871–72.

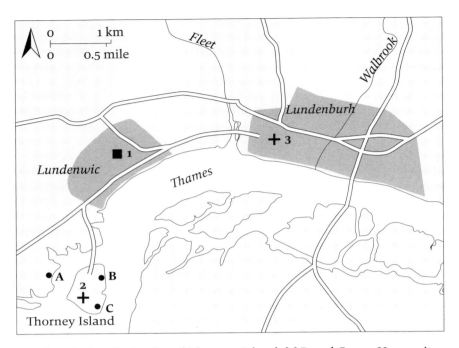

Lundenwic, Lundenburh and Thorney Island: [1] Royal Opera House site; [2] Westminster Abbey; [3] St Paul's Cathedral; [A] findspot of a possible gaming piece; [B] likely site of Westminster Bridge hoard; [C] findspot of Westminster sword.

Finally, there is one other burial which, with the Great Army signature, may plausibly be associated with the events of 865–75. At Kiloran Bay on the island of Colonsay in the southern Hebrides a Viking grave was discovered in sand dunes in 1882. A male warrior had been buried in a stone enclosure and a small boat had been placed over the grave [pl. 12]. Two slabs at either end were marked with crosses, perhaps Christian emblems added to a pagan burial, or Christian grave-markers reused from nearby. Outside the enclosure a horse was buried, its metatarsal severed by a massive blow. Was this, like the warriors buried at Repton, someone hedging his bets by being buried with both Christian and pagan symbols, or a lapsed convert? In addition to the usual accompanying weapons of sword, spear, axe and shield (the latter of Irish type), the warrior was buried with a set of bronze scales, comprising a balance beam, two pans and six decorated lead weights [pl. 13]. There were three early to mid 9th-century Northumbrian stycas: one of Æthelred II (841–44); one of Wigmund of York (c. 837–54); the third illegible. The two dated coins had been perforated and thus demonetized, perhaps for use as insets on lead weights given the centrally placed holes; the burial itself has been dated to the late 9th century.[49] A lead object, originally also interpreted as a weight, resembles crowned gaming pieces and is comparable to those from Torksey. Was this the burial of a proud warrior and trader, once a member of the Great Army that had camped at Torksey, whose journey north had led him to settle on this remote Hebridean island, where he was buried with the signature collection of artefacts typical of the Army's winter camp?

In conclusion, it is highly probable that many of the small number of known Viking burials in England made in the 870s can be associated with the Great Army. Given the huge size of the Army, there must have been many deaths each winter, and these individuals would most conveniently be buried within or close to the camps, as at Nottingham, Thetford, Torksey and Reading. Within the Repton/Foremark/Heath Wood complex, however, the two larger cemeteries appear to have been used over several years. The burials in these cemeteries can be seen as war graves, where warriors were brought together to be buried, possibly from some distance. There may have been larger cemeteries linked with the other Great Army camps, still waiting to be found, but Heath Wood seems to have had a special role, given its central and commanding location overlooking the floodplain of the Trent. The prominence at the Heath Wood cemetery of pagan funerary practices such as cremation with full weaponry, animal sacrifice and mound burial suggests that members of the Great Army who were buried there were making a deliberate statement about their Viking warrior identity. As we shall see in the next chapter, these practices largely disappeared as the Army began to settle permanently in England and warrior cremation gave way to Christian inhumation in churchyards.

7
Raiders to Settlers

The Anglo-Saxon *vill* at *Cotum* lies amidst the rolling chalk uplands of the Wolds of eastern Yorkshire, at the head of one arm of a dry valley, and near the later medieval village of Cottam. A small settlement was established here sometime in the 8th century AD, a dependency of the Northumbrian royal residence at *Driffelda* (near modern Driffield).[1] The *vill* comprised a pair of modest timber halls and a cluster of workshops set within a ditched enclosure, built adjacent to the ancient burial mound of a Bronze Age chieftain, which may have provided an imagined ancestral link to the distant past. The settlement also lay alongside a sunken trackway, one of many that had crossed the chalk uplands from at least the Iron Age. To the north this trackway ran down from the Wolds into the rich agricultural clay soils of the Vale of Pickering; south of *Cotum* it continued across the chalklands, ultimately descending to the Humber estuary, while another arm went eastwards to what are now the holiday resorts of the Yorkshire coast. The trackway continued to bring farmers onto the Wolds during the Roman period, and, after the legions abandoned their fortresses in York and Malton, it brought shepherds and their flocks up from lowland farms in the Vale to graze in summer pastures on the Wolds. Following the collapse of the northern Roman province of Britannia Inferior, permanent settlements on the Wolds largely disappeared, and clumps of woodland reappeared, providing an ideal habitat for wild deer.

Cotum was one of many such small settlements founded in the 8th century as the post-Roman population started to recover in size and the Wolds were recolonized. Its Anglo-Saxon name literally means 'at the cottages', but just a kilometre to the south-west there was a second cluster of Anglo-Saxon buildings at Cowlam (*Colmun,* 'at the hill tops'). Primarily agricultural, these sites acquired multiple functions as centres for taxation and the dispensation of justice, as well as for craft production and hunting. At *Cotum* small fairs and periodic markets were held on specific days of the year, attracting traders who sold decorative jewellery and fine bone and antler combs, all under the control of the local lords, keen to extract their sales tax. The medieval villages that ultimately succeeded these two Anglo-Saxon settlements went into decline in post-medieval times and today both Cottam and Cowlam are known by archaeologists as Deserted Medieval Villages (DMVs). Cottam is now only a series of grassy banks and mounds and Cowlam was bulldozed away by an overzealous farmer in the 1960s.

Julian first came to Cottam in 1992, with metal-detectorist Dave Haldenby, who had been detecting the site since 1987. Over five years Dave and his friends had found some 64 Anglo-Saxon dress pins, 34 strap-ends, and 22 Northumbrian stycas in a field immediately to the west of the modern Burrow House Farm. The high concentration of finds had led archaeologists and numismatists to call Cottam a 'productive site', not because they believed that metalwork was being manufactured there, but simply because it produced so many metal objects. Julian had been excavating at a more famous site on the Yorkshire Wolds at Wharram Percy to investigate the Anglo-Saxon origins of another DMV there, and he now wanted to extend his research to other known productive sites, such as Cottam, to see if they followed a similar pattern.

Julian and Dave had come to Cottam to meet Roger Bannister, the landowner and farmer. Potatoes were his primary business and the deep ploughing needed to grow them in the shallow chalk soils was disturbing the tops of Anglo-Saxon pits and ditches that had been buried for centuries, bringing the objects to the surface. Julian wanted to excavate Roger's field to see what traces of Anglo-Saxon settlement survived. Fortunately, Roger said yes, and over the last 20 years Julian and Dave have been researching the sites at Cottam and Cowlam, assembling a remarkable story that throws new light on the Viking Great Army and its impact on Northumbria.[2]

We have already seen that after leaving their camp at Repton the Great Army split in two, with one force under its leader Healfdene heading back to Northumbria. The *Anglo-Saxon Chronicle* records that in 876 'Healfdene shared out the land of the Northumbrians, and they proceeded to plough and support themselves'.[3] This short sentence underpins decades of academic debate about the impact of Scandinavian settlement on eastern England. It epitomizes the transition from Viking raiding, in search of silver and slaves, to the seizure of land for settlement, and the great land partitions imposed by the Viking leaders on the vanquished Anglo-Saxon kingdoms. Healfdene's appropriation of Northumbria set the pattern for the rest of the decade. The Wessex-based scribe of the *Anglo-Saxon Chronicle* records these momentous events with typical economy: in late summer of 877 'the army went away into Mercia and shared out some of it, and gave some to Ceolwulf' while in 880 'the army went from Cirencester into East Anglia, and settled there and shared out the land'.[4] Thus is described the death knell of the great Anglo-Saxon kingdoms of Northumbria, Mercia and East Anglia.

Archaeological study of Cottam has now helped to illuminate this transition from raiding to settlement. Fortunately, Dave was not like most metal-detectorists in the 1980s. He appreciated that the precise location of finds could be important, even when objects were recovered from disturbed plough-soil. Although this was in the days before hand-held Global Positioning Systems (GPS), he took care to record where he found each object, pacing out the distance of each findspot perpendicular to a modern fence-line to the east, and in relation to a gatepost. Gradually, using paper and coloured pencils he drew up a detailed map of all his finds, revealing that they were in two main concentrations, some 100 m (330 ft) apart. The southern cluster was right on top of the Anglo-Saxon enclosure, already revealed by the plotting of crop marks, which in dry summers were visible from the air as darker patches and lines where the crops were thicker over the deeper soils of the Anglo-Saxon ditches and rubbish pits. Our excavations confirmed the existence of a small Anglo-Saxon settlement here, including a pair of small timber halls and several workshops. The northern cluster was a mystery, however, as nothing was visible in the crop marks, apart from a single feature. Yet most of the 10th-century metalwork had

Distribution of metal-detected finds from Cottam superimposed on modern field boundaries and features plotted from aerial photography. The shaded area shows the extent of the geophysical survey of the northern settlement area.

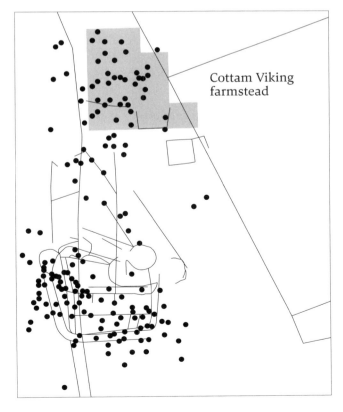

Cottam Viking farmstead

Anglo-Scandinavian
copper-alloy bell found at
Cottam, decorated with
ring-and-dot ornament.

been found in this area, including a pair of Anglo-Scandinavian bells. Surface collection of pottery sherds also revealed a concentration in the same area of a distinctive type of wheel-thrown pottery with a hard, black, pimply surface. This is known as Torksey ware and it was not made until the last quarter of the 9th century. We shall discuss its importance in Chapter 10.

Geophysical survey of this area confirmed that there were indeed settlement traces corresponding with the northern cluster of finds on Dave's map. Excavation demonstrated why they had remained invisible from the air. The features here were incredibly shallow – many only a few centimetres deep – because years of ploughing had removed the original ground surface, leaving the archaeological remains of the settlement too shallow to affect crop growth, apart from one gated timber entrance with a massive rampart and ditch on either side. Our excavation and survey revealed a type of settlement that had never been seen before. Beyond the imposing gatehouse was a series of small rectangular enclosures, with ephemeral traces of buildings represented only by the stubs of holes left by timber uprights as they rotted. In what appeared to be an empty field we had discovered the first Viking farmstead to be found in eastern England.

However, the story does not end there. Although we finished excavating at Cottam in 1995, we had only dug a small proportion of the settlements. Dave carried on metal-detecting and, by June 2015, 1,082 of his finds had been catalogued, 851 of which belong to the 8th to 10th centuries. Dave's finds are now in Hull Museum, but our detailed dating and plotting of them now reveals that there were actually two phases of Viking activity at Cottam, allowing us to tell the full story of what happened when Healfdene returned to Northumbria.[5]

Sometime in the late 870s, an offshoot of the Great Army arrived at Cottam. Maybe they were travelling north, gathering what loot they could on the way; maybe they had travelled out from *Jorvik*

Interpretative plot of the geophysical survey of the northern settlement area at Cottam, showing the sub-rectangular enclosures, and the entrance-way at bottom centre.

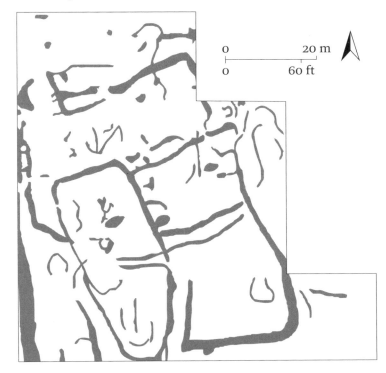

0   20 m

0   60 ft

and were reconnoitring Anglo-Saxon estates to seize. Whatever the reason, they appear to have looted the Anglo-Saxon *vill*, which was subsequently abandoned, its judicial function destroyed. An execution post or *heofod stoccan* (lit. 'head-stake'), which may have stood near the Bronze Age mound, was pulled down and a skull that had been mounted on it as a warning to other wrongdoers was unceremoniously tossed into a rubbish pit. The raiding party did not stay long but they left behind other evidence of their visit, spread over a wide area: a broken spear; the hilt of a sword; a fragment of a silver dirham; a silver sceat, which had been 'pecked' to test its silver content; and a globule of molten silver. Also left behind were the balance arm from a set of hand-scales, and a number of lead weights, probably employed to share out the precious metal that had been gathered en route. There were also pieces of 8th-century metalwork that had been crudely chopped up, including a piece of a gilt-bronze mount from the cover of an Anglo-Saxon book, cut along one edge. And in the rubbish pit, with the human skull, was a roughly broken fragment of a silver penny of Æthelberht of Wessex (858–*c.* 862/64), collected by a member of the raiding party in southern England and now casually lost in East Yorkshire.

However, just a couple of years later, maybe even sooner, the Vikings returned to Cottam and established their own farmstead just 100 m (330 ft) north of the abandoned Anglo-Saxon *vill*. The artefacts from this phase are tightly concentrated over the settlement area and they denote peaceful settlement, not raiding: spindle whorls, wool combs, two Anglo-Scandinavian bells and various dress accessories. Perhaps a member of the same group that had first raided Cottam saw its potential and returned, or maybe Healfdene had chosen to reward one of his other followers with the gift of this particular estate. Whoever he was, the new landholder decided to mark his ownership in the flamboyant style of the nouveau riche. His farmstead lacked any substantive defences – he had no need of them, with a succession of Viking rulers now in charge in *Jorvik* – although he built a gatehouse with a timber palisade.

Broken spear found
at Cottam.

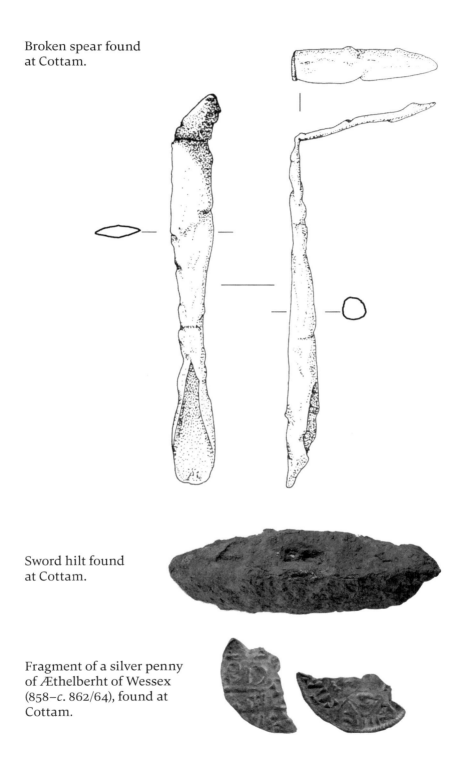

Sword hilt found
at Cottam.

Fragment of a silver penny
of Æthelberht of Wessex
(858–c. 862/64), found at
Cottam.

An 11th-century text attributed to Archbishop Wulfstan II of York (1002–23) describes such a gatehouse (*burh-geat*) as an important status symbol:

> And if a *ceorl* prospered so that he had fully five hides of his own land, [church and kitchen], bell [house] and *burh-geat* [gatehouse], seat and special office in the king's hall, then was thence forward entitled to the rank of a *thegn*.[6]

Cottam's new owner had a commanding view southwards, along the trackway to the abandoned ruins of the Anglo-Saxon farm and market, and beyond that to the Humber estuary and the North Sea, whence he had come. But for this Viking there was to be no going back to Scandinavia – he was here to stay and, given the female jewellery found at Cottam, it seems that he took an Anglo-Saxon wife. Not for her the traditional pair of oval brooches, such as those worn by the Norwegian immigrant buried at Adwick-le-Street, near Doncaster.[7] Instead she chose to decorate her cloak with a copper-alloy disc-shaped brooch in Anglo-Saxon style, bought from a metalworker in *Jorvik*, and decorated not with Anglo-Saxon ornament, but with a Scandinavian backwards-biting dragon, in what art historians term the Jellinge style. The brooch was neither Anglo-Saxon, nor Viking, but mass-produced in the workshops of *Jorvik* in a hybrid style, which archaeologists now call Anglo-Scandinavian.

This story of settlement dislocation, with the abandonment of an Anglo-Saxon settlement and its replacement by an Anglo-Scandinavian one, generally in a new location some short distance away, is repeated many times throughout eastern and northern England in the late 9th century. Indeed, at most excavated rural sites in these regions the latest finds date to the late 8th or 9th centuries, and occupation then abruptly ceases. This pattern has been confirmed by many major landscape excavations of the last 50 years, whether we look at Catholme in Derbyshire, Flixborough in North Lincolnshire or West Heslerton in North Yorkshire.

ABOVE Pair of oval brooches from female grave, Adwick-le-Street, South Yorkshire.

RIGHT Copper-alloy brooch, decorated with backwards-biting dragon in Jellinge style, Cottam.

The pattern is also mirrored in the evidence from metal-detected sites, in much larger numbers. Anglo-Saxon sites in Yorkshire are rich in finds of bronze dress pins and strap-ends, as well as Northumbrian stycas. The majority of these 'productive sites' show a sudden cut-off after the 9th century, with no artefacts that can be dated later than that.[8] As we have seen in Chapter 5, however, a second, much smaller group of metal-detected sites, including Roxby-cum-Risby, Swinhope, Stamford Bridge and Yapham, not only have aspects of the Great Army 'signature' but also a broader range of domestic artefacts and dress accessories associated with permanent settlement. The miniature Anglo-Scandinavian bells are diagnostic of this settlement phase, while lead spindle whorls for the spinning of wool are more prosaic examples of settlement finds. Such spindle whorls were frequently crudely finished and are conical or domed, usually with a flat top. They are found at many Viking sites, including thirteen on Coppergate in York, and it is believed that they were manufactured in York. They are not found at Anglo-Saxon sites, where spindle whorls are made of bone or ceramic, but they are common in Viking Age Scandinavia, representing 30 per cent of spindle whorls from Kaupang, for instance.[9]

Like Cottam, it appears that many of these sites with Anglo-Scandinavian artefacts were initially visited by members of the Great Army for raiding or trading but then occupied by Scandinavians into the 10th century. In the Yorkshire Wolds, for instance, metal-detected data provides evidence for visits by members of the Great Army leading to many settlements being abandoned, but with a smaller number of sites continuing in use with a 10th-century Scandinavian presence.[10] This is not to deny the importance of wider changes in settlement patterns and land ownership that were already under-way in 9th- and 10th-century England, including the break-up and privatization of royal and ecclesiastical estates. Nonetheless, by the late 9th century most Anglo-Saxon sites in Yorkshire had been in existence for 100–150 years and, as reflected by the introduction of the styca coinage, the Northumbrian economy was thriving. It cannot be coincidence that the abandonment of each site is associated with the appearance of objects that can be linked to the Viking Great Army. This demonstrates the major impact of the land partitions by leaders of the Great Army, and the consequent disruption of Anglo-Saxon settlement patterns. It is clear that the Viking winter camps led to many individual land takeovers after AD 876. Throughout southern Northumbria the new evidence tells a story of looting and the abandonment of farmsteads, traditional marketplaces and estate centres.

The site at Wharram Percy in North Yorkshire, explored over many decades, provides a rare excavated glimpse of a full settlement sequence. The Wharram project began in 1950 when the economic

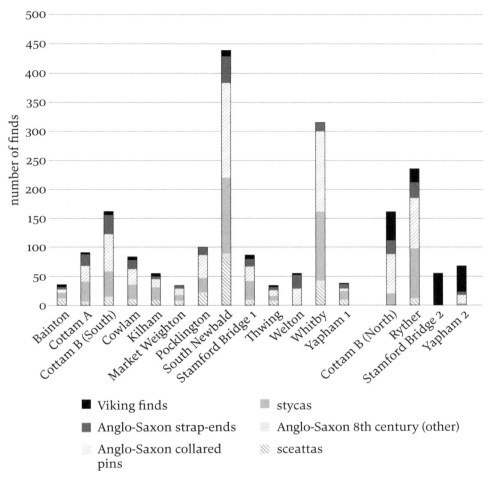

Graph comparing proportions of specific categories of finds at a range of Northumbrian Anglo-Saxon and Anglo-Scandinavian/Viking sites.

historian Maurice Beresford brought some of his students on the bus from Leeds to Malton and then walked several miles to a quiet, dry valley where St Martin's church nestled alongside a pair of 19th-century brick railway cottages. Armed with buckets and spades, he was able to demonstrate that the grassy humps on a gently sloping plateau overlooking the abandoned church hid the remains of rough chalk building foundations, indicating that there had been a much larger village at Wharram Percy, now essentially deserted. Fortunately, in 1951 Beresford's wall-chasing was brought under the control of Ministry of Works archaeologist John Hurst, who had been trained in the latest continental approaches to open-area excavation. Over the next 40 years, this unlikely duo explored the site, investigating not only the causes of the demise of the village but also its origins, and its place in the wider landscape. They and their collaborators found a number of small Anglo-Saxon settlement enclosures scattered across Wharram and adjacent parishes. As elsewhere in Yorkshire, the majority of these settlements had been abandoned in the 9th century. At Wharram, however, one such enclosure, which held a timber hall and the workshop of an ironsmith, continued in use and ultimately became the focus of the medieval manor house. By the late 9th or early 10th century the smithy housed a weapon-smith, producing swords as fine as those made in *Jorvik*, and the planned medieval village had begun to take shape, with the boundaries of what became the peasant tofts and crofts defined in the chalk and earth banks. At Cottam, the new Anglo-Scandinavian farmstead was abandoned within a generation or two, its owner moving to a new site known as either *Cotum* or *Cowlum* by the time of *Domesday Book*. At Wharram, however, the new Anglo-Scandinavian lord stayed put, and the settlement he founded developed into a nucleated village. Within a few decades he, or his descendants, adopted Christian beliefs and built a small timber church in the valley below the manor house, the precursor to St Martin's. When this founder-lord died he was buried adjacent to the apse of the church, and above his grave was placed a stone cover, reused from a sarcophagus looted from some nearby Roman villa. The grave cover was not flat, as in the style of Anglo-Saxon graves, but bowed, like those of the Viking kings buried among the ruins of the Roman headquarters building in York, adjacent to the great minster church of King Edwin.[11]

As the 9th century came to a close, the dispersed members of Healfdene's army, and those who followed, founded new estates, each with a private chapel, throughout the Vales of Pickering and York, and across the Wolds of Yorkshire. Some may have been relatives and friends of first-generation settlers who came direct from Scandinavia; others may have come from Ireland, particularly after the expulsion of Scandinavians from Dublin in AD 902.[12] They gave up their pagan burial customs and created new monuments – stone crosses – sometimes decorated with Jellinge-style intertwined monsters, but also depicting themselves, seated in their halls and surrounded by the weapons they had used to seize the lands of the Anglo-Saxons: a crudely sculptured sword, shield, axe and spear. Others built recumbent monuments known as hogbacks, arched in the centre and with house-like roofs decorated as if timber-shingled, sometimes with muzzled bears gripping either end. These were not Viking monuments – stone crosses and hogbacks were unknown in Scandinavia – but new hybrid types. As with their jewellery, the settlers combined elements of Irish, Anglo-Saxon and Scandinavian cultural identity to create new forms, and new identities.[13]

For decades scholars from different disciplines have debated the scale of Scandinavian settlement that would have been required to achieve such sweeping cultural changes. Place-name scholars have always argued for a major influx of settlers in the wake of the Viking armies, as reflected in the high proportion of Scandinavian-influenced place-names in eastern and northern England. In the former East Riding of Yorkshire, for example, 48 per cent of place-names recorded in *Domesday Book* suggest a Scandinavian connection; in the North Riding, 46 per cent; and in the West Riding, 31 per cent. Four main categories of place-names have been taken to indicate Scandinavian influence. Firstly, there are some 850 -*by* names across eastern and northern England, such as Aislaby, Balby, Brandsby, Dalby, Ferriby, Kirby and Selby, containing the Old Danish word *by*, meaning a farmstead or village. The Old English equivalent was the ending -*tun* (or -*ton*), as in Beeston, but the new word passed into English and is still used in the term 'by-law' to mean the law of the village. We can compare, for example, the place-names Osmondiston and Aismunderby, representing Osmund's *tun* and Asmund's *by*, respectively. There are some 220 *-by* names in Lincolnshire, and some 210 in Yorkshire. In Lincolnshire they are concentrated in the Wolds; in Yorkshire they are concentrated in the Vale of York. Many of the *-by* names are compounded with a Scandinavian personal name. In Yorkshire, of the 119 *-by* place-names that include a personal name element, 109 (over 90 per cent) are Scandinavian personal names, 7 are Old English and 3 are Old Irish.

The second English place-name ending that suggests a Scandinavian settlement is *-thorp*, as in Bishopthorpe, Danthorpe, Fridaythorpe, Newthorpe and Towthorpe. The Old Danish word *thorp* is generally taken to indicate some form of secondary settlement, and these sites may represent subsequent exploitation of marginal land, or outlying dependencies that became cut off from their distant estate centres by the Vikings. In Yorkshire there are some 155 place-names ending in *-thorp* recorded in *Domesday Book*, and 109 in Derbyshire, Nottinghamshire, Lincolnshire and Leicestershire. The *-thorp* names are less frequently linked with a Scandinavian personal name, and have therefore been regarded as being later than the *-by* names.

Thirdly, there is a class of place-names known as 'Grimston hybrids', which combine a Scandinavian and an Anglo-Saxon element, such as a Scandinavian personal name with the Old English *-ton* in Burneston, Scampston and Wiggington as well as Grimston itself, or *-hide* (an Anglo-Saxon land unit), as in Olaveshide. Each of the counties of Derbyshire, Leicestershire, Lincolnshire, Nottinghamshire and Yorkshire has some 50 Grimston hybrids. These names are often thought to represent Anglo-Saxon villages that were acquired by Scandinavian settlers, but perhaps remained outside direct Scandinavian control.

Finally, changes in the pronunciation of Anglo-Saxon place-names, to avoid un-Scandinavian sounds, have also been taken

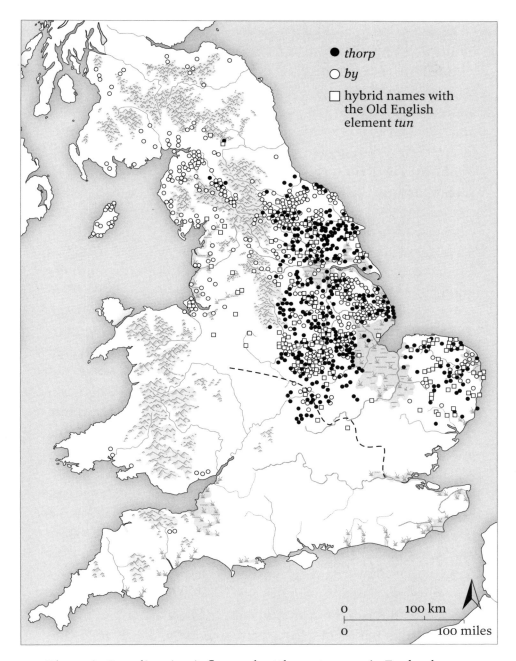

The main Scandinavian-influenced settlement names in England. The dotted line indicates the presumed boundary established by the treaty between Alfred and Guthrum in the 880s.

as evidence for Scandinavian settlement. Thus the Anglo-Saxon *Shipton* becomes Skipton, and *Cheswick* becomes Keswick.

It has also been argued that other linguistic evidence provides clear proof that the Anglo-Scandinavian settlements were part of a large-scale migration of people. Scandinavian pronouns, verbs and everyday words such as 'husband', 'knife' and 'window' were adopted into the English language. However, wider studies of population migration show that it is misleading to draw conclusions about numbers of immigrants on the basis of such linguistic changes, as the degree to which one language influences another often depends on their relative social status, and whether there is a need to borrow words to describe new things. Recent studies have also shown that Old English and Old Norse were mutually intelligible languages and that this may have meant that where Scandinavians settled in parts of northern and eastern England, these regions became effectively multilingual. Cases of intermarriage between speakers of the two languages may have created bilingual families. It is notable, in contrast, that Old Norse had only minimal influence on written forms of language, with Latin and Old English continuing to be the language of administration, the law, coinage and chronicles, reflecting the way in which status and power can inform language use.[14]

The proportion of individuals bearing Scandinavian personal names has also been used as a measure of the density of Scandinavian settlement.[15] In *Domesday Book* 40 per cent of the personal names compounded with settlement names in Derbyshire are Scandinavian, and 50 per cent in Nottinghamshire and in Cheshire. Of course, name-giving habits change with fashion, and are prone to influence from the elite, as testified by the number of children today named after royalty, media stars or footballers. Scandinavian names may have increased in popularity following the settlement period, and by the time of *Domesday Book* we see members of the same family with a mixture of both Scandinavian and Anglo-Saxon names. Written sources are restricted to the elite group and most of those individuals mentioned in *Domesday Book* are referred to as manor holders. Name-giving may reveal as much about class allegiance as ethnic identity.[16]

A contemporary source for 9th- and 10th-century personal names is provided by the coinage. Coins record the names of the moneyers who produced them. The proportion of Scandinavian names increases from none under Alfred to 3 per cent under Edward the Elder (899–924), 5 per cent under Æthelstan (924–39) and then 15 per cent under Eadred (946–55) and his successors. Regionally there is considerable variation. In York, *c.* 75 per cent of names are Scandinavian by the reign of Æthelred II (978–1016); in Lincoln, *c.* 50 per cent; Chester, *c.* 25 per cent; and in London only *c.* 7 per cent.[17] Yet even if all these individuals were born in Scandinavia they hardly represent a cross-section of 10th-century England, as they were drawn from an urban class who moved in elite circles. Name-giving habits may well have been profoundly affected by the Scandinavian settlement, but Scandinavian names may still have been confined to the land-owning and mercantile classes.

Nonetheless, for the first half of the 20th century Sir Frank Stenton and other leading Anglo-Saxon historians assumed that the significant Scandinavian influence on English language, legal institutions, culture and society could only have resulted from large-scale migration and settlement.[18] However, in 1958 historian Peter Sawyer published a short paper that challenged the conventional wisdom concerning the scale of the Viking settlement of England.[19] In this paper, and in his subsequent book *The Age of the Vikings* (1962), Sawyer examined the evidence for mass migration and pulled it apart (see Chapter 3).[20] Aside from questioning the reliability of the written sources, he emphasized that Scandinavian cultural influences on personal and place-name traditions were not recorded until *Domesday Book* was compiled some two centuries later, and that they reflected much later cultural borrowings and name-giving habits that had developed after the creation of Cnut's Anglo-Danish kingdom in the early 11th century.

Sawyer's minimalist views found favour among archaeologists, who in general had dismissed the 'invasion hypothesis' as an explanation of culture change in most periods of British prehistory. Indeed, archaeological evidence for large-scale Viking settlement in England had always been elusive, especially when compared with the very obvious changes in material culture, settlement and burial forms in the immediate post-Roman period.[21] Even where traces of Scandinavian influence could be found, such as on coins or stone sculpture, they were always integrated with Anglo-Saxon imagery and symbolism. In the late 1990s studies began to explore how Scandinavian settlers in England adapted to their new circumstances and how they and the communities in which they settled adopted aspects of each other's cultures. The numbers game came to be seen as largely illusory, with cultural impact not corresponding to relative population sizes.[22] These nuanced views of Anglo-Saxon cultural assimilation were explored in a volume we edited in 2000, entitled *Cultures in Contact*, in which several contributors denied that there was a clear link between culture and genetic heritage and argued for a socially created Anglo-Scandinavian identity.[23]

Nonetheless, the debate about the scale of settlement never completely went away, especially among place-name scholars.[24] Indeed, the contributors to our volume did not, on the whole, seek to downplay the scale of the settlements, only to question how we might identify it. In the last decade new forms of evidence have contributed to the view that there was, after all, large-scale settlement, as the pendulum swings back from the minimalist approach, and there is increased confidence that there are ways of identifying Scandinavian settlement in the archaeological record. Moreover, as Dawn has argued in a recent paper, this does not rest purely on scientific evidence such as stable isotopes, since, for example, specialist craftworking skills and traditions can provide distinctive markers of the activities of migrants (as we will see in Chapter 10).[25]

The popularity of metal-detecting in recent decades, and the large quantities of Anglo-Scandinavian and Scandinavian metalwork subsequently reported to the PAS have been the greatest upset to the minimalist position. The PAS database reveals a rich concentration of Scandinavian influenced dress-accessories in the Danelaw, the area of eastern and northern England heavily influenced by Scandinavian settlers. Jane Kershaw, in her study of the jewellery found by metal-detectorists, has taken this further and distinguished between Anglo-Scandinavian hybrid brooches, which may reflect the response of indigenous Anglo-Saxon women to Scandinavian fashions, and brooches in a more purely Scandinavian style, which represent 'the presence of significant numbers of Scandinavian women, dressed in a traditional Scandinavian manner'. The preponderance of Scandinavian artefacts, or objects associated with Scandinavian activity, in eastern and northern England, and particularly the large quantities of low-value female dress accessories, counter the idea that the Viking invasions in the 9th century only led to a change in the leaders to whom you paid your taxes. On the contrary, there must instead have been a widespread cultural shift in the rural as well as the urban population of Anglo-Saxon England.

Others have turned to archaeological science to estimate how many Scandinavian settlers there were. Genetic evidence for the scale of Viking settlement has proved ambiguous, given that large-scale studies have to rely on DNA sampling of modern populations, and the fact that both Anglo-Saxon and Danish immigrants originated from much the same area of the Continent, making their contributions to England's modern genetic profile difficult to distinguish. The latest large-scale study – the Oxford University *People of the British Isles* project – concluded that there was 'no clear genetic evidence of the Danish Viking occupation and control of a large part of England'.[26] However, Jane Kershaw and Ellen Røyrvik have challenged this interpretation. They estimate that the Danish Viking contribution to the Anglo-Saxon population was 10–50 per cent and, based on overall population estimates for the Danelaw of 150,000–450,000 (scaled down from *Domesday Book* numbers), they conclude the 'probable number of original migrants to be in the region of 20,000–35,000 over the course of the settlement period' in the late 9th and early 10th centuries.[27] Back-projecting from modern data to the 9th and 10th centuries rests upon contested assumptions about the rate of genetic change, and the population movements that could have led to genetic mixing. Stable isotope analysis, indicating the area in which an individual lived during childhood, is a more direct way of identifying origins of ancient populations, but is hampered by the similar geology of eastern England and modern Denmark. It can, however, identify settlers born in parts of Scandinavia with granitic bedrock, such as much of Norway.[28] A recent study of Anglo-Saxon cemeteries demonstrated that some individuals buried without any notable Scandinavian objects may still have been born and spent their childhoods in south-west Norway, contributing to the long-standing debate about the rarity of Viking-style burials in England. The authors conclude that isotope analysis 'can both identify individuals who migrated and start to quantify the scale of migration'.[29]

Finally, as we saw in Chapter 4, the investigation of the Great Army winter camp sites also supports the view that there were large numbers of settlers. The D-shaped enclosure at Repton, once thought to house a small force of three or four ships and a few hundred warriors, in accord with Sawyer's minimalist view, has been shown to represent just a fraction of the camp. The camp now revealed at Torksey is much more in keeping with the large-scale forces reported by the Anglo-Saxon chroniclers.

We can ultimately never know how many people of Scandinavian ancestry settled in England in the 9th and 10th centuries. We do know that the Great Army was made up of various groups, and may have gathered enterprising warriors in Ireland, France and even in other parts of England. We also know that while there was significant disruption to land-holding patterns, and a major transfer of land from kings and churches to new owners with Scandinavian names, it is unlikely that this was accompanied by major population displacement. The Ulfr who held the manor of *Cotun* by 1086, as recorded in *Domesday Book*, and the Ketilbjorn who held *Colmun* may have been descendants of Healfdene's warriors, but it is equally possible that they were of mixed ancestry, or that their forebears were Anglo-Saxons who identified with an Anglo-Scandinavian elite and adopted Scandinavian naming customs. Nonetheless, we can now be much more confident of the impact of the Great Army on the everyday lives of the Anglo-Saxons.

It is even harder to know if the warriors who sailed their long-ships onto the beaches of East Anglia in 865 planned to stay. Clearly they already knew a lot about the country they entered. Decades of contact and trade, as well as smaller raiding expeditions, had no doubt resulted in Viking travellers returning to Scandinavia with tales of the gold and silver in the Anglo-Saxon churches and mon-asteries, as well as of the fertility of the land. Certainly the initial intent was to accrue portable wealth that would help the young warriors gain status back home. But the Viking leaders also had a long-term strategy, and their rapid movements across England were not random, but were designed to oppress opposition, and to destroy the Anglo-Saxon kingdoms one by one. As the decade passed, their strategy evolved, and to consolidate their position they took on many of the trappings of Western European kingship themselves, including a new religion and the minting of coins, while their leading warriors decided to acquire land, taxing their tenants instead of stealing their silver as a long-term business plan.

✢

One Friday in late May 2016, Neil Parker, one of the detectorists we work with at Torksey, heard a particularly strong signal – from iron, not copper-alloy or silver. Digging down, he uncovered a dif-ferent sort of treasure: an iron ploughshare, its sides bent upwards to form a pair of cheeks that would have accommodated a timber beam. Returning to the hole after removing the ploughshare, he found that the signal was still just as strong. Puzzled, Neil reached down into the hole he had dug and pulled out two more plough-shares: a smaller one and a larger one, the two apparently slotted together with their points oriented in opposite directions. Anglo-Saxon and Scandinavian ploughshares are much the same, and we cannot know whether these had been brought from Scandinavia, or acquired from a local. The fact that they were not retrieved by their owner suggests that whatever his original plan for them had been, it was disrupted. Maybe they were too heavy to take on the road, or plans changed. There were fragments of calcined bone embedded in the iron – possibly the ploughshares had been burnt on a funeral pyre with their owner, who died before he had a chance to use them. This parallels the ploughshare found in an area of burning at Foremark in 2018, not far from the Viking cre-mation cemetery at Heath Wood.[30] Whatever the story behind the three ploughshares cached at Torksey, it is difficult not to conclude that, as early as the winter of 872–73, at least some members of the Great Army were already planning to seize land, and to plough and support themselves.

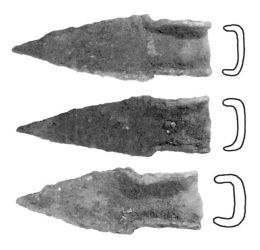

Three iron ploughshares found at the Viking winter camp at Torksey.

8

York and the Viking Camp at Aldwark

By the late 9th century York, or *Eoforwic*, as the Anglo-Saxons called it, was an important royal, ecclesiastical and trading centre, and the only major town in Northumbria. The Roman fortress walls, though in disrepair, were still standing and their gateways limited access to the interior of the fort, enclosing an area of 20 ha (50 acres). Inside the walls, the major building, then as now, was the minster church established by King Edwin in AD 627. Although we do not know for sure, it was possibly on or near the site of the present York Minster, and above or adjacent to the former Roman headquarters. It is likely that other Roman buildings survived, as many walls were not robbed for stone until it was needed for the building of the medieval city in the 12th century. There was probably a royal hall near the cathedral, and a residence for the archbishops. Much of the fortress interior was an open area. New diagonal roads joined the gateways as many of the Roman roads fell out of use. Outside the fortress there was a trading and manufacturing site at the confluence of the Rivers Ouse and Foss, close to what is today Fishergate, and probably the location of the documented Anglo-Saxon *wic* of *Eoforwic*. Here excavations have recovered sherds of continental pottery associated with the Rhenish wine trade, imported glass and lava quern stones, as well as evidence for metalworking, although its scale is not comparable with continental trading sites such as Dorestad. There was also Anglo-Saxon activity in the area of the former Roman *colonia*, or civilian settlement, on the other side of the River Ouse from the fortress, and perhaps an Anglo-Saxon monastic complex in the Bishophill area. It is likely that by the mid-9th century York had a population of *c.* 2,000, making it the greatest concentration of people north of the Thames. The Northumbrian economy was thriving, and apparently fully monetized, facilitated by the production of the low-denomination styca coinage, of which York was the only mint north of the Humber.[1] The kingdom had its problems, with successive kings dying in battle, murdered or overthrown, but this was nothing compared with what was about to happen, when the Great Army first arrived in York on All Saints' Day in AD 866.

York, *c.* AD 866. The shaded area indicates concentrations of Anglo-Saxon finds.

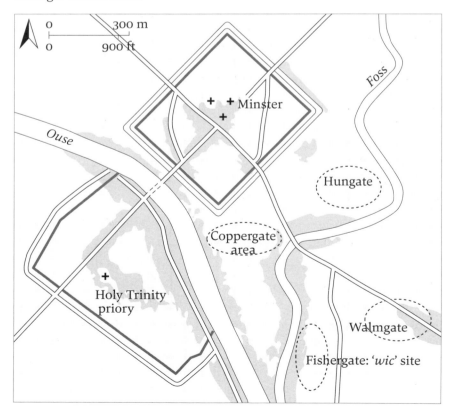

It was a major Christian feast day and the unsuspecting Northumbrians were at prayer. The speed with which the Viking force had reached York seems to have taken its inhabitants by surprise and, according to Symeon of Durham, a chronicler and monk writing in the early 12th century, once in the city they 'ranged hither and thither, filling everywhere with blood and lamentation.' Symeon continues that the Army 'destroyed monasteries and churches far and wide with sword and fire, and when they departed they left nothing but roofless walls.'[2] He recounts how Wulfhere, archbishop of York, fled to the church's rural estate at Addingham in West Yorkshire. It was not until 21 March 867 that the rival claimants to the kingdom of Northumbria, Ælla and Osberht, were able to set aside their differences and organise a response in the face of the common Viking enemy. Their combined forces broke back into the city but, having smashed their way in, they found themselves trapped within its walls. The *Anglo-Saxon Chronicle* relates that 'an immense slaughter was made of the Northumbrians, some inside and some outside, and both kings were killed.'[3] The capture of York is remembered in several later English accounts, but Scandinavian legend adds some gory details about the personal conflict between Ælla and Ivar the Boneless who, as we saw in Chapter 3, was one of the legendary sons of Ragnar Loðbrók. In the Icelandic saga tradition, Ælla had captured Ragnar and put him to death in a snake-pit. In revenge, according to Sigvatr Thórðarson, an Icelandic poet writing in the 1020s or 1030s, 'Ivar, who resided at York, had Ælla's back cut with an eagle', in which his lungs were pulled out and arranged in the shape of an eagle's wings.[4] The veracity of the blood-eagle ritual has been much-debated, and the story is most likely to have been embellished through multiple retellings and later Christian inventions about the barbaric behaviours of pagan peoples. Nonetheless, the events surrounding the fall of York in 866–67 clearly had a long-lasting impact on the historical imagination in both England and Scandinavia.

✛

In the last chapter we examined the impact of the Army on the Northumbrian countryside; it is now time to look at what happened in the Northumbrian towns. After disposing of both claimants to the Northumbrian throne, Osberht and Ælla, the leaders of the Great Army installed a series of Anglo-Saxon puppet kings, who ruled York for them for a decade, starting with Egbert. The Army presumably maintained a garrison in York, although in 872–73 it returned in force to quash a fresh Northumbrian uprising. Although no new coins were minted under the puppet kings, it is probably an oversimplification to suggest that under the Vikings Northumbria completely reverted to a bullion economy until the Viking kings of York created their own silver coinage from *c.* 895. Nonetheless, York clearly experienced major economic and political disruption.

Six hoards of stycas can be dated to *c.* 865, the eve of the attack. All were found during 19th-century development; they probably represent just a fraction of what was buried and never recovered. Two styca hoards were deposited on the north-east bank of the Ouse, along what is now Coney Street; three were found dug into or near the Roman ramparts in St Leonard's Place, and another was discovered on Walmgate.[5] Maybe it was also the threat of Viking attack that led to an Anglian helmet being buried in a back yard behind what would soon become the street of Coppergate. The putative *wic* site at Fishergate seems already to have been in decline before the Army arrived and it was certainly abandoned by the late 9th century. None of the ubiquitous late 9th-century pottery known as York ware has been found at Fishergate, but there is plausible evidence for a visit by members of the Great Army in a terminal from a penannular brooch and a silver penny of Æthelberht of Wessex, the latest coin from the site.[6] The only other Æthelberht coin found in Northumbria is that from Cottam, mentioned in Chapter 7.

In 875, Healfdene returned to Northumbria, introducing direct Scandinavian rule in the region, although the impact of this in York itself is difficult to discern. The large-scale excavations at Coppergate provide the most detailed picture of Viking Age York, as now presented in the Jorvik Viking Centre. In the Anglian period this area appears to have been unoccupied. The earliest dated post-Roman feature is a furnace or hearth with an archaeo-magnetic date of 860±20, associated with a cache of Roman glass for remelting found nearby. A styca of Eanred (*c.* 810–40/41) and sherds of Anglo-Saxon Ipswich ware suggest some activity, but it is impossible to say if it pre- or post-dates 866. No Anglo-Saxon buildings were found within the boundaries of the excavation, although a fragment of late 8th- or early 9th-century cross found in the north-east corner of the site may relate to the Anglo-Saxon predecessor of All Saints church and an associated cemetery. Indeed, there is a scatter of haphazard burials within the Coppergate excavation area, including that of a male aged 36–45 who was dumped unceremoniously in a pit in the late 9th century, and could have been a victim of the

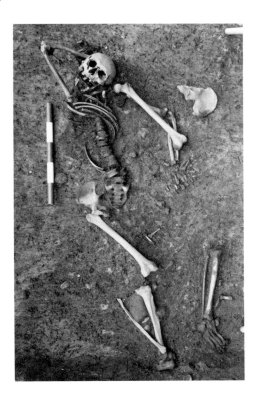

Late 9th-century burial
of male aged 36–45,
Coppergate, York.

Great Army. However, it is not until at least *c.* 900 and possibly as late as *c.* 930–35 that we can see the creation of boundaries within the excavation area, suggesting that Coppergate, the street of the cup-makers or wood-turners (Old Norse *koppari*), was not laid out until this period. Furthermore, it is not until *c.* 930–55 that the four tenements are distinguishable, with their post-and-wattle houses-cum-workshops at the street frontage and gable-ends facing onto the street. In form they are actually reminiscent of Anglo-Saxon buildings, with nothing particularly Scandinavian about them, and the dating of *c.* 930 would link them to the capture of York in 927 by Æthelstan, grandson of Alfred (see Chapter 9).

The redevelopment of Viking York as a trading and manufacturing town, therefore, did not take place until at least a generation after the arrival of the Great Army. In which case, if the Vikings did not really occupy York until the early 10th century, where were they? Where was the winter camp of 866–67, and when Healfdene returned to Northumbria in 875, where did he go?

At least part of the answer lies at Aldwark, in North Yorkshire, *c.* 20 km (12 miles) north-west of York. Here a huge mass of Viking plunder, directly comparable to that from Torksey, has been recovered over the last 20 years, allegedly amounting to *c.* 7,000 items [pl. 19–22]. Like Torksey, the camp is adjacent to a navigable river, in this case the River Ure, near the point where its name changes to the River Ouse. The place-name is also rather suggestive, as it is derived from the Old English *ald weorc*, or 'old fortification', and excavation by York Archaeological Trust revealed a large sub-rectangular enclosure of possible early medieval date. Gareth Williams has dated the finds assemblage, principally from numismatic evidence, to the later 870s and has associated it with the move of Healfdene's part of the Great Army back into Northumbria, noting that the smaller total area of this camp, occupying *c.* 30 ha (75 acres), can be explained by the splitting up of the Army recorded in 874.[7] Aldwark was once known by the portmanteau name of Ainsbrook (from the surnames of the metal-detectorists who identified the

View of the Viking camp at Aldwark from the west bank of the River Ure.

Map showing the location of Aldwark in relation to York, with key Roman routeways.

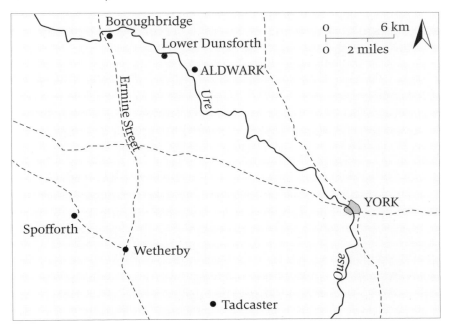

site) and more recently as 'a riverine site in north Yorkshire' or 'a riverine site north of York', abbreviated as ARSNY.[8] This secrecy and confusion stems from the chequered history of the site and the fact that it was found not by archaeologists but instead, like so many sites visited by the Viking Great Army, by metal-detectorists.

Mark Ainsley and Geoff Bambrook were from the north-east of England and had been metal-detecting at Aldwark since 1996. They were aware it was a rich Viking site, but they were initially reluctant to report their finds, fearing that other detectorists would find out and would loot what they regarded as their site. Over the years they had found thousands of objects and although they had kept some records, we may never know precisely how many items they removed from the site as they had sold many of the finds, including hundreds of stycas, on the online marketplace eBay. They had landowner permission, but in the eyes of some archaeologists they were 'night-hawks' – metal-detectorists who search for artefacts in secret, often under cover of darkness (hence the name), and sell their finds for monetary gain without reporting them.

That changed in late 2003. Mark recalls that it was a cold day, and he didn't want to go out, but was persuaded to by Geoff. He found a silver Saxon coin lying on the surface, and soon a second one, inches away, and then a third. Over successive days a range of objects appeared: four cubo-octahedral weights, four lead circular weights, a Thor's hammer amulet refashioned from the beam of a copper-alloy balance, eleven pieces of hacksilver, a dirham fragment, a silver-gilt mount (possibly from a bowl) inset with blue glass, a gilt copper-alloy mount, a whetstone, a ringed pin, an iron belt buckle, a strap-end, a possible shield grip, fragments of two Viking swords, and several more coins [pl. 19]. Mark and Geoff believed they had found a hoard. However, they also encountered human bone, and it was this that persuaded them to report their finds. With some apprehension they went to the Yorkshire Museum, where they met Simon Holmes, the local PAS Finds Liaison Officer. Simon gradually won their trust and persuaded Mark and Geoff

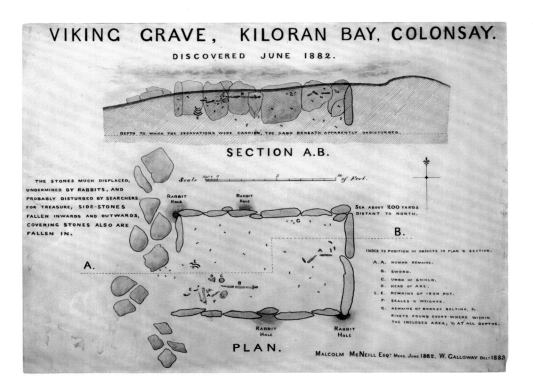

VIKING GRAVE, KILORAN BAY, COLONSAY.

DISCOVERED JUNE 1882.

SECTION A.B.

THE STONES MUCH DISPLACED,
UNDERMINED BY RABBITS, AND
PROBABLY DISTURBED BY SEARCHERS
FOR TREASURE; SIDE-STONES
FALLEN INWARDS AND OUTWARDS,
COVERING STONES ALSO ARE
FALLEN IN.

DEPTH TO WHICH THE EXCAVATIONS WERE CARRIED, THE SAND BENEATH APPARENTLY UNDISTURBED.

Scale

RABBIT HOLE

SEA ABOUT 200 YARDS DISTANT TO NORTH.

A.

B.

INDEX TO POSITION OF OBJECTS IN PLAN & SECTION.

A.A. HUMAN REMAINS.
B. SWORD.
C. UMBO OF SHIELD.
D. HEAD OF AXE.
E.E. REMAINS OF IRON POT.
F. SCALES & WEIGHTS.
G. REMAINS OF BRONZE BELTING, &c.
RIVETS FOUND EVERY-WHERE WITHIN
THE INCLOSED AREA, ½ AT ALL DEPTHS.

RABBIT HOLE

RABBIT HOLE

PLAN.

MALCOLM McNEILL ESQ.ʳ MENS. JUNE 1882. W. GALLOWAY DEL.ᵗ 1883

12, 13 Viking burial at Kiloran Bay, Colonsay, in the Inner Hebrides, discovered in 1882. A male warrior, who may have once fought with the Great Army, was buried in a stone enclosure. A small boat, represented by clench nails, had been placed over the grave. The warrior had also been buried with a set of scales and six decorated inset lead weights. The seventh lead object, with a 'crown', may have been a gaming piece that doubled as a weight.

14, 15, 16 Viking cremation cemetery at Heath Wood, near Repton, Derbyshire. *ABOVE* Mound 16. The unfilled hole in the centre of the mound suggests that this was one of the five barrows opened by Thomas Bateman on 22 May 1855. *OPPOSITE, ABOVE* Mound 50 under excavation in 1998. *OPPOSITE, BELOW* The location of the pyre is framed by the two striped ranging poles, each 2 m in length.

17, 18 Silver sword-hilt grip and shield clamp, both found within the cremation hearth, Mound 50, Heath Wood.

19, 20 Finds from the Viking camp at Aldwark, North Yorkshire.
TOP Lead inset weights (top left) and copper-alloy cubo-octahedral
weights (below centre), complete and pierced silver coins, hacksilver
and three parts of a sword hilt (right), now in the British Museum.
ABOVE Selection of Aldwark finds now owned by a private collector in
the USA, including four inset lead weights (top centre left), silver ingots
and other hacksilver and a piece of hackgold. Many of the finds from
Aldwark were recovered by metal-detectorists and sold privately.

21 Fragment of a decorative copper-alloy mount, found at Aldwark and now in a private collection, decorated with two crudely inscribed intertwined snake-like beasts with biting heads.

22 Terminal from an 8th-or 9th-century bridle mount of Irish manufacture, found at Aldwark and now in the Metropolitan Museum of Art, New York. The copper-alloy mount is in the form of a spread-eagled animal with a downward-facing head. Its front legs are birds in profile and its hind legs are animal heads. The mount may have been intended for reuse as a woman's brooch.

23 Objects recovered from the Leominster hoard included a 9th-century gold finger-ring with eight external facets decorated with alternating rosettes or flower petals set in a black niello background, and a 5th- or 6th-century crystal sphere mounted in a gold setting, looted from an Anglo-Saxon or Frankish treasury.

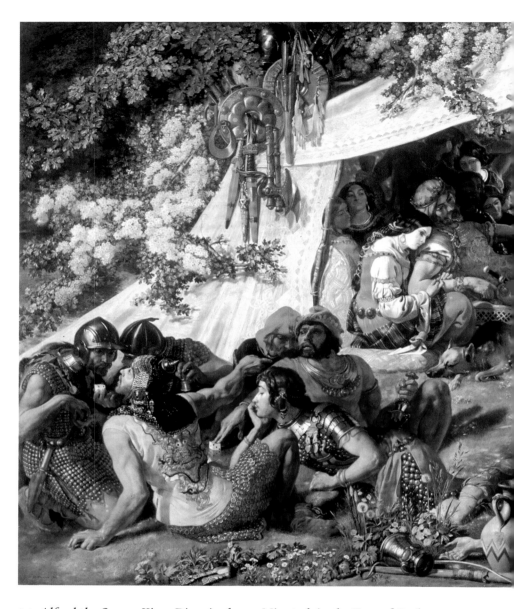

24 *Alfred the Saxon King, Disguised as a Minstrel, in the Tent of Guthrum the Dane*, by Daniel Maclise (1806–1870). This artwork, painted *c.* 1852, lacks historical accuracy but typifies the romantic mythology that developed around Alfred in the 19th century.

25 *OPPOSITE* The Alfred Jewel, thought to be the end of a reading-pointer associated with King Alfred's education programme, was found on the estate of Sir Thomas Wroth at North Petherton, Somerset in 1693. It passed to his uncle Colonel Nathaniel Palmer who bequeathed it to Oxford University in 1718. It is now in the Ashmolean Museum.

26 Torksey ware cooking pot, 10th century, with characteristic sandy black fabric, excavated in York.

27 Stamford ware pitcher, 11th century, with distinctive white fabric and yellow lead glaze. This example is believed to have been excavated from the site of the Angel Inn in Oxford High Street in the 19th century, and was presented to the British Museum in 1887, as part of the Franks bequest.

to take him to the site. They had also found a small group of iron nails, and when Simon plotted them, he thought they had found a boat burial, although it later transpired that the nails were actually from chests.

Simon recognized the importance of the finds and contacted Richard Hall, Viking specialist, and Deputy Director at York Archaeological Trust (YAT). Richard then talked to English Heritage, in order to acquire funding to mount an exploratory excavation. The British Museum was also informed – the concentration of precious-metal objects meant that the finds were legally classified as Treasure and became known as the Ainsbrook hoard. This meant that the Museum had the option to purchase the finds, at a price determined by the Treasure Valuation Committee, with the reward split 50:50 between the finders and the landowner. The press found out about the discovery and the television programme *Time Team* also became involved. It was agreed that they could film the excavation so long as they did not disclose its location, for a *Time Team Special* entitled 'Codename Ainsbrook', which was broadcast in 2008.

A small team from YAT started digging at Aldwark in March 2004. Two trenches were excavated to look for evidence of the boat burial in the area where Mark and Geoff had recovered the 'hoard'. There was no sign of a boat, but there was a large hole, 3.6 × 2.4 m (12 × 8 ft) across and 0.8 m (2.6 ft) deep, dug by the detectorists to extract the objects, as well as some later medieval features. Meanwhile, English Heritage undertook a geophysical survey of a much larger area, revealing a large sub-rectangular ditched enclosure, as well as possible rubbish pits. Mark and Geoff then admitted that the 'hoard' was not their first discovery at Aldwark, and that they had in fact been working it for many years, recovering finds from a much wider area. One spot they described as a 'blacksmith's shop', where they had recovered iron ingots; another they called 'Silver Alley'. They also went back to the hedgerows where they had discarded many iron objects as being of little interest, and now handed them

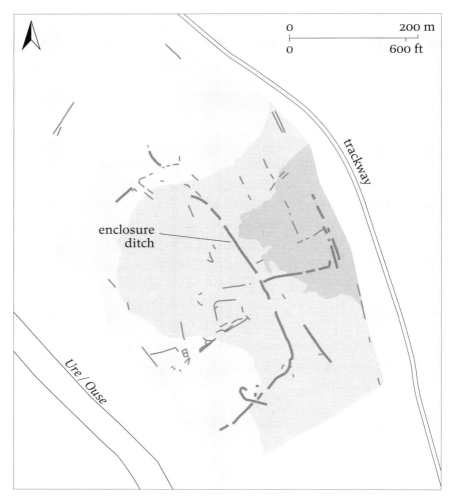

Interpretative plot of the geophysical survey of the camp at Aldwark, showing the enclosure ditch.

over to the archaeologists. The site clearly comprised more than the burial of a treasure hoard; in fact, Aldwark is one of the most important Viking sites to be discovered this century.

English Heritage agreed to fund exploratory excavations, to be undertaken by YAT, but it was a large area to investigate, and only 0.5 per cent of the total area of the site was excavated. Six initial trenches dug in July 2005 found nothing of the Viking period, and a trench across the enclosure ditch found only one sherd of Bronze Age pottery. The only early medieval finds made during the excavation were recovered by Mark and Geoff, from the plough-soil. In October – November 2005 YAT returned to dig new trenches inside the enclosure, with a focus on a possible entranceway, making 21 trial trenches in total. A number of pits were excavated but few contained finds, other than a piece of folded lead sheet and a nail. In the north-eastern part of the site a spread of burnt sand, charcoal and burnt cobbles was located. Metalworking debris was recovered from this area, including a layer of casting sand, iron slag, a possible iron punch, a weight and clench nails. There were also eighteen fragments of burnt clay, thought to be from an oven-lining.[9]

A number of trenches were dug within the enclosure. In one of the highest parts of the site a layer of wind-blown sand was cut by two pits. The first contained a lot of animal bone, a plated key, an iron ring and nail head, iron slag and a styca. In the second was a large quantity of animal bone, silver and copper-alloy waste and iron slag, and a Burgred coin (852–74). Nearby was a dump of sand containing a quern fragment and a lead weight. Two severely disturbed human skeletons were also found in this trench, but there was no trace of any grave cuts. Radiocarbon samples from the lower half of one of the bodies have been dated to AD 890–1020, with a 95 per cent probability, which would make them later than the camp.[10]

In another trench a pit contained a Roman bracelet, an amber bead, a metalworking punch or awl, two iron rivets and a styca of Archbishop Wulfhere (c. 854–900). A third trench was positioned to examine a rectilinear enclosure identified by the geophysical survey, and here the ditch was found to contain a possible anvil stone, and butchery waste. Two pits mainly contained more butchery waste, but an early medieval iron bell, an iron handle and iron slag were also found in one of them. In the second was a variety of early medieval finds, including an iron spike for textile-working, a key, a copper-alloy wire ring, a lead spindle whorl and a whetstone, as well as lead and copper-alloy metalworking waste.[11] In total, ten radiocarbon dates were derived from these pits and ditches, providing a broad date range of AD 610–770 for the start of activity, and AD 700–920 for the end. The other trenches produced nothing of early medieval date; the features were prehistoric or Roman.

The results of the excavations were seen as disappointing; there was little trace of the Viking treasure that had been recovered by Mark and Geoff, and little sign of any structures. However, in the light of our research at Torksey, and the later identification of Aldwark as a Viking camp, this is actually not surprising. For a site occupied for only a short period one should not expect substantial archaeological features – the pits of butchery waste and metalworking debris at Aldwark are entirely consistent with metalwork processing, ship repair and supplying a large army. The ground conditions were also almost identical to those at Torksey, comprising a mixture of sandy till covered by small patches of glacial sand and gravel. Extensive wind-blown sand may have both eroded and buried archaeology, and this has been exacerbated by truncation caused by modern deep ploughing, cutting into the Viking occupation layers, leaving only the bases of the deeper pits and ditches, and distributing the majority of objects into the plough-soil.

At the time of the excavation, however, the significance of Aldwark as a Great Army site was not fully appreciated and both the archaeologists and detectorists were frustrated. Mark and Geoff thought Richard had been digging in the wrong place; Richard was suspicious of what they were telling him. This tension was captured by the *Time Team* cameras, and their 'Special' programme was turning into a fiasco; presenter Tony Robinson was clearly annoyed by what he described as 'the cloak and dagger stuff' and commented that it was 'not just bizarre', but 'actually rather irritating'. To make matters worse, the British Museum's Treasure Valuation Committee came back with a price for the Ainsbrook hoard, which they finally valued at £3,750 for the coins and £1,250 for the other artefacts. The *Time Team Special* showed Mark and Geoff as deeply disenchanted; they believed that the coins alone, which included several rare types, were worth *c.* £40,000. Overall, they appeared to regret having gone public in the first place; they were also vilified by some on social media and withdrew from contact with archaeologists. The British Museum acquired a few items from the hoard but Mark and Geoff went on to sell most of their collection privately, and it has subsequently become distributed among a number of private collectors, although some of it turned up in an exhibition in the Atkinson Galleries in Southport in 2018.

Publication of the excavations and what information could be salvaged about Mark and Geoff's finds has also been slow. Richard Hall tragically died in 2011, although the Aldwark site has now been brought to publication by a team led by Gareth Williams at the British Museum. Unfortunately, because of an agreement that had been made between YAT, Mark, Geoff and the landowners, the site location has been withheld in the publication, which has used the acronym ARSNY. In our view this is unnecessary, as its identity is now widely known. Indeed, using information already placed in the public domain by the team (for instance, that the site was on a river within a day's walk north of York) several people armed with basic maps had already worked out where it was, including many detectorists and collectors. The clue was in the name all along!

Given the international importance of Aldwark, and the need to know its landscape context in order to appreciate its significance and its relationship with York, we believe it is essential that its location is placed in the public domain, as we did in our 2016 Torksey report. Without archaeological context this is simply a random collection of treasure that cannot contribute to future research and knowledge.[12] As is also the case with Torksey, any threat to the site is now minimal as it has been so intensively detected, and both sites have now been covered with recycled waste that contains large quantities of metal fragments, making it extremely difficult to find any more Viking objects.

So what can be learned from this sorry tale, other than that the relationship between archaeologists and metal-detectorists can be tricky? Aldwark is clearly a very similar site to Torksey. It is located on a navigable river, at a natural landing place and the next strategic crossing point upstream from York. It differs in having traces of an enclosure although the dating of this feature is uncertain and it could pre-date the Viking activity. It is also smaller, at 31 ha (77 acres), but this can be attributed to the fact that the Army split after Repton. It seems probable, given the radiocarbon date range and some of the earlier finds, that there was Anglo-Saxon activity on the site, although it is uncertain if it was occupied immediately prior to the Viking occupation. As with Torksey, the Anglo-Saxon coins allow us to date this activity very precisely. There are several coins of the lunette type, issued jointly as part of the monetary and political alliance of Alfred and Burgred between 871 and 874; the presence of examples of a particularly rare type suggests an earliest possible date for the coin assemblage of 873–74, very close to the end of the circulation period for this type, c. 875.[13] The dirham fragments are not so precisely datable, but they are also consistent with a focus of activity in the mid-870s. The main activity at the Aldwark site lasted for no more than a few years, possibly less, but the typology of some of the metalwork suggests continued activity on a smaller scale, possibly into the early 10th century. Thereafter, there is no evidence to suggest any further occupation or non-agricultural activity. In summary, it seems highly likely that the majority of material reflects short-lived activity on a Viking winter camp, as was the case with Torksey. Some may be associated with the original attacks on York in 866 and 867, but most finds are probably connected to Healfdene's return north in 875–76.

The published finds from Aldwark are very similar to those from Torksey, providing the same characteristic Great Army signature. Gareth Williams has catalogued 90 Northumbrian stycas, although Mark Ainsley alleges that he and Geoff had found hundreds. While these coins would be less out of place on a Northumbrian site than at Torksey, the majority date from the 840s or later, with surprisingly few from the reign of Eanred (c. 810–c. 850). The stycas thus seem to have been deposited over a comparatively short period of a few years rather than indicating continuous occupation of the site throughout the 9th century. A high proportion are also blundered, suggesting they may have been Viking attempts at minting or forging coinage. Williams initially recorded some 283 weights (including 24 cubo-octahedral weights, and several lead weights with decorative insets), 14 dirham fragments, 69 finds of silver (including hacksilver, an ingot and metalworking debris), and 2 pieces of hackgold.[14] As well as the excavated finds, the 2020 publication also notes the presence of over 50 'hedgerow finds' – metal-detected objects, mainly of iron, which had initially been discarded at the field edge by Mark and Geoff – as well as over 300 new finds that the pair brought in for recording in February 2008. It should also be noted that although the 'Ainsbrook hoard' finds are kept separate in the publication, they should really be seen as part of the overall assemblage. The collection is not like any other known hoard of the period and it is likely that it simply represents the first group of finds that the detectorists decided to declare, albeit a selection that they found in one area of the site.

Viewed together, the metal-detected and excavated finds demonstrate that a broad range of craftworking and manufacture was being undertaken at Aldwark. Ten samples of litharge cake, weighing 1.4 kg (3.75 lbs), were found by Mark and Geoff. These are waste products of the cupellation process for refining debased silver. The silver alloy is melted with lead and then heated in a small flat hearth or container together with something absorbent, like crushed bone. The silver does not oxidise and remains as a silvery droplet or button on the surface, which can then be picked off. This leaves behind a flat-based, dense 'cake', sometimes with a noticeable dished central area where the silver had been. About 6.5 kg (14 lbs) of metalworking slag and other waste was recovered from the excavation trenches. Five of the ironworking slag samples appear to have been formed at the base of working smithing hearths, but there was also slag derived from non-ferrous metalworking, including pieces of vitrified furnace lining, one of which has copper-alloy deposits within it. Five pieces of copper-alloy waste were probably casting waste. In addition, three copper-alloy ingots reported in 2008 can be added to another three published by Mark Blackburn in 2001 that are believed to have come from Aldwark.[15] As is the case at Torksey, most of the fragments of lead waste or objects were very small and probably spillages from casting. At Aldwark, the different material types were scattered without particular concentrations in specific trenches, suggesting that several different types of metal-working took place at a variety of locations around the camp. Other items were associated with textile production, notably spinning, and a total of 28 lead spindle whorls were recorded. There was also evidence for woodworking, including an iron axe-head, two spoon bits and a punch. Combined with the clench nails and iron smithing these may indicate the repair of ships. There were also two possible leatherworking awls.

A wide range of dress accessories was also recorded, although most of the 40 strap-ends recovered by the detectorists are likely to have been brought to Aldwark as raw materials for copper-working, particularly as only ten dress pins were found, a similar ratio to that at Torksey. In addition, there were two buckle plates, nine belt slides, various annular and penannular brooch fragments, pieces of disc and trefoil brooches and four hooked tags.[16] Among the more distinctive Viking objects is a lead-alloy amulet in the form of a Valkyrie figure and a crude drawing of Fenrir on a piece of scrap

Three copper-alloy ingots believed to be from Aldwark. This auction-catalogue photograph from 2001 is the only record to survive.

lead.[17] Fenrir was a mythological wolf who bit off the right hand of the god Týr, and it was foretold that he would kill the god Odin during the events of Ragnarök, at the end of the world. Other finds included two intertwined snakes carved on a strap-end [pl. 21], as well as two hexagonal copper-alloy bells, and several examples of Irish metalwork. Most of this is of 8th- or 9th-century date and probably arrived at Aldwark as the result of plunder, tribute or trade, reinforcing that members of the Great Army had previously been active in Ireland. Weaponry and horse equipment are well represented. In addition to the three swords found in the 'hoard', seven iron hilt fittings and part of a sword blade were recovered. There was a spectacular bridle mount of Irish manufacture, dating to the 8th or 9th century [pl. 22], as well as pieces of four prick-spurs.

In gathering information from various collectors and dealers we have been able to identity other artefacts that Mark and Geoff detected from Aldwark and sold, including many more dirhams, as well as additional spindle whorls and a large number of lead gaming pieces, many of which were previously identified as weights.[18] Care has to be taken in these enquiries as the name of Ainsbrook has become so well known that it has been used as a provenance to add caché value to finds that may actually have been recovered elsewhere. Nonetheless we have been building up our own catalogue of finds that we are confident originated from Aldwark.

Despite the fact that we have incomplete information from both Aldwark and Torksey, the finds assemblages from these locations are large enough to be representative of the nature of the Viking winter camps and the range of activities that took place in them. Adding more finds would not alter the basic picture. They also indicate what we should expect to find at Foremark/Heath Wood/ Repton, and at other camps of the Great Army. Aldwark, with its proximity to York, is of particular interest. The winter camps men-tioned in the *Anglo-Saxon Chronicle* were probably named after the closest widely known settlement. When the chronicler says that the Great Army stayed at York, that does not have to mean they

RIGHT Lead amulet in the form of a Valkyrie-like figure, found at Aldwark. Her face is shown in profile with her hair tied up or knotted and hanging down her back. She is depicted wearing a long dress and holding a round shield. The object appears to have been folded in antiquity, and later straightened out.

ABOVE Fragment of scrap lead from Aldwark on which a depiction of the mythological wolf Fenrir has been crudely inscribed. Fenrir is apparently carrying a sword, and the legs of a human figure can be seen between his jaws.

were all within the fortress walls of the city, or even immediately outside them. It is a reasonable hypothesis that Aldwark is actually the site of the Great Army's winter camp at York. The Army's relationship with the local population appears to have been rather hands-off, at least at first, as reflected in the installation of puppet kings. As we have seen, there is no evidence for a significant Viking presence in the city of York until some 30 years later, in the early 10th century. The fact that the Army did not immediately choose to occupy the town provides a new perspective on their contribution to the development of towns in the 10th century, which we will return to in Chapter 10.

Meanwhile, what happened to Healfdene himself after he returned to York and he and his followers began to settle in Northumbria after

876? He largely disappears from the historical record in England, although early 12th-century sources written in Durham allege that he was abandoned by his part of the Great Army:

> For as insanity afflicted his mind, so the direst torment afflicted his body, from which there arose such an intolerable stench that he was rendered odious to his whole army. Thus despised and rejected by all persons, he fled away from the Tyne with only three ships and was never seen again.[19]

Whether we choose to believe this late account of his offensive personal hygiene and troubled mind, it is erroneous in at least one respect, as Healfdene appears to have fled to Ireland, where he was, in fact, seen again. As we mentioned in Chapter 6, he may be the Albann who, according to the *Annals of Ulster*, killed the son of Olaf (Amlaíb) 'king of the Norsemen' in 875, but was himself killed in 877 in a battle between 'the fair heathens and the dark heathens' at Strangford Loch (Co. Down).[20] This turn of events, when considered alongside the evidence of Ivar and Olaf operating on both sides of the Irish Sea, suggests that the ambitions of the principal Viking leaders in the 860s and 870s were to acquire land and power across Britain and Ireland. It may have been unrealistic to aim to control such a wide territory, but the scale of the threat posed by the Great Army was considerable.

We know little of what happened in Northumbria between the late 870s and *c*. 900. Our most important written source is the 11th-century *History of St Cuthbert*, the story of the late 7th-century bishop of Lindisfarne and his community. It describes a series of miracles associated with Cuthbert after his death, the landholdings of his episcopal community and its fate after it fled Lindisfarne around 875. Thereafter, the monks of the community of St Cuthbert spent the best part of a decade travelling around the north of England, carrying the body of the saint, and attempting to protect themselves and their properties from Viking raiders. A hoard deposited in the early 870s near the church at Gainford on the River Tees reflects Viking activity on one of its estates (Chapter 3), and may have been one of the events that prompted the community to set out to protect its lands. In the early 880s they came to an arrangement with a Viking army, assisted by a vision from the saint:

> At that time St Cuthbert appeared in the night to the holy abbot of Carlisle named Eadred, firmly commanding him as follows: 'Go', he said. 'Over the Tyne to the army of the Danes, and tell them that if they wish to be obedient to me, they should show you a certain young man named Guthred son of Harthacnut, the slave of a certain widow. In the early morning you and the whole army should offer the widow the price for him, and at the third hour [take him] in exchange for the price; then at the sixth hour lead him before the whole multitude so that they may elect him king, and at the ninth hour lead him with the whole army upon the hill which is called *Oswigesdune* and there place on his right arm a golden armlet, and thus they shall all constitute him king. Tell him also, after he has been made king, to give me all the land between the Tyne and the Wear.'[21]

Guthred, which is an Old English version of the Old Norse name Guthfrith, was duly made king. Peace was sworn over the body of St Cuthbert, and over the coming years Guthred proved a useful ally for the religious community, which acquired numerous properties in the north of England from him.[22] It is not possible to be sure who Guthred was; nor is it clear whether Eadred had come to an arrangement with an offshoot of the Great Army or another Viking force. Yet what is alleged to have transpired is certainly reminiscent of the Great Army's behaviour. The army described in the *History of St Cuthbert* drew on the power and influence of the Anglo-Saxon Church to establish itself in northern England, adapted to a Christian style of kingship, and acquired land; it was also clearly riven by rivalries that a wily local leader was able to exploit.

This source of information is late and there may well be embellishments in the interests of the community of St Cuthbert. Quite how Abbot Eadred was able to march up to a Viking army and make demands of it is not explained and this aspect of the account may be a little far-fetched. Nonetheless, there is other evidence to suggest there is a grain of truth in this story. For example, a late 10th-century version of the *Anglo-Saxon Chronicle* by an ealdorman called Æthelweard, reports the burial of a king called Guthfrith in the 'superior church' in York in 895, while a coin found in a hoard at Ashton, Essex, also dated to around 895, may have been minted in his name, as it bears the inscription 'GUDEF ...'.[23] It is also similar to coins minted south of the Humber, suggesting that Guthred/Guthfrith had extensive territorial control. Æthelweard records that an Anglo-Saxon delegation was sent from Wessex to Northumbria in 894, following raids on land near Stamford, Lincolnshire, and while we do not know for certain that this delegation met with Guthred, it appears to be another indication of a ruler in York with authority beyond the Humber in the mid-890s. As we will see in Chapter 9, Vikings in Northumbria assisted raiders in East Anglia in 893, providing further evidence for the continuation of wide-ranging Scandinavian ambitions for territorial control in England.

Our main evidence for political authority in York in the years that followed are silver coins minted in the period *c.* 895–905 in the names of two kings with Old Norse names, Siefrid and Cnut. Their coins are very diverse and overtly Christian, bearing various types of cross and with inscriptions in Latin. Many also incorporate abbreviated liturgical inscriptions, such as DNS DS REX (*Dominus Deus Rex*, 'The Lord God is King') and DNS DS O REX (*Dominus Deus Omnipotens Rex*, 'The Lord God Almighty is King'), while others cite Psalm 98, *mirabilia fecit* ('He has done marvellous things'). It seems likely that these two Scandinavian kings brought with them moneyers from the Continent; indeed, some of the coins contained the letters KRLS at each end of a cross, which stands for *Karolus* or Charles, and this design mirrors coins of the Frankish king Charles the Simple (r. 897–922). It has been suggested that the use of the name *Karolus* on coins of Cnut may reflect that this was his baptismal name, and we know that a Viking force on the River Seine accepted baptism from Charles in 897.[24]

It is uncertain what role Archbishop Wulfhere played in accommodating the new kings, but there are grounds for suspecting that he helped to legitimize their rule. The messages conveyed by the coins of Siefrid and Cnut demonstrate that Christianity had become important in the symbolism of royal authority and the archbishop is likely to have been central to this, and perhaps even influenced the design of the coins. While this is speculation, Wulfhere, who had been archbishop of York since 854, clearly had developed a knack for accommodating successive kings, whatever their backgrounds. During his episcopacy he had seen 'great civil strife' leading to the first Northumbrian king under whom he served, Osberht, being deposed *c*. 862 in favour of Ælla; the two kings then joined forces to face the Great Army and were both killed in York in 867. Wulfhere then collaborated with a king subsequently appointed by the Great Army, Egbert, and had been forced to flee with him to Mercia in 872 when there was an uprising against the puppet-king. The next king under whom he served was Ricsige, about whom we know little, but whether serving a Great Army appointee or a legitimate Northumbrian king, Wulfhere remained in post (see Chapter 3). He must have had to deal at some point with Healfdene, when his part of the Great Army set up camp at Aldwark, and would have witnessed their arrival in York. He must surely have been involved in the decision to bury Guthred in York Minster. It is, then, hardly surprising that he should have been able to respond to the arrival of Siefrid and Cnut, with his influence over their reigns simply the latest example of his ability to respond to changed circumstances. For the Vikings, Wulfhere was another case of an Anglo-Saxon leader with whom they could do deals.

PART III

The Making of a Nation

9
Wessex Fights Back and the Origins of England

Having traced the establishment of Scandinavian rulers in York, we now return south to explore how Guthrum adapted to the challenges of becoming a king in England. During his reign in East Anglia (c. AD 880–90) he was clearly influenced by King Alfred, and the two kings found a means of working together, with Christianity central to their cooperation. Ultimately, however, this was to pave the way for the absorption of East Anglia into the kingdom of Wessex in the early 10th century. We will also see how Alfred used the strategic marriage of his daughter Æthelflæd to gain control over Mercia. Our chronological account ends with the conquest in the early 10th century by Alfred's descendants of large parts of the kingdoms where the Scandinavians had settled. These actions of Alfred's children Edward and Æthelflæd, and his grandson Æthelstan, consolidated the role of the kingdom of Wessex in the making of England, but it is Alfred – and his wars against the Great Army – that live on in popular imagination and national origin myths.

While Healfdene returned to Northumbria in 874 after spending the winter in Repton, the remainder of the Army, under its kings Guthrum, Anwend and Oscetel, headed back to East Anglia, spending the winter of 874–75 at Cambridge. They then moved into Wessex, to Wareham in Dorset, which Asser described as a fortified site and the location of a nunnery.[1] Here, in 876, the *Anglo-Saxon Chronicle* reports that Alfred 'made peace with the enemy and they gave him hostages, who were the most important men next to their king in the Army, and swore oaths to him on the holy ring – a thing which they would not do before for any nation – that they would speedily leave his kingdom'.[2] The forging of peace between the Great Army and local rulers is frequently mentioned in the *Anglo-Saxon Chronicle*, but this is the first time we discover what one of these peace agreements entailed. However, while the *Chronicle* suggests this peace involved swearing on a Viking ring, in his account Asser replaces the ring with Christian relics: 'they took an oath, on all the relics in which the king placed the greatest trust after God Himself (and on which they had never before been willing to take an oath to any race)'. In this way, Asser was taking care to craft Alfred's reputation as a defender of Christianity, and as a king who used religion in his response to the Viking threat. In contrast, the Vikings were portrayed as untrustworthy: according to Asser the Army slipped away from Wareham, 'paying no heed to the hostages, the oath and the promise of faith', and headed to Exeter, where it spent the winter.[3] Alfred went in pursuit, but was unable to catch up with them before they reached their fortress. Nonetheless, the *Chronicle* reports that 'they gave him hostages there, as many as he wished to have, and swore great oaths and then kept a firm peace'.[4] This may not have been a sincere change of heart, however, as the raiders had just lost a large part of their fleet at sea during a storm, and so they may have wanted to avoid battle.

In 877 the Army left Exeter for Mercia, which suggests that the treaty with Alfred required it to leave his kingdom. Æthelweard's late 10th-century version of the *Chronicle* records that in the Mercian town of Gloucester the Army built 'booths', or 'huts', presumably for trading. Later that year Mercia was divided between the Army and Ceolwulf II, who, as we saw in Chapter 3, had been assisted by the Vikings in becoming king when the Army spent the winter at Repton in 873–74.[5] He was now to discover what the price of collaboration with the Great Army meant: the loss of half his kingdom.

Its position strengthened, and emboldened by its conquest of eastern Mercia, the Army returned to Wessex, and based itself at the royal estate at Chippenham, Gloucestershire. The *Chronicle* tells us that the West Saxons submitted to the Army, or were driven 'across the sea', except for Alfred who 'journeyed in difficulties through the woods and fen-fastnesses with a small force'.[6] Asser elaborates on this, providing the basis for the heroic stories that later developed around Alfred, placing the events in the marshes of Somerset, where 'He had nothing to live on except what he could forage by frequent raids, either secretly or even openly, from the pagans as well as from the Christians who had surrendered to the authority of the pagans.'[7] In effect, Alfred was in hiding. While this was perhaps a humiliation, it was a better fate than that of his contemporaries Osberht, Ælla and Edmund, who were slaughtered, or Burgred, who had been exiled to Rome. And his kingdom was still intact, which was more than Ceolwulf II could say.

At this time, in early 878, another Viking force landed in Devon led by 'the brother of Ivar and Healfdene', whom later sources identify as Ubba, the same man who had played a part in the death of King Edmund.[8] It is possible that this force, said by Asser to have come from overwintering at Dyfed in Wales, arrived in support of Guthrum's efforts to subjugate Wessex. Asser placed the ensuing battle between the West Saxons and Ubba's force at Countisbury Hill, Devon, recounting that the West Saxons based themselves in a stronghold that was 'unprepared and altogether unfortified'. Here they were besieged by the Vikings, who thought that they could starve them into giving in, but the West Saxons 'were divinely inspired and ... burst out unexpectedly at dawn against the pagans', and defeated them.[9] The *Anglo-Saxon Chronicle* adds that 'there was captured the banner which they called "Raven"'.[10] In Viking mythology ravens were associated with the god Odin and with warfare, as scavengers of human remains on the battlefield. The capture of this potent symbol would have been a bitter blow to the raiders. Ubba was also killed in this encounter but was to live on in legend alongside Ivar as one of the most ferocious leaders of the Great Army. Roger of Wendover, writing in the early 13th century, describes the nuns of Coldingham in the Scottish borders cutting off their noses and upper lips to repel the raiders, to which Ubba and Ivar responded by burning the nunnery and killing all inside.[11]

Meanwhile, Alfred stayed in the marshes at Athelney, gathering his forces and preparing to engage Guthrum in battle. In early May of 878, Alfred journeyed out to 'Egbert's stone'; the precise location is unknown, but suggested as being to the east of Selwood Forest, on the Dorset/Wiltshire border. There Alfred was met by 'all the people of Somerset and of Wiltshire and of that part of Hampshire which was on this side of the sea' who rejoiced to see him.[12] The tide was turning and two days later Alfred's forces arrived at Edington, now famed as the site of a crucial battle against the Great Army that was Alfred's most important victory. The West Saxons put the Army to flight, and then besieged them in their fortress, which was probably at Chippenham. This proved decisive, and, according to Asser, 'thoroughly terrified by hunger, cold and fear, and in the end, by despair' Guthrum sought peace. The terms of the peace treaty required that Guthrum convert to Christianity, and three weeks later he and 30 of his men arrived at Aller, near Athelney:

> King Alfred raised him from the holy font of baptism, receiving him as his adoptive son; the unbinding of the chrisom on the eighth day took place at a royal estate called Wedmore. Guthrum remained with the king for twelve nights after he had been baptized, and the king freely bestowed many excellent treasures on him and all his men.[13]

This marked an important change in Anglo-Saxon dealings with the Great Army and was critical to its integration into English society, as we shall see. First, however, we turn to newly discovered evidence that has transformed our picture of the events of the late 870s. Two coin hoards from Watlington and Leominster, found just months apart in 2015, show the origins of England in a different light. They also show two very different sides of modern metal-detecting.

✛

On 8 October 2015 metal-detectorist James Mather was searching a field near Watlington, in Oxfordshire. He'd been in the field for five hours, but had found nothing and was about to head back home. James was an experienced detectorist – it had been his hobby for some 25 years, and he'd had over 100 artefacts recorded on the PAS database, although no major finds. That was about to change. Returning to his car, James spotted an area of higher ground, terrain often favoured by detectorists, and started to make a zig-zag search pattern across it. Almost immediately he got a good signal, and exposed what looked like a flat, squashed silvery cigar about 7 inches down. He started to move away to continue his search, but then realized he had seen something like it before – a silver ingot from the Cuerdale hoard in Lancashire, the largest Viking hoard ever found in the British Isles. Retracing his steps, James started to search a larger grid around the find-spot, and now found a coin of what he recognized to be an Anglo-Saxon or Viking type. Within minutes he had uncovered what appeared to be a great mass of coins.

At this point James realized that he had stumbled across something important, and called the farmer. They discussed whether they should try to remove the coins in the failing light, or come back the next morning. Fortunately they did the right thing. On a mobile with a low battery and dodgy connection James called his PAS contact, David Williams, the Finds Liaison Officer for Berkshire. David told James to stop digging, and that he would visit the site himself to excavate the find archaeologically. But David could not get there straightaway as his diary was packed. What was to be done to protect the discovery in the meantime? James and the farmer considered parking a piece of farm machinery over it – but would a tractor sitting in the middle of the field simply draw attention to it? In the end they settled for making a small heap of stones over the find spot. Then followed the longest five days in James's life.

On 13 October David Williams arrived with Emma Cooke, an experienced excavator from the Surrey Archaeological Society who had worked with David before. James had got to the field early, but with a sense of rising panic realized that he couldn't find his marker stones. Had someone robbed the site? He retraced his steps, and finally found the cairn, discovering for the second time what would be known as the Watlington hoard. David and Emma set to work and found that the hoard was fairly shallow, maybe 20–30 cm (1 ft) below the surface. They identified the hole in which it had been buried, but no other features. The hoard was large and the coins were fragile; if they tried to excavate it *in situ*, they risked damaging objects and losing information. They decided to lift it as a solid block and excavation continued in the Conservation Laboratory of the British Museum, where the Treasure Valuation Committee valued it at £1.35m. Thanks to a public fundraising appeal it is now back in Oxfordshire, and on display in the Ashmolean Museum.

A study of the Watlington hoard by Jane Kershaw and John Naylor has confirmed that it consists of whole or parts of fifteen silver ingots, six silver arm- or neck-rings with southern Scandinavian parallels, a single small piece of hackgold and a fragment of a hooked tag. The complete silver rings and ingots correspond to the Scandinavian weight unit of 25 g (*c.* 1 oz), whereas each of the cut pieces are about one-third of that weight. Several of the objects show high levels of nicking, where the silver content had been checked as they changed hands. The closest parallels for the hacksilver are from the smaller hoard recovered from Croydon, and dated to the London overwintering of 871–72 (see Chapter 3), although there are also similarities with finds from Aldwark and Torksey. It is noteworthy, however, that the hoard contains complete ingots and rings, unlike the winter-camp finds, which had largely been cut up. The hoard also

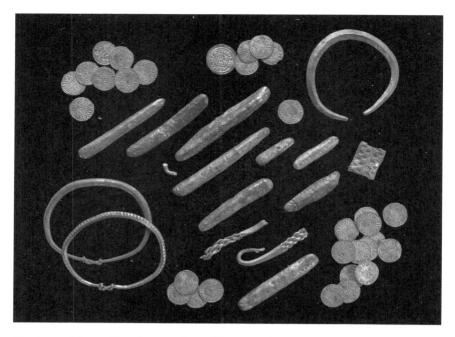

The hoard from Watlington found by metal-detectorist James Mather in 2015.

includes 192 coins, of which the majority were minted for Alfred, of the so-called cross-and-lozenge variety which, as we have already seen, crops up with Great Army associations at Aldwark, Dunsforth and Roxby-cum-Risby. There are also some coins of Ceolwulf II and two of Archbishop Æthelred of Canterbury, the majority minted in London, with some from Canterbury and Winchester. The core of the hoard was therefore clearly brought together in south-east England, although there are two Carolingian coins of the 870s, both minted in Milan, but probably acquired in the Netherlands: one each of Charles the Bald and Louis the Stammerer. The presence of a 'Two-Line' type of penny dates the hoard to the late 870s, after the Battle of Edington. Following their defeat by Alfred the remnants of the Great Army probably used the ancient trackway known as Icknield Street, which passes through Watlington close to where the hoard was found. A member of the Army, planning to return, buried his personal treasure hoard away from the road.

Fortunately for James Mather, and for our knowledge of this critical period, he never made it back, although we will never know why.[14]

‑‑‑‑

The Watlington hoard demonstrates the value of metal-detectorists reporting their finds to archaeologists and the PAS. The second important metal-detected discovery in 2015 relating to the Viking Great Army is a very different tale, however – one that culminated in hefty jail sentences for the finders and their accomplices. In June of that year two Welsh detectorists, George Powell and Layton Davies, secretly dug up a hoard in a field in Eye, near Leominster, Herefordshire, close to the Welsh border. Davies was an experienced detectorist: he held a certificate for 'best find in Wales' in 2014 and had been a member of various metal-detecting clubs for many years, although Powell, the younger man, was said to have taken the 'leading role'. The hoard was the largest find either of them had ever made, comprising more than 300 silver coins, several silver ingots, a 9th-century gold ring, a dragon's-head gold bracelet and a rock-crystal pendant, with a total worth estimated to have been over £3 million [pl. 23]. If they had declared it under the Treasure Act, as British law requires, they would have been entitled to a 50 per cent share with the landowner. However, they decided not to tell the farmer, the landowner or the museum, and instead contacted two coin dealers: Simon Wicks and Paul Wells, who had a stall at the Pumping Station antiques centre in Cardiff. It was agreed the coins should be taken to London, where Wicks tried to sell them to Mayfair auctioneers Dix Noonan Webb. The auctioneers were suspicious, however, and rumours began to circulate. On 6 July – a month after their discovery – the Herefordshire FLO, Peter Reavill, contacted Powell and Davies and gently asked if they had anything to tell him. They initially denied finding anything more than a couple of damaged coins, but later decided to declare to the National Museum of Wales the gold ring and the bracelet, the crystal pendant and two more coins. But the net was closing in.

A 'Two Emperors' silver penny from the Watlington hoard, showing Alfred and Ceolwulf II seated side by side below a winged figure.

Police visited Wells's house and when he showed them five coins from the hoard that had been stitched into his magnifying-glass case he was arrested. Meanwhile, Wicks admitted that he had sold several of the coins 'to a friend', who bought them in a deal at a service station, paying £28,000 cash in three brown paper packets. Police also recovered deleted photos on Davies's phone showing the hoard intact in a freshly dug hole. In November 2019 Powell and Davies were convicted of theft and concealment at Worcester Crown Court and jailed for 10 and 8½ years, respectively. Wicks and Wells were found guilty of concealment and also jailed. However, some 300 coins are still missing; apart from the jewellery, only 31 coins have been recovered. The nature of the hoard suggests that it had been looted from an important church, and hidden by a Viking warrior in 879, one year after the defeat of the Great Army at Edington. The presence of the coins near Leominster suggests that part of the army was in the area before moving east via Watlington.[15]

As Viking hoards go, the Leominster and Watlington finds were not particularly large. The Leominster hoard comprised c. 300 coins; the Watlington hoard, 192 coins. The Watlington hacksilver weighs 1.1 kg (2.4 lbs), which is not much compared to the Cuerdale hoard of c. 905, with its 31 kg (68 lbs) of silver and 7,000 coins. Given that an Anglo-Saxon sheep was worth around 8 g (0.2 oz) of silver, the Watlington hoard had the value of a small flock of 125 sheep, or 62 pigs, or 31 cows. It would have covered only one-eighth of the *wergild* (ransom money) of a high-ranking Dane or Anglo-Saxon, maybe around £18,500 in today's money. Nonetheless, these hoards are hugely significant for the story of the Great Army because they contain so many coins of Alfred and Ceolwulf II of Mercia. We know little of Ceolwulf II's reign after the Army installed him as the new king of Mercia in place of Burgred in 873. However, there is growing evidence that contrary to the *Anglo-Saxon Chronicle*'s description of him as a 'foolish king's thegn', he proved both an acceptable and effective king. He was joined in witnessing charters granting land by the leading lords and ecclesiastics of his kingdom, and the Leominster and Watlington hoards provide a new perspective on his collaboration with Alfred. The Watlington hoard contains thirteen examples of the rare 'Two Emperors' penny that shows Alfred and Ceolwulf seated side by side below a winged figure representing either Victory or an angel. The image on the coins suggests an alliance between the kingdoms of Wessex and Mercia. It therefore challenges the *Chronicle* account that dismisses Ceolwulf as a puppet of the Vikings (see Chapter 3). We know little more than that he ruled for five years, 874–79, and we do not know the circumstances under which Ceolwulf's reign came to an end, or how he died. It is apparent, however, that Alfred's successors wrote Ceolwulf II out of history, contributing to our tendency to privilege Alfred in accounts of the origins of England.

It is now time to go back to the late 9th century and to continue the story of Guthrum. After converting to Christianity, Guthrum and his followers stayed at Cirencester in Gloucestershire and then, in 880, they moved on to East Anglia, 'settled there and shared out the land'.[16] The Great Army had now succeeded, through one means or another, in securing territory in three of the four Anglo-Saxon kingdoms. However, Alfred was determined that the same fate would not befall Wessex and famously drew up a treaty with Guthrum. This treaty divided out their areas of authority, and made arrangements for relations between their followers concerning legal disputes, trade and the movement of people, and prohibited their followers from joining each other's armies. The treaty also defined a boundary between the two realms: 'up the Thames and then up to the Lea, and along the Lea to its source, then in a straight line to Bedford, then up the Ouse to Watlington Street'. This boundary has informed modern maps of the so-called Danelaw but we do not know if the border persisted for very long. At first appearances, the treaty demarcates the areas of jurisdiction of Alfred and Guthrum, but it can also be seen as yet another instance in which Alfred drew the Great Army into new ways of doing things – his way! Guthrum and his Scandinavian followers were from a region where written diplomacy was unknown, so the creation of a written treaty was part of the process by which Guthrum was integrated into the legal, social and economic structures of the Anglo-Saxon communities among which he and his followers now lived.[17]

In drawing up this treaty, Alfred stated that he was supported by the *witan* (king's council) of the *Angelcynn* (English), and there may have been an attempt in his use of language to speak on behalf of people over whom he in fact had no authority. The creation of a notion of Englishness emerges strongly throughout Alfred's career. For example, in 886, the *Chronicle* records that Alfred went into London and 'all the English people [*all Angelcynn*] who were not under subjection to the Danes, submitted to him'.[18] This seems to have been a symbolic acknowledgment of the uniting of the West Saxon and Mercian realms under Alfred, who must have gained control over London a few years earlier; he besieged it in 883 and was already minting coins there in the early 880s.[19] London had formerly been part of Mercia, and from this time was placed under the jurisdiction of the Ealdorman Æthelred, who had ruled Mercia since the death of Ceolwulf II, perhaps around 879. Æthelred married Alfred's daughter, Æthelflæd, and, although we do not know when, it is widely suspected that it was in 886, coinciding with Alfred's ceremonial visit to London.[20] While Mercia retained a separate identity for the remainder of Alfred's reign, Wessex and Mercia were being drawn ever closer together and, as Asser records of the events of 886, 'all the Angles and Saxons – those who had formerly been scattered everywhere and were not in captivity with the pagans turned willingly to King Alfred and submitted themselves to his lordship'.[21]

From this time onwards, Alfred signed charters as *rex Angul-Saxonum* rather than *rex Saxonum*, reflecting his claims to speak on behalf of a wider area than just his kingdom of the West Saxons. The term *Angelcynn*, though not new, appears with increasing frequency in the 880s and 890s, especially in texts associated with Alfred's educational reforms.[22] For instance, an Old English translation of Pope Gregory the Great's (590–604) *Pastoral Care* was written during Alfred's reign, reportedly by the king himself, and when it was circulated it was prefaced by a letter in which he addressed his subjects as *Angelcynn*.[23] Alfred asked his bishops to teach 'all the free-born young men now among the *Angelcynn*' to read English, and said that he had arranged for a selection of Christian and philosophical texts that were 'the most necessary for all men to know' to be translated into English.[24] When introducing his law-code, compiled from earlier West Saxon and Mercian laws, Alfred invoked the two kingdoms' shared history, referring to them as the *Angelcynn*, and emphasizing their common Christian heritage to unite them conceptually into one people – to 'shape an English imagination' as Sarah Foot has put it.[25] Unquestionably, the threat of the Great Army created circumstances in which a unified kingdom of the English became possible. It is unlikely that Alfred could ever have created this kingdom by himself, but he may have imagined it, and a sense of the English as a unified people was to become close to a reality in the coming decades.

Meanwhile, Guthrum was establishing himself as king of East Anglia. We have no documentary evidence directly about his reign, but there are hints of continuing tensions with Wessex. For example, in 885 the *Chronicle* records that:

King Alfred sent a naval force from Kent into East Anglia. Immediately [when] they came into the mouth of the Stour they encountered sixteen ships of Vikings and fought against them, and seized all the ships and killed the men. When they turned homeward with the booty, they met a large naval force of Vikings [*micel sciphere wicinga*] and fought against them on the same day, and the Danes had the victory.[26]

Æthelweard's late 10th-century version of the *Chronicle* records that a newly arrived Viking army from the Continent received assistance from the East Angles and this may explain why, in retribution, Alfred sent his force into East Anglia.[27] There may also have been a territorial dispute at stake, because the River Stour formed the ancient boundary between East Anglia and the kingdom of the East Saxons, which had been nominally incorporated into Wessex in the early 9th century but still retained a sense of separate identity.

The coins minted in Guthrum's realm illustrate the style of kingship adopted by this former Viking leader. Some of the earliest coins imitated those minted by Alfred, sometimes even copying the names of Alfred's moneyers, even though they would not have been minting coins for another king, especially not with numerous spelling mistakes. Indeed, the poor levels of literacy on Guthrum's coins suggest that the mints under Scandinavian control did not have the official oversight and consistency characteristic of those in Wessex, and this enables us to distinguish genuine Alfredian coins from East Anglian copies. Another difference is the slightly lighter weight of Guthrum's coins, which is consistent with earlier East Anglian practices, and different from those in Wessex where Alfred had reformed his coinage and increased the weights and proportion of silver in the mid-880s, in co-operation with Ceolwulf II. Having converted to Christianity, Guthrum adopted an Old English baptismal name, Æthelstan, revealed in the brief entry in the *Chronicle* noting the death in 890 of 'Guthrum, whose baptismal name was Æthelstan', and he used it on some of his coins. Coins issued by Guthrum as 'Æthelstan' were at the traditional East Anglian weight. Some, however, were based on Frankish designs, minted using a

Coin of Guthrum minted
in his baptismal name of
Æthelstan.

die from the trading centre at Quentovic, near the mouth of the River Canche in France. This suggests that some of his moneyers must have come from the Continent and that Guthrum was being presented on his coinage as a king with wide-ranging connections.

In the years after Guthrum's death, coins were minted commemorating Edmund, the former King of East Anglia who had been killed at the hands of the Great Army in 869. We do not know who was ruling East Anglia at this time but it seems likely that the Edmund coins were minted for Scandinavian rulers who were attempting to integrate into East Anglian society. This overtly Christian coinage, treating Edmund as a saint, mirrors that of Guthrum in following the usual East Anglian weight standard and displaying poor standards of literacy. It was minted at several locations across East Anglia, including Norwich and Shelford, and reflects a continuing sense of distinctive regional identity. The miracles associated with Edmund's body, particularly the capacity of his decapitated head to call out, may have held a powerful appeal for Christianized Scandinavians, as a sign of a ruler whose powers were able to transcend death. The early miracles also seem to have focussed on vengeance against thieves and an arrogant East Anglian nobleman called Leofstan. Abbo of Fleury's account of the life of St Edmund (see Chapter 3) described how Leofstan, 'rich in worldly things but ignorant of God', doubted that the saint was still whole and demanded to see the body, after which 'he went mad, and raged cruelly, and ended wretchedly in an evil death'.[28] Being both Christian and a warrior who remained powerful in the afterlife may have made Edmund a heroic figure for both Scandinavian settlers and East Anglians to rally around as they crafted a common identity.[29]

Such regional identities continued to prove troublesome to Wessex. Newly arrived Viking armies received assistance from East Anglia and Northumbria in 893, despite them having previously given oaths and hostages to Alfred. One of these Viking forces, led by Hæsten, had a base at *Benfleet* (possibly on what is today Canvey Island), where it left its women and children, presumably believing them to be safe in a region where they had previously received help, although a West Saxon force subsequently captured some of them. Shoebury, near Southend, was also used as a base in 893 by Viking armies, who subsequently received reinforcements from both East Anglia and Northumbria. Together they raided westwards as far as Buttington in Powys (Wales), where they were besieged and starved so much that they took to eating their horses. After suffering a heavy defeat to the West Saxons, the survivors returned to their fortress in Essex and 'collected again before winter a large army from the East Angles and Northumbrians, placed their women and ships and property in safety in East Anglia, and went continuously by day and night till they reached a deserted city in Wirral, which is called Chester'.[30] While this force was also besieged and defeated, the events of 893 revealed that any ambitions Alfred may have had for a kingdom of the English still had some way to go.

Engaging the Great Army in battle was only one of Alfred's strategies. An early 10th-century Anglo-Saxon document called the *Burghal Hidage* lists 33 fortifications or *burhs* in southern England, along with the land (hides) and men required for their maintenance:

> For the maintenance and defence of an acre's breadth of wall sixteen hides are required. If every hide is represented by one man, then every pole [5 m or 16.5 ft] of wall can be manned by four men. Then for the maintenance of twenty poles of wall eighty hides are required.[31]

Archaeological evidence suggests that the *Burghal Hidage* describes a defensive network that was created in the late 9th century. In some cases, Roman defences were adapted, as demonstrated by excavations at Winchester in Hampshire, Bath in Somerset and Chichester in Sussex. Elsewhere, new defensive circuits were built, such as at Wallingford in Oxfordshire, Wareham in Dorset and Cricklade in Wiltshire, where the rectilinear design of the structures mimicked the layout of Roman towns.[32] This network of fortifications, none more than 65 km (40 miles) apart, suggests a well-planned and coordinated response to the Viking threat in late 9th-century Wessex. Perhaps Alfred's repeated experiences of engaging unexpectedly in battle with the Army, exacerbated by those weeks spent holed up in the Somerset marshes, persuaded him of the need for a new strategy.[33]

This new defensive network was a more systematic means of protecting Wessex from Viking raiders. The kingdoms of Wessex and Mercia certainly had earlier defensive systems in the form of linear earthworks, look-outs and defended places, but these were regionally specific and evidently not entirely successful in responding to the threat posed by the Great Army, which moved at speed along the inland waterways and major routeways of England. As discussed in previous chapters, the Army had good intelligence about the Anglo-Saxon kingdoms, catching those it raided off-guard, and it was adept at seeking out bases for the winter, exploiting the defensive possibilities of riverine sites and islands, and taking advantage of well-stocked estate centres. While not always victorious in pitched battles, it nonetheless succeeded in bringing to an end three royal lineages, and was clearly intent on conquest and settlement. The West Saxons were unable to drive out the Army, and while an accommodation was reached with Guthrum, hostilities continued. A new response was required from the last remaining kingdom, and it is in this context that we need to place the West Saxon defensive system described in the *Burghal Hidage*.

In facing the Great Army, the Anglo-Saxon military responses had largely been locally organized, but in the 890s, when there were renewed attacks on England by Viking armies that had been

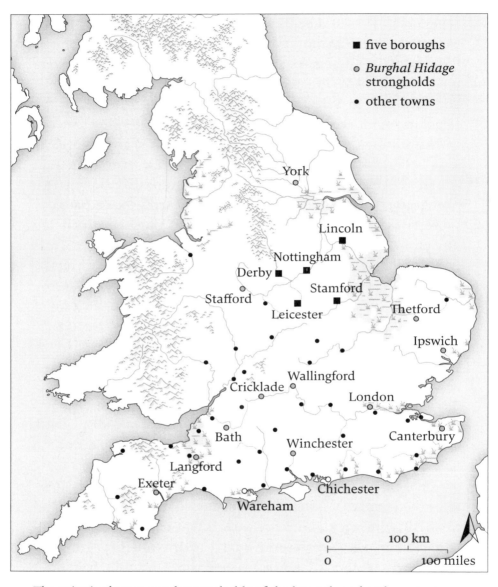

The principal towns and strongholds of the late 9th and 10th centuries.

on the Continent, the West Saxon response was led by King Alfred himself. The *Chronicle* entry for 893 reveals that Alfred had created a standing army, or *fyrd*: 'The king had divided his army into two, so that always half its men were at home, half on service, apart from the men who guarded the boroughs.'[34] This suggests a more coordinated system of defence than had previously been in place, with regulation of military forces and standing defences at strongholds, close to strategically important routeways. A system must also have existed to provision the garrisons. The regular presence of part of Alfred's army in these fortifications would have prevented them from being seized easily by passing Viking forces, which had previously happened when the Great Army was travelling through the countryside, sometimes taking refuge in existing fortifications, as it did at Nottingham. When faced with a Viking attack Alfred was now able to mobilize the necessary forces rather than relying on local responses. In 893 this new system worked effectively. When the newly arrived Viking forces made their way into Wessex and 'captured much booty', they were intercepted at Farnham, in Surrey, as they headed north to retrieve their ships in Essex, and Alfred's force 'put the enemy to flight and recovered the booty'.[35]

Alfred also took the battle to the enemy, building his own fleet in 896, as recorded by the *Chronicle*:

> Then King Alfred had 'long ships' built to oppose the Danish warships. They were almost twice as long as the others. Some had sixty oars, some more. They were both swifter and steadier and also higher than the others. They were built neither on the Frisian nor the Danish pattern, but as it seemed to [Alfred] himself that they could be most useful.[36]

Once again, Alfred is presented as the architect of a successful defence of the kingdom of Wessex and of England more generally. Yet the Vikings had been opposed at sea before, as happened in encounters that occurred in 875 and 882.[37] Moreover, although

Alfred's new fleet was clearly noteworthy, its crew suffered numerous casualties in the ensuing battle in an unnamed estuary on the south coast, possibly Poole harbour. The fatalities included one of Alfred's reeves and another member of his household, but many Frisians were also killed, and it has been suggested that Alfred was required to bring in naval expertise from Frisia.[38] There is therefore much reason to doubt the claim that Alfred founded the English navy, and it is uncertain whether this new ship design endured, as there is no subsequent reference to it. Anglo-Saxon written sources suggest that Alfred's great-grandson Edgar (r. 959–75) was far more important in the development of the English naval capabilities but in modern imaginings of the origins of the English navy Alfred has proven 'a more romantic national figure than Edgar'.[39]

Alfred died on 26 October 899, aged about 50, possibly of Crohn's disease, given Asser's description of his symptoms.[40] He was succeeded as king of Wessex by his son Edward the Elder, who faced a momentary threat to his rule from his cousin Æthelwold, son of Alfred's older brother Æthelred I, when Æthelwold seized the royal residences at Wimborne in Wiltshire and Christchurch in Hampshire. Æthelwold was besieged in an encampment at Badbury near Wimborne by Edward, but managed to escape by night and travelled north where he gained the support of 'the Danish army in Northumbria' and, according to one version of the Chronicle, was accepted as king.[41] Coins minted in York in the name of ALVALDUS are almost certainly for Æthelwold. In 902 he landed with a fleet in Essex, which yet again was providing a useful base for opponents of Wessex, and then 'induced the army in East Anglia to break the peace'.[42] In an ensuing battle, at Holme in Cambridgeshire, his forces were victorious against those of Edward the Elder, but Æthelwold was killed alongside Eohric, a Scandinavian king of East Anglia. Also dead was Brihtsige, almost certainly from one of the Mercian royal families that had vied for control with the lineage from which Ceolwulf II seems to have descended. Æthelwold had gained support from Northumbria, East Anglia and Mercia, and had he not been killed there was a very real possibility that he could have challenged Edward the Elder. English history might have been very different if Æthelwold had succeeded.

Meanwhile, Mercia remained under the control of Ealdorman Æthelred, but we hear little of him in the *Chronicle* after the mid-890s; it is believed that he suffered ill-health, dying in 909. It was his wife, Æthelflæd – Alfred's daughter, and of Mercian royal descent herself through her mother, Ealhswith – who was increasingly in a position of authority in Mercia. The West Saxon version of the *Chronicle* has little to say about her, but fortunately a chronicle known as the *Mercian Register* provides an account of her achievements as the so-called Lady of the Mercians, details of which were later incorporated into some of the *Chronicle* manuscripts. The early 10th century saw Æthelflæd and her brother Edward capture territory under Scandinavian control. The offensive seems to have begun after 909 when a peace that Edward had agreed with the Scandinavian settlers in Northumbria and East Anglia was breached. The English forces were subsequently victorious in a battle at Tettenhall in Staffordshire. Over the following decade Edward and Æthelflæd began to secure their territories and to conquer land under Scandinavian control, ordering new *burhs* to be built at more than fifteen locations throughout the Midlands, while existing *burhs* at Huntingdon and Colchester were 'repaired and restored'. At some places with an existing *burh*, such as Hertford, Stamford, Nottingham and Bedford, a second was constructed, on the opposite bank of the adjacent river. At Buckingham Edward had two *burhs* built, one on either side of the River Great Ouse. In the *Chronicle* entries in these years, encounters between the forces of Edward and Æthelflæd and the Vikings are depicted as occurring at *burhs*, which is also where Scandinavians, still described as armies, submitted to them: hence in 917 'the army which belonged to Cambridge chose [Edward] especially as its lord and protector'.[43]

During this period Æthelflæd was clearly a formidable campaigner and powerful leader in Mercia. Alongside the many *burhs* founded in her reign, she built churches and established saints' cults. For example, in 909 the relics of St Oswald, a 7th-century Northumbrian king, were taken from the monastery of Bardney in Lincolnshire, deep in Scandinavian-controlled territory in east Mercia, to her foundation at Gloucester. Her authority extended into Wales, where she sent a force in 916 after one of her abbots had been killed there. The royal site of *Brecenanmere* (probably on Llangorse lake in Powys) was destroyed and the wife of the King of Brycheiniog and 33 others were taken captive. Two years later she extended her authority into Northumbria, and 'the people of York had promised her – and some had given pledges, some had confirmed it with oaths – that they would be under her direction'. However, she died shortly afterwards, and was buried in her church at Gloucester; the *Annals of Ulster*, while ignoring the deaths of her father and brother, record her demise, describing her as *famosissima regina Saxonum* ('renowned Saxon queen'). Mercia had retained a separate identity under Æthelflæd, but Edward moved quickly to counter any threat from her daughter, Ælfwyn, who was 'deprived of all authority in Mercia and taken into Wessex', and the long history of Mercia as an independent kingdom was over. We are not to know what might have transpired had she outlived her brother, but Æthelflæd was certainly capable of bringing multiple kingdoms under her authority.

It is, however, important to balance this account by acknowledging that Edward seems to have exerted his authority in Mercia by fighting battles, forging peace treaties and granting land there, as well as minting coins, something that Æthelflæd and her husband never did; nonetheless, there is no question that both Æthelflæd and her brother played critical roles in moving forward Alfred's vision of a kingdom of the *Angelcynn*. Yet it was to be Edward's son Æthelstan who consolidated this, extending his rule into Northumbria and capturing York in 927, after which 'he brought under his rule all the kings who were in this island', including Hywel, king of the West Welsh, Constantine, king of the Scots, Owain, king of the people of Gwent, and Aldred, son of Eadwulf from Bamburgh.[44]

This was not the end of the matter, however, and in 937 Æthelstan defeated a combined force of Vikings and Scots in a monumental battle at *Brunanburh*. Its location has never been securely identified but the battle is commemorated in a poem, inserted into the *Anglo-Saxon Chronicle*, which records the scene as Æthelstan's forces departed victorious from the battlefield:

> They left behind them the dusky-coated one, the black raven with its horned beak, to share the corpses, and the dun-coated, white-tailed eagle, the greedy war-hawk, to enjoy the carrion, and that grey beast, the wolf of the forest.[45]

Æthelstan was now 'King of the English' – even 'King of the British' in some charters – although the distinctive identities of the separate kingdoms were to persist for decades and the Viking threat was far from over. There were numerous steps to come in building an English nation, but the contribution of Alfred in seeing off the Vikings was fundamental. This period and this king, above all others, would capture popular imagination in centuries to come, and the stories that emerged around Alfred and the Great Army have played a significant role in shaping English identity.

The mythology about King Alfred began in his own lifetime, and Asser's *Life* was central in this.[46] Asser's royal biography portrayed Alfred as having been marked for greatness from childhood: he was more loved by his parents and 'more pleasing in manner, speech and behaviour' than any of his brothers; from the cradle onwards he showed a desire for wisdom and a love of literature, winning a book of poetry from his mother which she offered to whichever of her sons could learn it the fastest. As an adult, Alfred is said to be a skilled huntsman, with a keen desire for book learning. In 887 when Alfred begins to read Latin and translate it for the first time, Asser depicts the skill as coming through divine inspiration, seemingly overnight. Asser extolls Alfred's many virtues, and assigns his successes against the Viking marauders to his personal qualities and to divine assistance, as he 'struggled like an excellent pilot to guide his ship laden with much wealth to the desired and safe haven of his homeland, even though all his sailors were virtually exhausted'.[47]

When Alfred died the *Anglo-Saxon Chronicle* noted simply that he was king 'over the whole English people except for that part which was under Danish rule, and he had held the kingdom for one and a half years less than thirty'.[48] The late 10th-century chronicler Æthelweard, a descendant of Alfred's older brother Æthelred, was more lavish in his praise: 'Then in the same year, there passed from the world the magnanimous Alfred, king of the Saxons, unshakeable pillar of the western people, a man replete with justice, vigorous in warfare, learned in speech, above all instructed in divine learning.'[49]

Other chroniclers developed the mythology over the following centuries, with the 11th-century *History of St Cuthbert* recounting a tale of Alfred in the marshes of Athelney sharing bread with a pilgrim who turns out to be St Cuthbert; the saint tells the king 'I will be your shield and your friend and the defender of your sons' and prophesies that Alfred will be victorious against the Vikings.[50] This story was replicated in numerous later sources and became widely known across England. A similar story occurs in the *Life of St Neot*, composed in the late 10th century at the monastery of St Neot's in Huntingdonshire, about the 9th-century hermit-saint from Cornwall; in this version it is St Neot who appears in a vision to Alfred, this time promising God's mercy if he changes his ways. The famous story of Alfred allowing the cakes of a swineherd's wife to burn when he should have been watching over them appears here, and it is because Alfred takes the scolding he receives without complaint that St Neot returns and promises to help him against the Vikings.[51] These two stories about Alfred, in unrelated manuscripts, are believed to have originated at the royal court of Wessex, perhaps in the early 10th century when Alfred's grandson King Athelstan was making grants of land to the community of St Cuthbert as he extended his authority over Northumbria.[52]

Chroniclers of the 12th century incorporated information drawn from Asser into their histories, spreading knowledge of the king's achievements. They also embellished their accounts with their own inventions. William of Malmesbury was the first to tell the story of Alfred disguising himself as a minstrel to enter the camp of Guthrum to find out the Army's plans. The Norman chronicler Orderic Vitalis claimed that Alfred was 'the first king to hold sway over the whole of England'. Traditions that Alfred founded Oxford University emerged in the 14th century, and the University was later to make much of this, commissioning numerous portraits of him. In 1718 this endeavour was aided by a bequest of a spectacular late 9th-century Anglo-Saxon jewel made of enamel and quartz encased in gold filigree, around the sides of which is the inscription AELFRED MEC HET GEWYRCAN ('Alfred ordered me to be made'). This item, probably the jewelled end of a pointer to aid a reader in following text on the page, may have circulated with a manuscript of one of the books that Alfred had directed to be translated into Old English, since such an object is described in his Preface to *Pastoral Care* as accompanying distribution of the text. Known as the 'Alfred Jewel', the object was discovered near Alfred's monastic foundation at Athelney and, with its unquestionable link to the king and his institutional reforms, revived popular interest in Alfred when it was put on display in the University's Ashmolean Museum, where it can still be seen [pl. 25].

The figure of King Alfred was adopted by the 18th-century Hanoverian kings of England as a model prince, and over the course of the 18th and early 19th centuries he was put to numerous political uses, and entered the realm of Romantic hero as the subject of many plays and poems, history books and paintings. Some of these were, however, dreadful, with Simon Keynes noting of an epic poem about Alfred composed by John Fitchett, a lawyer, in 1808: 'It is organized in 48 books, occupying a total of about 3,000 pages or about 131,300 lines, making it approximately 41 times longer than *Beowulf*. It must indeed be one of the longest poems in the English language, and might even qualify as the most unreadable.'[53]

During the reign of Queen Victoria, and the rise of the British Empire as a consequence of its maritime prowess, Alfred's role as founder of the English navy was emphasized and the mythology surrounding him was further developed. After the Houses of Parliament were destroyed by fire in 1834, competitions were held to design new decorative schemes for the rebuilding. Alfred inspired several submissions depicting his alleged foundation of the English jury system and opposition to the Vikings. One cartoon submitted by the artist Daniel Maclise as a design for a fresco showed Alfred in the camp of the Danes. Although Maclise's fresco was not commissioned for Parliament, he painted this design under the title *Alfred, the Saxon King, Disguised as a Minstrel, in the Tent of Guthrum the Dane*, which went on display at the Royal Academy in 1852 [pl. 24]. In 1877 a statue of Alfred was unveiled in his birthplace at Wantage by the Prince of Wales, showing the king with his axe at his feet and a parchment role containing his laws in his hand. Subsequent historical analysis has put Alfred and his achievements into more measured context, and it is now clear that the English constitution, legal and political institutions do not solely derive from Alfred. Yet his achievements have unquestionably transcended those of all other Anglo-Saxon kings in popular culture, including his appearance in a *Ladybird* children's book. At the heart of the popular appeal of Alfred's story are his struggles with the Great Army. The same political propaganda that developed the Alfredian mythology from the 9th to 19th centuries presented the Anglo-Saxons as the true ancestral English while the Scandinavian settlers were cast as outsiders. Nonetheless, in the next chapter we will consider how the Viking Great Army was itself a catalyst for the economic and industrial foundations of England.

10

The First Industrial Revolution

Today Torksey is a sleepy village nestled between the River Trent and the Foss Dyke, popular with barge owners who often pause at the cafe before passing through the lock that regulates water levels between the river and canal. But in the 11th century Torksey was a major town of eastern England, larger even than Nottingham. It had a mint and, by 1066, 213 burgesses with their own court. It was an important place on long-distance routeways between London and York. *Domesday Book* records that 'if the king's messengers should come thither the men of the same town should conduct them to York with their ships and their means of navigation' and the sheriff was required to feed them. In this chapter we will reveal the role that the Great Army played in the transformation of Torksey into a town, and its wider contribution to urbanization and trade across eastern and northern England. We will show that the response of the rulers of western Mercia and Wessex to the Viking threat was also a catalyst for urban growth, as they established *burhs* and captured the strategic bases at which members of the Great Army had settled. Together these influences made a major contribution to the development of medieval England's society and economy.

We begin our account in 1960, when the Adult Education Department of the University of Nottingham embarked on a series of summer excavations for its students. Their first target was two fields to the south of the village of Torksey. Here Maurice Barley and his students had been hoping to find out more about medieval Torksey. Written sources revealed that it had once been a thriving town, but it had fallen into decline towards the end of the Middle Ages, as the Foss Dyke silted up and trade from Lincolnshire began to be focussed on the east coast port of Boston. Barley was drawn here by the 16th-century antiquarian John Leland who wrote that:

> The old buildings of Torksey were on the south of the new town, but there now is little scene of old buildings, more than a chapel, where men say was the parish church of old Torksey, and on Trent side the earth so balkith up that it showeth that there by likelihood hath been some wall, and by it is a hill of earth cast up: they call it the Windmill Hill, but I think the dungeon of some old castle was there.[1]

In excavations over three years Barley found few traces of this medieval town, but he did, however, uncover two pottery kilns. Their products included bowls, cooking pots and storage jars, some decorated with the thumb impressions of the potters [pl. 26]. He was unsure of their date, but was aware of sherds of this sort of pottery in the Nottingham town ditch, which had been filled in during the late 11th century.[2] Over the next six years, Barley and his students returned each summer to Torksey and uncovered another five pottery kilns at the southern edges of the village, which suggested that pottery production may have commenced in the early 9th century. Barley drew attention to similarities of the pottery with continental products and thought that the industry originated during the era of the Mercian Supremacy, in the 8th or 9th century, although 'it was the circumstances of mobility and enterprise created by the Scandinavian settlements which enabled it to flourish'.[3]

Following our work on the winter camp of the Great Army north of the village we found ourselves drawn to this earlier work and the possibility that the pottery kilns provided the key to understanding

The Anglo-Saxon town at Torksey.

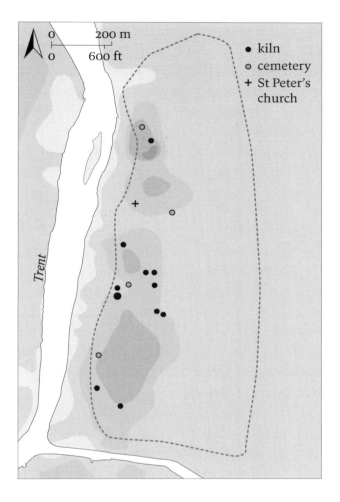

what brought the Great Army to Torksey. In fact, what we found was completely different, and it revealed that the overwintering led to an industrial revolution on the banks of the Trent.[4] Gareth Perry is a member of the Torksey research team and a pottery specialist who was a former PhD student of Dawn's. He had his doubts about the conclusions of Barley's earlier work, and particularly the belief that the pottery industry had commenced in the early 9th century. In one of our project meetings he pointed out that this conclusion rested on the presence of Torksey pottery at the rural settlement of Goltho, some 32 km (20 miles) to the east, but that this site had since been re-dated to the 10th century. As far as Gareth was aware, the earliest secure contexts in which Torksey pottery had been found were late 9th-century layers at Lincoln and York. He was also unconvinced that there had been sufficient analysis of the Torksey pottery to know how it was made, or from where the potters who established the new industry had come. It became clear that we needed to undertake a new investigation of its dating and origins, which were critical to understanding the development of the town. At one of our team meetings we discussed whether it was plausible that continental potters would turn up at just the right place to find the types of clay needed for this industrial level of pottery production, which saw pots fired to very high temperatures. For Gareth the answer to that question was obvious: an experienced potter would have a keen eye for landscape and would easily be able to find the right type of clay outcropping on the surface. That meeting was to lead to Gareth spending many hours walking around Torksey, the river banks and fields, retracing the steps of the potters of a thousand years ago. What emerged from this work was ground-breaking.

Gareth set off with augur in hand to collect clay samples from around the village to learn more about the raw materials available to potters. It was immediately apparent that there were at least five different types of clay available in the immediate vicinity from which kilns could be constructed and pots made. So, to find out which sources they had used, he took clay samples, formed them into bricks and fired them in kilns at the University of Sheffield. For comparison he collected a selection of Torksey sherds excavated by Barley that are now in University of Nottingham Museum, and fragments of a kiln lining excavated in 2007 at the northern edge of the village.[5] Thin sections of pottery, kiln linings and fired clay were taken and examined in the laboratory under a high-powered microscope. From this Gareth was able to reconstruct how pottery was made in Torksey, which revealed that the site must have seen the arrival of highly experienced potters, used to making pottery in a very different way to the local Anglo-Saxon communities. There had been a veritable industrial revolution.[6]

It emerged that the potters had selected two different types of clay. The kilns were made of the clay on which they were built, adjacent to the Trent. Given the large amounts of clay needed, as well as the requirement for lots of water, this was a sensible choice of location. Being adjacent to the river also gave the potters ready access to one of the major routeways into midland England, while they could use the Foss Dyke to take their products to Lincoln. The pottery itself was made from a different band of clay, from an outcropping more than a kilometre east of the village. Looking back at Barley's records, Gareth noticed that he described a pit next to one of the kilns as 'filled with green clay', which is the colour of the freshly dug clay that the potters had sourced, showing that they collected their clay and stored it close to where they were working. Barley had presumed that the potters must have had to acquire quantities of sand to mix into their potting clay to protect it from thermal shock during firing. But microscopic analysis revealed that this clay source had naturally occurring sand inclusions. This confirmed to Gareth that the potters who selected that clay source

Artist's reconstruction of a Torksey ware kiln, shown in cutaway cross-section.

were experienced and able to select just what they needed from the array of raw materials at their disposal. The Torksey pottery was manufactured in a completely different manner to local pottery. The local pottery had been made by building up coils of clay to form vessels, whereas Torksey ware was thrown on a fast potter's wheel, of a type not seen in Britain since the Roman period. This manufacturing process could be identified under the microscope where the elongated grains of sand were uniformly parallel to the edges of the pottery sherds. This orientation of the sand happens as a consequence of a pot spinning on a wheel as the potter squeezes and stretches the clay walls upwards. It was also apparent that the potter's wheel turned anti-clockwise and, therefore, that they were right-handed. Grooves from throwing the clay were found on the inside of the pots but not their outsides, showing that the potters then smoothed the outer surfaces. A roughly rectangular stone that had been trimmed to a curve on one side was found near one of the kilns and interpreted as a potter's rib for shaping the outside of vessels. Close analysis of both the colour of the pottery and the shape of the pores in the clay, which are affected by heat and oxygen levels, suggested it had been fired to very high temperatures, at least 800–850°C. This, again, showed a marked contrast with the earlier handmade wares, which had been fired in small batches in open bonfires, whereas the Torksey pots were fired in large numbers in kilns, using technology completely new to 9th-century England.

Torksey ware cooking pot, excavated at Castle Farm, Torksey in 1994. The large crack shows this was a waster, damaged during firing.

Gareth was also struck by comments in a number of reports that suggested that the Torksey industry had inspired a range of other potteries across the country, which would account for the wide distribution of what they called 'Torksey type' pottery. So he analysed samples of this 'Torksey type' pottery from York and Lincoln, as well as from Julian's excavations at Cottam and Dawn's excavations at West Halton near the confluence of the Trent with the Humber, and concluded that this pottery, too, was made from the clays in Torksey. Given how frequently 'Torksey-type' pottery is reported from excavations across Lincolnshire and Yorkshire the likelihood was emerging that Torksey was not simply an influencer of pottery production but was the centre of a major industry providing pottery to large swathes of eastern and northern England from the late 9th to late 11th centuries. The findings were revolutionary.

To throw more light on this industry we undertook a geophysical survey and fieldwalking in the same field where Barley had conducted his first three seasons of excavation. The field was covered in wasters from pottery production, which suggested that there might have been more kilns than the two identified by Barley. Our magnetometer survey revealed a very strong discrete magnetic anomaly where Barley uncovered his Kiln 1, and similar features elsewhere in that field may indicate the location of perhaps as many as another ten kilns. In the spring of 2019, we were alerted to the presence of yet more kilns, when Dawn was contacted by Stephen Dean at the Environment Agency, which was investigating the flood defences at Torksey Lock. The Agency had commissioned a programme of geophysical survey, and in the light of our work had realised that some of the anomalies were probable kiln sites.[7] Torksey was clearly the hub of a massive pottery industry, with over 20 kiln sites traced in the field to the south of the village and another thirteen found elsewhere in the village by Barley or developer-funded excavations. More kilns of the later Anglo-Saxon period have been identified here than at any other town in England.

Our survey also identified a rectangular ditched enclosure at the highest point of the field above the River Trent floodplain. It appears to have surrounded a sizable cemetery, as our fieldwalking recovered remains of ploughed-out burials from its interior and badger activity along the field bank continues to disturb the graves. Barley had reported finding burials on the western edge of the field in the early 1960s, some of them cut into a pit that he interpreted as a lime kiln used in the construction of a church. This may also be where Leland reported a chapel in the early 16th century, but no traces of it were found by Barley, and our fieldwalking did not recover any stonework there. Barley dated the graves to the 13th century, but our radiocarbon dating of the human remains has shown that the cemetery originated at least as early as the 10th century.

Dawn had previously undertaken research on the burial practices of the later Anglo-Saxon period, and was alert to the fact that towns typically had multiple burial locations. She decided to focus on this aspect of the development of Torksey for her paper at the 2013 Viking Congress in Shetland.[8] Her exploration of unpublished excavation reports revealed further burial places in Torksey, in keeping with its growing urban status. Two were located at the north and south end of the village respectively, and also associated with pottery kilns, from which they were separated by ditches. The juxtaposition of cemeteries with pottery kilns at three separate locations in Torksey may indicate that the different potting communities had their own burial places, within which men, women and children were interred. In contrast, what appears to be a high-status cemetery, unrelated to any known kilns, was excavated in the centre of the village. Here a group of at least 20 burials have been found, some of which were in stone-lined graves. One individual had been buried wearing fine clothing as traces of gold thread survived. This is close to the documented location of the lost medieval church of St Mary's, and near to the surviving parish church of St Peter's, whose cemetery probably also originated at this time. A 12th-century source refers to a third parish church in Torksey, All Saints, but there is no clear evidence where this was. Nonetheless, by the 11th century there were three churches and at least five cemeteries in Torksey, demonstrating its growing size and importance.

+

Looking across eastern England, pottery industries similar to that at Torksey can be identified at Stamford, Lincoln, Thetford, York, Nottingham, Newark, Northampton and Leicester. All of these locations were towns in the later Anglo-Saxon period. Furthermore, all are in those regions of East Anglia, eastern Mercia and Northumbria where Scandinavians began to settle following the division of those kingdoms by the Great Army. Indeed, some of these wheel-thrown pottery industries are found at precisely the places where the Army had spent the winter. Just one thing did not quite make sense, however. In Scandinavia very little pottery was used in this period, with even less produced there, and certainly there was no tradition of making pottery on a fast potter's wheel or using kilns like those excavated at Torksey. The parallels are, rather, on the Continent, in northern France and the Low Countries. These are exactly the regions in which at least some members of the Great Army had been raiding in the years before arriving in England. Just as the Scandinavian kings who took control of territory in England from Guthrum onwards relied on moneyers from the Frankish realm, so it now seems that the pottery industries of eastern England saw the arrival of another group of continental craftworkers. Perhaps they had been part of the Great Army, or had simply followed in its wake, but either way they took advantage of the possibilities opened up by the Army's territorial conquests.

Encouraged by these findings about the introduction of pottery production into the regions of Scandinavian settlement in England, we began to consider the impact that this may have had on the origins and growth of towns. This has been a longstanding debate among historians and archaeologists of Anglo-Saxon England, who now agree that the network of Roman towns did not survive the 5th-century withdrawal of the Roman imperial authority and economic infrastructure, but have presented competing explanations for when towns re-emerged. Debate has focussed on whether it was the Mercians, in the 8th and 9th centuries under kings such as Offa (r. 757–96), or the West Saxons in the 9th and 10th centuries, whose power and ambitions fostered urban growth. Much attention has focussed on royal palaces and monasteries as providing the impetus for urbanization, since these were pre-existing centres of power. However, as Martin Carver has pointed out, these power centres do not, on the whole, lie underneath or adjacent to the new Anglo-Saxon towns, and while there is some historical evidence to suggest there were 8th- and 9th-century fortified sites, 'there is no good reason for assuming they were in exactly the same places as the later burhs'.[9] The towns that grew in the decades from c. 900 did not represent continuity from earlier arrangements, but something new and dynamic concentrated in the regions of Scandinavian settlement. Many of the places at which the new wheel-thrown pottery industries developed have other evidence for urban activity in the years on either side of AD 900, and most of these settlements seem to have been transformed at this time.

Lincoln was the Roman city of *Lindum Colonia*, and a provincial capital. There is little evidence, however, for its occupation within the crumbling remains of the Roman walls in the Anglo-Saxon period, beyond a few cemeteries and churches, even though it was possibly the seat of the bishop of Lindsey. While there is slight evidence of occupation on the opposite side of the Witham at Wigford, this site appears to have been abandoned in the 9th century (Chapter 1). There is tentative evidence that members of the Great Army were based in Lincoln in the 870s. A small collection of finds from the church of St-Paul-in-the-Bail in the upper part of the town is characteristic of material found at other Great Army sites, including four silver pennies from Wessex dating to the early 870s, a Carolingian belt buckle and a Trewhiddle-style strap-end and belt buckle. Other evidence for Scandinavian activity in Lincoln comes from coinage.

There was a mint in Lincoln under Scandinavian control before the end of the 9th century, producing copies of Alfred's coins in which the monogram representing the name of London was modified to represent Lincoln. St Edmund coins minted under Scandinavian control in East Anglia have also been recovered from the town.[10] It is around then, at the end of the 9th century, that evidence for urban life in Lincoln, in the form of trade and manufacture, emerges for the first time since the Roman period.

Early medieval pottery kilns have been identified in the lower part of the former Roman city on both Flaxengate and Silver Street, and by the mid-10th century their products were distributed all over Lincoln and further afield in Lincolnshire. Lincoln was a centre of several different types of pottery production, each characterized by distinctive forms, fabrics and firing regimes, and pottery continued to be produced there into at least the 11th century. Buildings were constructed facing Flaxengate, Silver Street and nearby Danesgate. Since none of these streets align with the former Roman walls and streets, it suggests a reconfiguration of the layout of the town, providing further indication of the lack of continuity in urban life. Flaxengate seems to have been heading down the hill towards the River Witham from where finished goods may have been transported. By the mid-10th century Lincoln was a thriving town, with evidence around Flaxengate not only for pottery production but also for glass-working and metalworking. Coins were minted in Lincoln in the 920s dedicated to St Martin, a 4th-century Roman soldier who rejected his weapons and refused to fight on account of his Christian faith, and with whom miracles were subsequently associated. There are echoes of the fascination that Scandinavian converts had for another martyr, St Edmund, and both saints' lives share the theme of a warrior's martyrdom leading to supernatural powers after death. The popularity of St Martin in both Frankia and Ireland may also have influenced the choice by Scandinavian rulers who would have encountered his cult there.[11] In the decades following the arrival of the Great Army, Lincoln was transformed into a thriving centre of manufacture and trade. Settlement expanded into Wigford again, which seems to have become a focal point for manufacture and trade adjacent to the Witham. It is notable that over 80 per cent of the 10th-century funerary monuments known in Lincoln come from two newly founded churches in Wigford, suggesting that the trading community was expressing itself through ecclesiastical foundations and funerary display. By 1066 there were over 1,270 tenements in Lincoln, most held by burgesses, and it has been estimated that there may have been as many as 12,000 people living there, and at least 30 churches.[12]

A similar transformation can be identified further south in Lincolnshire, at Stamford, where Ermine Street crossed the River Welland by a ford, the 'stone ford' (Old English *stan, ford*) of its name. Stamford was clearly another strategic point in the transport network, at the boundary between the shires of Lincolnshire and Northamptonshire and the royal lands of Rutland. At the time of *Domesday Book* Queen Edith, wife of Edward the Confessor, held 70 tenements in Stamford that were part of Rutland, located adjacent to the church of St Peter in the west of the town. Rutland is thought to have been the dower land of the Anglo-Saxon queens, given to them for the duration of their marriage, and possibly deriving from a Mercian royal estate. In any case, the lands west of Stamford must have been seen to be of strategic importance, given that Alfred sent envoys to Northumbria in 894 to negotiate over this territory after it had suffered Viking raids. Little is known of Stamford prior to the late 9th century. An enclosure comprising three concentric ditches with a palisade surrounded the church of St Peter, which is believed to have been a pre-Viking foundation. Two of the ditches contained kiln wasters and pottery, while one also contained a Scandinavian imitation of a coin of Alfred. On this evidence the enclosure seems to date to the second half of the 9th century, but it is difficult to be sure whether or not this predated the arrival of Scandinavian settlers.[13] The pottery kilns in Stamford produced the most distinctive of the new wheel-thrown wares, manufactured from the locally available white clay, and its products were diverse, including bowls, jars, pitchers, cooking pots, crucibles for metalworking and lamps [pl. 27]. Much of the pottery was lead-glazed, sometimes with red-painted decoration, and it has similarities with the products of industries in northern France. The glazing reveals that the potters would have needed to have been supplied with large amounts of lead. The most obvious source for this would have been the lead mines in the Derbyshire Peak District, in a part of eastern Mercia that must have come under Scandinavian control in the partition with Ceolwulf II in 877. These mines were certainly being exploited in the early 9th century, when an Abbess Cynewaru, possibly from Repton, made a grant of land in Wirksworth on condition that the recipient sent an annual payment of lead to Canterbury Cathedral.[14] Aside from pottery production, excavation in Stamford has also revealed contemporary evidence for ironworking hearths and stone quarrying.[15]

When Stamford was captured by King Edward the Elder in 918 it was reported by the *Anglo-Saxon Chronicle* that the people who belonged to the 'northern *burh* submitted to him and sought to have him as their lord'.[16] This *burh* must have been constructed during the period of Scandinavian control on the north banks of the Welland.[17] The street layout to the east of St Peter's church has been used to identify the rectangular form of the *burh*, which was roughly 6 ha (15 acres) in area. Traces of a timber defensive structure have been excavated there, along with buildings arranged in a rectilinear street pattern facing onto the later High Street.[18] A small hoard of coins dating to *c.* 890 was found in the northern *burh* in 1902 by workmen who were digging a trench on St Leonard's Street. It was broken up before it could be properly recorded, but was clearly a Scandinavian hoard, as it included copies of Alfred's coins minted in Lincoln and Leicester, as well as two from York and one of the Carolingian king Charles the Bald. Many of the coins in this hoard had been nicked or pecked, consistent with their having passed through Viking hands. Some of the St Edmund pennies are known to have been struck in the north-east midlands, and Stamford may have been the location of this mint.[19]

The arrival of Edward and his army in 918 played a further part in the development of Stamford, as he took control and 'ordered the borough on the south side of the river to be built'. As a result of this initiative the town grew on either side of the river, in a development that is mirrored at several towns where Edward founded *burhs*, such as Nottingham, Bedford and Hertford. By the mid-10th century Stamford was one of the major *burhs* in Mercia, when this former kingdom was 'redeemed' from Scandinavian control by Edward the Elder's son King Edmund, including 'five boroughs, Leicester and Lincoln, Nottingham and likewise Stamford, and also Derby'.[20] It had one of the most prolific mints in later Anglo-Saxon England and by the time of *Domesday Book* it had become a large town comprising 406 properties and four churches. It is difficult to avoid the conclusion that the arrival of the Great Army and the potters who followed in its wake were crucial to the transformation of Stamford, with the subsequent conquest by Edward contributing to its further expansion.

Like Torksey, Thetford is a place where the Great Army is recorded as having spent the winter and where a major pottery industry subsequently emerged. It was also located at a strategically important place, at a fording point over two rivers, the Thet and the Little Ouse, and where they were crossed by the Roman Icknield Way. Occupation of Thetford in the 7th and 8th centuries was largely concentrated to the west of the medieval town. It was during the late 9th and 10th centuries that Thetford grew into a sizable settlement. In addition to furnished 9th-century burials (Chapter 6), there are traces of Viking influence in the form of Scandinavian and continental metalwork found there, including a Borre-style brooch, a trefoil brooch, four of continental type and a strap-end with interlace decoration. A Thor's hammer was found, made of lead rather than silver, and so may have been a model to be used during the casting process. Three pieces of steatite, or soapstone, must have come from Norway or Scandinavian settlements in Shetland. Steatite is a common find on Scandinavian settlement sites as it is a soft stone that could be readily carved into bowls. The recovery of five Northumbrian stycas in Thetford is striking given their rarity this far south and, as we have seen, these are part of the 'signature' of the Great Army. A mid-9th-century Carolingian coin minted by King Lothar in Dorestad has been cited as rare evidence of activity in the town prior to the arrival of the Great Army, but these coins are unusual finds in England, and it is more plausible that it was brought to Thetford by a member of the Great Army, as probably was also the case with another continental coin found in Thetford, one minted for the West Frankish King Charles the Bald between 864 and 877. Five St Edmund pennies, minted in East Anglia during the period of Scandinavian control, have also been recovered from Thetford, providing additional evidence for its occupation at this time.[21]

The form of the Great Army's camp at Thetford is uncertain from the archaeological record. The late 10th-century version of

Thetford, showing approximate areas of known late Anglo-Saxon industrial activity (hatched), including pottery kilns which were concentrated on the western side of the town, with contemporary burial sites marked by dots.

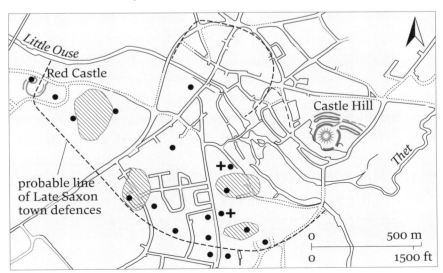

the *Anglo-Saxon Chronicle* by Ealdorman Æthelweard implies an orderly structure when he writes that they 'laid out a camp in the winter season at Thetford', but it is a late source and such details are not necessarily reliable. Excavation has revealed a ditched enclosure on the south bank of the Little Ouse, enclosing an area of *c.* 60 ha (150 acres), but the ditch fill suggests that it dates to the 10th century.[22] Furthermore, most of the finds that seem to be associated with the Great Army have been found outside of this enclosure, suggesting that the focal point of the Army's activity was to the south and east of the 10th-century town.

The principal evidence for Scandinavian influence in Thetford comes from the pottery industry that developed there in the late 9th century. More than ten kilns have been excavated, producing a standard range of bowls, storage jars, dishes, cooking pots, lamps, costrels and crucibles. Thetford ware is found widely across East Anglia and beyond. As in Torksey, the kilns were located adjacent to cemeteries. Further evidence for craftworking and manufacturing in Thetford includes crucibles for melting silver and copper alloy; chalk moulds for casting ingots; iron slag and metalworking tools; sawn antler tines and horn cores discarded as the waste products of bone- and antler- working; heckles (wool combs), spindle whorls and needles used in textile production; and a bone lucet used in cord-making. Iron awls and creasers used in leatherworking, and evidence for tanning, have also been identified. Over 200 pits of later Anglo-Saxon date have been excavated, associated with cess deposits, storage, quarrying of sand and gravel and rubbish disposal. Traces of multiple buildings were seen, and while not enough could be identified of their structures to be certain of their function, some were doubtless domestic dwellings and others used for storage and perhaps housing of animals. By the time of *Domesday Book* Thetford had 943 burgesses, plus 75 identified tradesmen, comprising bakers, brewers, tailors, washers, shoemakers, robemakers and cooks. There were also at least eleven churches. Excavation suggests that by this time the town had shrunk from its 10th-century extent, but even so it remained large. Again, it is difficult to avoid the conclusion that the arrival of the Viking Great Army at Thetford was a key factor in its transformation from a small settlement into a town.

+

There is nothing to suggest that places like Torksey, Stamford, Thetford and Lincoln were urban settlements when the Great Army arrived in the East Midlands and East Anglia. In each case, however, we have archaeological evidence to indicate the presence of members of the Great Army, which is also documented in our historical sources at both Torksey and Thetford. Our work at Torksey suggests that the Great Army was akin to a town on the move. The arrival of such a large population must have been the catalyst for urban development at numerous places. While there were to be many stages by which these centres developed into the 11th-century towns that were first recorded in detail in *Domesday Book*, the pottery industries were major contributing factors. The arrival of continental potters, from those regions of the Frankish realm where members of the Great Army had previously raided, cannot be a coincidence. This is reinforced by the fact that such industries scarcely developed outside of the areas of Scandinavian settlement. Indeed, the regional contrast in pottery production and use largely persisted until after the Norman Conquest. Throughout the 10th century, daughter industries of the earliest pottery production centres were founded at places such as Newark in Nottinghamshire, which made products identical to those at Torksey; and Langhale, Bircham and Grimston in Norfolk, which made pottery resembling that from Thetford. As late as the 11th century a pottery industry producing wares similar to those from Stamford was founded at Pontefract in West Yorkshire, exploiting similar types of white clay available locally. In the spread of industrialization, the legacy of the Viking Great Army of 865 was still being felt over 200 years later.

Immigrants and Artisans

The potter was a specialist at his craft. His workshop was on the southern edge of the growing Anglo-Saxon *burh* of Torksey, in a potter's field. There was plenty of clay here, so he didn't have to go far to dig up fresh supplies to reline the firing chamber of his kiln. Sometimes he found human bones from the old cemetery when he dug, and he didn't like that, but here he was well away from the settlement, so there was less risk of a chance ember being carried on the wind and settling in the thatched roofs of the halls. But for his pots he used a different clay, and for this he had to go about a mile east of the town, near the old Foss Dyke. The clay was special here – it was green and easily worked, and it contained grains of coarse sand that gave the pottery its rough texture. The Torksey potters had always brought their potting clay from here and stored it in pits next to their kilns.

He had inherited his wheel from his father, and learnt his trade sitting between his father's knees at that same wheel, firm hands pressing over his, showing him how to draw up the vessel sides. The wheel moved in the same direction as the rising sun and it was important to get the speed right. As the wheel turned, he used a shaped stone to give the pots their smooth curves, and his thumbs to pinch the rim. Once he was satisfied, he would wipe the pot with a damp rag and carefully slide a piece of cord underneath it to cut it from the wheel-head. Then he would turn the pot upside-down and stand it outside his workshop to firm up. The final touch was to use his fingers to press out the base from the inside so that it slightly sagged, making it easier for his customers to use on the cooking hearth.

His kiln had served him well for many years. It was a solid, circular structure, with vertical walls about as tall as him, and as wide. It had a central pedestal from which the fire bars radiated. These were made of clay, reinforced with wooden rods. On these he stacked his pots, and when the kiln was ready for firing, he placed the lid on top. It had a stokehole at the base and with a good fire underneath the kiln it got really hot – this made the pots hard. To make the pots come out an even dark grey-black, instead of mottled with red, he had been taught to add some damp fuel before they were completely fired, to fill the kiln with smoke, and then to block the flue, cutting out the air. Mostly he made cooking pots, but also bowls and storage jars, and some pitchers. They sold well, and he sometimes made the trip down the Trent and then across the Humber and up the Ouse to *Jorvik*, where the townsfolk would buy his whole boat-load.

The potter's family had been making pots on the banks of the Trent for four generations. He had heard tales of his great-grandfather sailing up that same river with a mighty Viking army. They had crossed the sea from the great Carolingian Empire, and made their camp at Torksey in the days of King Alfred. His great-grandfather had travelled with the longships, bringing his potting skills with him and, most importantly, his knowledge of the potter's wheel, which hadn't been used here since the time of the Romans. There were new markets in England where he could sell his pots, and plenty of work.

The potter was about to make another river journey, but this time he would not be coming back to Torksey. Edgar, king of all England, had died in AD 975, and there was a new Viking threat. But this time the raiders were not settling: they were demanding tribute money instead. It was time to move on, although he wouldn't be travelling as far as his great-grandfather. There was a new *burh* – they called it 'the New Work' – at Newark-on-Trent, 14 miles upstream. It was in another good location, at the point where the old Roman road, the Fosse Way, crossed the Trent. He had a business opportunity there. The markets for pottery from Torksey and Lincoln had mainly been to the north, in the old kingdom of Lindsey and into Northumbria. His family had never been able to sell in the south in Kesteven; the people of that region were different, and they got their pottery from Stamford. The Torksey potter had been made an offer. Those in charge of planning the New Work had promised him his own plot within the town defences. He would be the only potter and in return for a modest rent and the taxes on his sales the plot was his. Even better, he had found a good supply of potting clay, no further from his kiln in the New Work than his Torksey clay was from his old kiln. The potter was about to become the only maker of Torksey ware in Newark.

+

This tale of a Torksey potter relocating to Newark is based on new research by our colleague Gareth Perry.[1] The potter's great-grandfather would have been an immigrant potter from northern France, who in the 870s travelled in the 'baggage train' of the Viking Great Army to their winter camp at Torksey, settling there permanently. The story of how he and his children and grandchildren contributed to England's first industrial revolution seems a good place to end our own journey. Along the way we have shown the importance of connections between warriors, traders and craftworkers, but also the value of collaboration between archaeologists, historians, numismatists and metal-detectorists. There have been heroes and villains in the 9th century, and also in the 21st century – the latter including metal-detectorists who fail to report their finds but also, to be fair, those archaeologists who fail to publish their excavations.

It is highly unusual to be able to provide a year-by-year record of events over a thousand years ago, but metal-detecting evidence interpreted in the light of the annual entries in the *Anglo-Saxon Chronicle* for the years 865–76 has provided us with extraordinary chronological resolution. This has allowed us to provide a detailed account, for the first time, of this critical period in English history. The Viking Great Army was active in England for little more than a decade but even as recently as a decade ago not a lot was known about it, beyond the names of its leaders, the places it attacked and where it overwintered. Now that we understand the immense size of the winter camps, and the wide range of activities there, we are able to grasp the Army's impact on the places it visited and to see its archaeological signature at a much larger number of sites throughout England. Our story has shown how a quest for silver and slaves became a quest for land, how warriors became settlers and entrepreneurs, and how a late 9th-century Viking army came to have a long-lasting impact on the making of a nation.

Timeline

c. **789** First recorded Viking raid on England kills a royal official
named Beaduheard at Portland

793 Lindisfarne attacked and plundered by Vikings

794 St Columba's monastery on Iona attacked

810 Major raid on Frisia by 200 ships

814 Death of Charlemagne, aged 70; succeeded by Louis the Pious

824 Skellig Michael attacked

834 Dorestad laid waste by raid

835 'Heathens' ravage Isle of Sheppey in the first great raid
on Anglo-Saxon England

839 Large Viking raid into *Fortriu* in which local kings are killed

840 Viking force spends winter on Lough Neagh in Ireland;
Louis the Pious dies; his lands are divided between his sons,
Louis the German, Lothar and Charles the Bald

841 The *longphort* of Dublin is constructed

845 Paris plundered by Viking raiders in 120 ships

850 First recorded overwintering of a Viking army in England,
on Thanet

851 350 ships arrive at the mouth of the Thames; raiders attack
Canterbury and London

855 A Viking army overwinters on Sheppey

864 Charles the Bald reforms the Frankish army and creates
cavalry; orders construction of fortified bridges to block
Viking raids

865 Viking 'Great Heathen Army' lands in East Anglia; Æthelred I
becomes king of Wessex and Kent

866 Great Army seizes York

867 Northumbrian counter-attack on York defeated; kings Ælla and
Osberht both killed; Great Army overwinters in Nottingham

868 Great Army overwinters in York

869 Great Army kills Edmund, King of East Anglia; overwinters
at Thetford

870 Dumbarton Rock besieged and captured by Olaf and Ivar; Great Army overwinters in Reading

871 Battle of Ashdown; year of nine battles between Wessex and Great Army; King Æthelred I dies and is succeeded by his younger brother, Alfred; Great Army overwinters in London

872 Great Army overwinters at Torksey

873 Great Army overwinters adjacent to Mercian royal monastery at Repton; King Burgred of Mercia exiled

874 Great Army splits; one part led by Guthrum, Anwend and Oscetel, overwinters in Cambridge, and the other, under Healfdene, on the Tyne

875 The southern army evades Alfred and camps at Wareham; the northern army 'shares out the land of the Northumbrians'

876 Alfred makes peace with the Vikings; they evade him and reach Exeter

877 The Great Army moves from Cirencester and attacks Chippenham in midwinter; army shares out the land of the Mercians

878 Alfred flees into hiding in Somerset and builds a stronghold at Athelney; he defeats the Army at the Battle of Edington and makes a peace with Guthrum who converts to Christianity

880 Guthrum moves from Cirencester to East Anglia to settle and share out the land

886 All the Anglo-Saxons 'not under subjection to the Danes' submit to Alfred in London; Ealdorman Æthelred of Mercia marries Alfred's daughter, Æthelflæd, at around this time

890 Death of Guthrum

893 New Viking armies arrive in East Anglia; Alfred creates a standing army

896 Alfred builds his own fleet; Viking army disperses

899 Death of Alfred, succeeded by his son Edward the Elder

927 Æthelstan, Edward's son, captures York

937 Æthelstan defeats combined army of Vikings and Scots at *Brunanburh*

Notes

Chapter 1

1 Throughout this book we will use the term 'Viking' to refer to those raiders and raiding armies that originated from Scandinavia in the late 8th and 9th centuries. Where the raiders become settlers, we use the less pejorative term 'Scandinavian'. It is worth noting, however, that there are only five references to Vikings (*wicingas*) in the *Anglo-Saxon Chronicle*, our main contemporary source for England (Fell 1986; 1987). The use of the word then appears to have died out, apart from in 13th- and 14th-century Icelandic sagas, until it was reintroduced in the Romantic era, and it was only during the 19th century that 'Viking' became a standard term for Scandinavian invaders. Similarly, it was the 19th century, and specifically Wagnerian costume design, that saw the introduction of the horned helmet, which was borrowed from much earlier prehistoric antiquities and never actually worn by the Vikings. For England the Viking Age is generally accepted to run from *c.* AD 800 to 1066, although Scandinavian culture had a longer-lasting influence on the British Isles. The focus of this book, however, is on a much narrower period of just over 30 years, from the arrival in England of the Viking Great Army in 865 until the death of King Alfred in 899.
2 Tummuscheit and Witte 2018
3 Sindbæk 2008, 155
4 See Lund *et al.* 1984 and Sindbaek 2009 for Wulfstan.
5 For short summaries of the archaeology of Ribe, Hedeby, Birka and Kaupang see papers in Brink and Price (eds) 2008; for the latest information on excavations in Ribe see Sindbæk 2018; for Kaupang see Skre (ed.) 2007.
6 Jørgensen 2008
7 Nelson 1991, 44

8 The account of Ottar's travels is incorporated in the late 9th-century text known as the *Old English Orosius*, a translation, possibly made by Alfred himself, of a 5th-century Latin text by Paulus Orosius.
9 Lund *et al.* 1984, 18–22
10 See Bill 2008 for a summary of Viking ships; see Ravn 2016, 107–9 for Viking maritime organization.
11 For recent overviews and discussion of the causes of the Viking Age see Barrett 2008, 2010; Ashby 2015; Raffield *et al.* 2017; and Baug *et al.* 2019.
12 For the Salme ship burials see Price *et al.* 2016; for Staraya Ladoga and Viking activity in the East see Androshchuk 2008.
13 For general introductions to Viking Age England see Richards 2004 and Hadley 2006.
14 See Blair 2018, 179–308 for a recent survey of Anglo-Saxon settlement patterns.
15 See Blair 2005 for minster churches.
16 Andrews 1997
17 Morton 1992
18 Scull 2009
19 Atkin 1985; Wade 1988
20 The account of the Royal Opera House excavations is based upon Malcolm *et al.* 2003.
21 Colgrave and Mynors 1993, book II, ch. III
22 Malcolm *et al.* 2003
23 Blair 2018, 259

Chapter 2

1 This description of the Portland incident is based upon a combination of sources: the *Anglo-Saxon Chronicle* (Whitelock 1961, 35); the *Laws of Alfred* (in Whitelock 1979, 407–16); the *Chronicle of Æthelweard* (Campbell 1962, 27) and the *Chronicle of John of Worcester* (Darlington *et al.* 1995).
2 Ninth-century sources are imprecise in how they describe Viking raiders.

Heathens or pagans are the most common terms and national descriptors seem to be used interchangeably. Indeed, Denmark, Norway and Sweden did not exist as nation states in the 9th century. If the chronicler is correct that these raiders were from Hordaland, then these may have been Norwegian Vikings who were generally more active around Scotland and the Northern Isles.

3   Whitelock 1961, 36
4   Whitelock 1979, 843
5   Whitelock 1979, 775–77
6   Anderson 1922, 263–65
7   Mac Airt and Mac Niocaill 1983, 277, 281
8   Mac Airt and Mac Niocaill 1983, 293
9   Somerville and McDonald 2014, 218–21
10 Mac Airt and Mac Niocaill 1983, 299; Crawford 1987, 49
11 Whitelock 1961, 41–42
12 Mac Airt and Mac Niocaill 1983, 299–305
13 Ó Floinn 1998, 161–62
14 Mac Airt and Mac Niocaill 1983, 301
15 Smyth 1999, 7, 16–17, 21
16 Nelson 1991, 65
17 Kelly 2015
18 Sheehan 2008; Kelly 2015
19 Kelly 2015, 82–83
20 Simpson 2005; Purcell 2015, 42–44
21 Russel and Hurley 2014
22 Mac Airt and Mac Niocaill 1983, 303, 307
23 Nelson 1991, 66
24 Mac Airt and Mac Niocaill 1983, 249–51, 315
25 Ó Floinn 1998, 163
26 Mac Airt and Mac Niocaill 1983, 313; Crawford 1987, 41, 49–50
27 Mac Airt and Mac Niocaill 1983, 317–19
28 Nelson 1997, 19
29 Coupland 1991a
30 Coupland 1998, 89–93
31 Robinson 1921, 44
32 This is probably but not certainly Harald Klak.
33 Nelson 1991, 51

34 Nelson 1991, 69; Coupland 2001
35 Nelson 1991, 60
36 Nelson 1991, 58, 60; 1992, 144
37 Vita Faronis episcopi Meldensis ch. 123, as quoted in Coupland 2003, 190
38 Nelson 1992, 151–52; Coupland 2003, 190
39 Nelson 1991, 75–76
40 Nelson 1991, 95–99
41 Raffield 2016 discusses the significance of these brotherhoods for the organization of Viking armies.
42 Walther 2004, 175
43 Coupland 1991b
44 Nelson 1991, 87, 90–91, 95, 131, 174
45 Nelson 1991, 56
46 Nelson 1991, 95, 185; Purcell 2015, 48
47 Walther 2004, 173
48 Nelson 1991, 185
49 Nelson 1991, 128
50 Nelson 1991, 129
51 Nelson 2003, 14–15
52 Besteman 2004, 95
53 Besteman 2004, 95; Besteman 2006–7
54 IJssennagger 2013, 85–91
55 Coupland 2006, 243–48; Nelson 1991, 62

Chapter 3
1   Brooks 2010
2   Abels 2006
3   Whitelock 1961, 45
4   Keynes and Lapidge 1983, 74; Downham 2007, 64
5   Downham 2007, 66, 68
6   Whitelock 1961, 49; Short 2009, 156–57
7   McLeod 2014
8   Whitelock 1961, 76
9   South 2002, 51
10 South 2002, 51
11 Giles 1849, 190
12 Keynes and Lapidge 1983, 77
13 Keynes and Lapidge 1983, 77; Whitelock 1961, 46
14 Hall 2001, 146
15 Whitelock 1961, 46; Keynes and Lapidge 1983, 77–78
16 Blackburn 2001, 127
17 Winterbottom 1972, 65–87
18 Cubitt 2000, 63–64; see Chapter 9.

19 Keynes and Lapidge 1983, 78; McLeod 2006, 145
20 Keynes and Lapidge 1983, 78
21 Keynes and Lapidge 1983, 78
22 Keynes and Lapidge 1983, 78
23 Keynes and Lapidge 1983, 79
24 Keynes and Lapidge 1983, 79
25 Whitelock 1961, 47; Keynes and Lapidge 1983, 80
26 Giles 1849, 206
27 Giles 1849, 209
28 Whitelock 1961, 48
29 Keynes and Lapidge 1983, 82
30 Campbell 1982, 138
31 South 2002, 53
32 Keynes 1997, 59; Wilson 1976, 395; Townend, 2014, 165
33 Sawyer 1962, 120
34 Sawyer 1962, 120–27
35 Edgeworth 2008 has subsequently argued that the Viking fortress at Tempsford was not the rectangular earthworks known as Gannocks Castle (which are indeed likely to be much later) and that the fortress referred to in the Anglo-Saxon Chronicle may instead be a D-shaped island set within a larger enclosure at the confluence of the Rivers Ouse and Ivel.
36 Sawyer 1962, 127
37 Sawyer 1962, 127
38 Brooks 1979, 7
39 Brooks 1979, 11
40 Brooks 1979, 9
41 Brooks 1979, 11
42 Sherlock 1956, 395–96; Graham-Campbell 2004, 38
43 Astill 1984, 70, 73
44 Brooks and Graham-Campbell 2000
45 Christmas 1862, 302
46 Brooks and Graham-Campbell 2000, 92
47 Christmas 1862, 302–4
48 Evans 1866, 232–40
49 Blunt and Dolley 1959, 222–34
50 Brooks and Graham-Campbell 2000, 80; Whitelock 1979, 532
51 Graham-Campbell 2000, 92
52 Brooks and Graham-Campbell 2000, 84–85
53 Borrell and Hawkins 1840–41, 14
54 Graham-Campbell 2002, 54
55 Heywood 1884, 349; 'lunette' coins are so called because they have the moneyer's name in three lines across the reverse, with the upper and lower lines enclosed in lunettes, or half-moons.
56 Pagan 1965, 24
57 Metcalf 1958, 76–77
58 Brooke 1924, 322; Smith 1925, 135; Blunt and Dolley 1959, 220–21
59 Graham-Campbell 2004, 37
60 Blunt and Dolley 1959, 221; Brooks and Graham-Campbell 2000, 86
61 Pagan 1966, 190–91
62 South 2002, 49–51, 83–84
63 In Northumbria, tiny copper-alloy coins known as stycas provided the standard means of exchange, and indicate that prior to the arrival of the Vikings the economy was fully monetized.
64 Brooks and Graham-Campbell 2000, 90
65 Brooks and Graham-Campbell 2000, 89
66 Wilson and Blunt 1961
67 Brooks and Graham-Campbell 2000, 90; Graham-Campbell 2004, 37
68 Graham-Campbell 2004, 37; this figure excludes two Anglo-Saxon hoards discovered by metal-detectorists, at Hingham in Norfolk and Worlington in Suffolk, which were probably hidden in the late 860s as a result of Great Army activity in East Anglia (Pestell 2019, 15–16, 20–22)
69 Malcolm et al. 2003, 278–284
70 Biddle and Kjølbye-Biddle 1992, 57–58
71 Biddle and Kjølbye-Biddle 1992, 40
72 Biddle and Kjølbye-Biddle 1992, 40; Biddle and Kjølbye-Biddle 2001, 59 give an internal area of 1.46 ha, but recalculation by Guilbert 2004, 250, 254 n.17, and Stein 2015, 43, and comparison with Ordnance Survey maps, confirms that a figure of 0.4 ha is nearer the mark, suggesting that 1.46 ha is a misprint for 0.46 ha.
73 Abels 2003, 276

74 Halsall 2000, 269
75 It has been suggested that the camp at Reading lies beneath the site of the medieval abbey; see Graham-Campbell 2004, 34–35, 38.
76 For example, Edgeworth 2008, 13

Chapter 4
1 Manuscripts C, A and B contain the extended version: *Her for se here on Norþhumbre, and he nam winter setl on Lindesse æt Tureces iege, and þa namon Mierce friþ wiþ þone here*, while manuscript D notes only that 'In this year the army took up winter quarters at Torksey'; Whitelock 1961, 47.
2 The Portable Antiquities Scheme database can be accessed online at www.finds.org.uk
3 Blackburn 2002
4 Our account of the camp at Torksey draws upon the finds catalogue provided in Blackburn 2011, and the full report of our own research in Hadley and Richards 2016a, with finds catalogue in Richards and Hadley 2016. Figures for numbers of finds have been updated so that they were accurate in December 2019.
5 Edwards and Hindle 1991, 128 argue that the Trent was navigable as far upstream as Burton-upon-Trent (Staffordshire).
6 Sawyer 1998, 197
7 Stein 2013; 2015
8 Cole 1992; Coates 2008, 84
9 Stein 2015
10 Torksey is first recorded as 'Turoc's island' (Old English: *Tureces iege*), although later spellings are all consistently 'Turc's island' (*æt Turces ige*, or *in Turcesige*); Cameron and Insley 2010, 122–26.
11 Blackburn 2011, 225
12 Pirie 2000; Abramson 2018
13 Williams 2015, 99
14 Blackburn 2011, 229–30
15 Blackburn 2008, 52–53; 2011, 229; Kilger 2008
16 Blackburn 2008, 47–55
17 Naismith 2005, 194–95

18 Blackburn 2011, 230–35
19 Pestell 2013, 249–50
20 Pettersson 2009; Williams 2011, 354–55
21 Blackburn 2011, 242
22 Pedersen 2008, 121, 132–40
23 Graham-Campbell 2002; Blackburn 2009; Kershaw 2017
24 Blackburn 2007, 69–73
25 McLeod 2006; 2014, 186–98
26 Pelteret 1980, 106–7; Holm 1986
27 Hennius 2018
28 Hall 2016
29 MacLean 2009, 168; Dass 2007, 35, 83–85
30 Hadley and Hemer 2011, 64–65; Whitelock 1961, 55, 57; Graham-Campbell and Batey 1998
31 Hadley and Richards 2016a; the radiocarbon dates for two samples were AD 770–900/920–40 and AD 830–40/870–900 (at 95 per cent probability).
32 Skre 2008
33 Price 1991, 11–13; Hall and Williams 2020, 93–94
34 Lund 1986, 109–112
35 Nelson 1991, 95, 112, 164; McLeod 2006, 146; Stafford 1980.
36 Whitelock 1979, 406; a hide was the land required to support a peasant family.
37 Sawyer 1998, 246–52
38 Everson and Stocker 2007
39 Williams 2013, 17–19
40 Biddle and Kjølbye-Biddle 1988, 1–10
41 Biddle and Kjølbye-Biddle 1988, 7
42 Morris 1989, 268–69
43 Jarman 2018, 28–35
44 Britain's Viking Graveyard, Windfall Films; first broadcast Channel 4, 21 April 2019; Jarman 2019, 24–25

Chapter 5
1 Richards *et al.* 2009, Section 2.6
2 Richards and Naylor 2012, 135–39
3 PAS finds reference numbers are provided in a paper we published in Medieval Settlement Research (Hadley and Richards 2018).
4 Hadley 2000; Hadley *et al.* 2016
5 Pagan 1986, 209; Blackburn 1998
6 Little Carlton formed a case study

in a recent book by Adam Daubney (2016) addressing metal-detected evidence for the long-term use of the rural landscape in Lincolnshire.

7   Daubney 2016, 249–68; Willmott and Daubney 2019
8   Steedman 1994
9   Portable Antiquities Scheme identification number: NLM-8E52D1
10 Hadley and Richards 2020
11 Richards 2004, 192–93
12 Williams 2015
13 Hadley and Richards 2018
14 Woods forthcoming 2021; Williams 2014, 22
15 Ager and Williams 2014
16 Richards and Haldenby 2018
17 Cameron 1998, 117
18 The first element of the place-name is Middle English *brende*, 'burnt', and must relate to an event long post-dating the appearance of the Great Army in the vicinity; Cameron 1998, 21–22; Blair 2013, 188.
19 Blair 2018, 92–93
20 Abramson 2016; Hadley and Richards 2016, 39, 61
21 Hadley 2000, 277–78
22 Owen 1971, 29
23 Loveluck 2007, 154–57
24 Archibald *et al.* 2007, 422–24
25 Archibald *et al.* 2007, 413–20; Williams 2014, 22
26 Williams and Naylor 2016
27 Leonard 2015, 104–79
28 Schoenfelder and Richards 2011
29 Loveluck 2007, 155
30 Loveluck 1996
31 Johnson 2002
32 Webster 1991
33 Whitelock 1961, 43, 53
34 Whitelock 1961, 48
35 Kershaw 2013
36 Tester *et al.* 2014, 383–93
37 Archibald 1998; Kershaw 2016, 102–3
38 Halsall 2003
39 See Williams 2019 for a good account of Viking weaponry and battle tactics.
40 Whitelock 1961, 45–46
41 Baker and Brookes 2013, 137, 142, Fig. 28
42 Baker 2011; Baker and Brookes 2013, 143–46; Brookes 2013, 49–51
43 Baker and Brookes 2013, 172; Edwards and Hindle 1991
44 Langdon 1993; Baker and Brookes 2013, 173
45 Raffield 2014, 640
46 Whitelock 1961, 45
47 Dobat 2017, 602–3
48 Bogucki 2009; Gardela 2015, 219–20; Jagodziński 2010, 140
49 Reuter 1992, 93–94
50 Groothedde 2004, 116
51 Groothedde pers. comm.
52 Nicolaysen 1877

Chapter 6
1   Fell 1986
2   For an extended discussion of Norse burials and belief systems see Price 2019.
3   For discussion of Viking burials in England see Richards 2004, 189–212; Hadley 2006, 237–64.
4   See Richards 2004, 213–27; Hadley 2006, 258–62
5   Biddle and Kjølbye-Biddle 1992; 2001
6   Berg 2015
7   O'Connor 2000, 170
8   Gotfredsen *et al.* 2014
9   Biddle and Kjølbye-Biddle 2001, 65
10 Jarman 2019, 22
11 Downham 2007, 238
12 Strontium and oxygen isotope analysis shows that both grew up in the same place – in a region commensurate with values expected from southern Scandinavia (Budd *et al.* 2004).
13 Radiocarbon dating has narrowed the date for this double grave to AD 873–86 (Jarman *et al.* 2018, 194).
14 Biddle 2018, 56
15 Biddle, Blunt *et al.* 1986, where it is described as a finger-ring, but such rings with ring-and-dot ornament and wire loop are now more usually seen as earrings, an interpretation supported by its location in the grave.
16 Biddle, Blunt *et al.* 1986, 26–27
17 Bigsby 1854, 401–2
18 Macdonald 1929, 19

19 Hawkes *et al.* 2018, 198–205
20 Raxworthy *et al.* 1990
21 Biddle 2018, 38
22 Biddle *et al.* 1986, 111–19
23 Richards *et al.* 2004, 102–3
24 Biddle and Kjølbye-Biddle 2001
25 Jennbert 2004
26 Jarman *et al.* 2018, 194
27 Montgomery 2000
28 Surveyed in Eriksen 2013
29 Richards *et al.* 2004, 102–3
30 Jarman *et al.* 2018
31 Bateman 1861, 92–93
32 Richards *et al.* 2004, 46–47
33 These earlier archaeological investigations of the site are described in Richards *et al.* 2004.
34 Arbman 1969, 66–67
35 Hadley and Hemer 2011
36 The identification of the Scandinavian origins of the adult human and horse comes from recent unpublished PhD research by Tessi Loeffelmann at the University of Durham.
37 Whitelock 1961, 47; Keynes and Lapidge 1983, 80
38 Graham-Campbell 2004, 38
39 Rogerson and Dallas 1984, 53, 105–6
40 Rogerson 1995; Graham-Campbell 2001, 110–12; Pestell 2019, 34–37
41 Evison 1969, 342; Graham-Campbell 2001, 115
42 A ballast pit is a stone or gravel quarry used to provide stone for railway tracks.
43 Akerman 1867, 460–63
44 Evison 1969
45 Wilson 1965
46 Cowie 1988; Thomas *et al.* 2006, 40–46
47 Dunning and Evison 1961
48 Sloane *et al.* 1995
49 Graham-Campbell and Batey 1998, 118–22

Chapter 7
1 Loveluck 1996, 43; Richards 1999, 92; the *Anglo-Saxon Chronicle* records that Aldfrith, king of the Northumbrians died *on Driffelda* in AD 705.

2 The fieldwork at Cottam was published in Richards 1999, while the work at Cowlam and wider landscape is discussed in Richards 2013, with the latest publication of the metal-detected finds in Haldenby and Richards 2016.
3 Whitelock 1961, 48
4 Whitelock 1961, 48; Whitelock 1961, 50
5 Haldenby and Richards 2016
6 Whitelock 1979, 468
7 Speed and Walton Rogers 2004
8 Richards and Haldenby 2018
9 Richards and Haldenby 2018, 342
10 Richards and Haldenby 2018
11 For Wharram Percy see Wrathmell 2012 for the Anglo-Saxon to Anglo-Scandinavian transition; Stamper and Croft 2000 for the Anglo-Saxon manor excavations, and Mays *et al.* 2007 for the churchyard.
12 Mac Airt and Mac Niocaill 1983, 352–53
13 Richards 2004, 221–24
14 Ekwall 1930; Hines 1991; Page 1971; Townend 2000
15 Fellows-Jensen 1968
16 Hadley 1997
17 Smart 1986
18 Stenton 1943
19 Sawyer 1958
20 Sawyer 1962
21 Richards 2000; 2004
22 Hadley 1997
23 Hadley and Richards 2000
24 Abrams and Parsons 2004, 398–400
25 Hadley 2020
26 Leslie *et al.* 2015, 313
27 Kershaw and Røyrvik 2016, 1679
28 Buckberry *et al.* 2014
29 Buckberry *et al.* 2014, 430
30 Jarman 2019, 24

Chapter 8
1 For Anglian York see Rogers 1993, Hall 1994, 31–33, Tweddle *et al.* 1999, and Mainman 2019.
2 Rollason 2000, 97
3 Whitelock 1967, 45
4 Townend 2014, 25–28
5 Tweddle *et al.* 1999, 200–7
6 Rogers 1993, 1358, object no. 5333; Abramson 2016

7 Williams 2015, 19
8 See Hall and Williams 2020 for the publication of Aldwark, although there it is now known as 'A Riverine Site Near York'.
9 Hall and Williams 2020, 66–69
10 Hall and Williams 2020, 73
11 Hall and Williams 2020, 73–74
12 A few years previously, Julian had been given a tour of the site by Mark Ainsley, after the YAT excavations had finished, but before the *Time Team Special* had been broadcast. Fed up with YAT's small trial trenches Mark was trying to encourage Julian to excavate at Aldwark. Julian had first met Mark and Geoff in 2006, following an introduction from Simon Holmes. They had information about coins being night-hawked from an Anglo-Saxon site at Burdale, which Julian was excavating, and as part of their growing trust in archaeologists they helped Julian with details of material that had previously been looted. They also assisted with metal-detecting during the University of York's training excavations in 2006 and 2007. Indeed, some of the footage of Mark and Geoff detecting for Codename Ainsbrook was filmed at Burdale, to disguise Aldwark.
13 Subclass E – Williams 2008; Blackburn and Keynes 1998; Williams 2020; Blackburn 2001; Hall 2011, 78
14 Williams 2015, 99; Hall and Williams 2020, 19
15 Blackburn 2011, 235
16 Hall and Williams 2020, 50–58
17 The Fenrir drawing is one of the objects not mentioned in the Hall and Williams 2020 publication, but it was displayed in the Southport art gallery exhibition alongside other objects from Aldwark.
18 Lee Toone, *pers. comm.*
19 Johnson South 2002, 86–87
20 Mac Airt and Mac Niocaill 1983, 331–3; Ó Cróinín 2013, 254
21 Johnson South 2002, 53
22 Johnson South 2002, 53, 59, 87–89

23 Campbell 1962, 51; Blackburn 2001, 128
24 Blackburn 2004, 329–31

Chapter 9
1 Keynes and Lapidge 1983, 82
2 Whitelock 1961, 48
3 Keynes and Lapidge 1983, 83
4 Whitelock 1961, 48
5 Whitelock 1961, 49
6 Whitelock 1961, 49
7 Keynes and Lapidge 1983, 83
8 Whitelock 1961, 49
9 Keynes and Lapidge 1983, 84
10 Whitelock 1961, 49
11 Giles 1849, 191–92
12 Whitelock 1961, 49
13 Keynes and Lapidge 1983, 85; the 'chrisom' was a white christening cloth.
14 This account of the discovery of the Watlington hoard is based upon Williams and Naylor 2016 and presentations given at a conference held 15 November 2018 at the Ashmolean Museum in Oxford.
15 The account of the Leominster hoard and the conviction of the finders and dealers is derived from news reports on the *Guardian* and BBC websites in November 2019: https://www.theguardian.com/uk-news/2019/nov/21/detectorists-hid-find-that-rewrites-anglo-saxon-history; https://www.bbc.co.uk/news/uk-england-hereford-worcester-50461860
16 Whitelock 1961 50
17 Kershaw 2000
18 Whitelock 1961, 52
19 Blackburn 1998
20 Foot 1996, 27; Blackburn 1998
21 Keynes and Lapidge 1983, 98
22 Foot 1996
23 Keynes and Lapidge 1983, 125
24 Keynes and Lapidge 1983, 126
25 Foot 1996, 34
26 Whitelock 1961, 51
27 Campbell 1962, 45
28 Winterbottom 1972, 826
29 Christie 2004, 145–55; Cubitt 2000, 63–64

30 Whitelock 1961, 56
31 Baker and Brookes 2013, 32–33; another manuscript lists thirty-one *burhs* and it is thought that the other two were added later.
32 Baker and Brookes 2013, 6
33 Abels 1988, 62
34 Whitelock 1961, 54
35 Whitelock 1961, 54
36 Whitelock 1961, 57
37 Whitelock 1961, 48; 50
38 Hooper 1989, 203–4
39 Swanton 1999, 21–22
40 Craig 1991
41 Whitelock 1961, 59
42 Whitelock 1961, 59
43 Whitelock 1961, 60–67
44 Whitelock 1961, 68–9
45 Whitelock 1961, 69–70
46 This discussion of the mythology surrounding Alfred draws on Keynes 1999.
47 Keynes and Lapidge 1983, 101
48 Whitelock 1961, 58
49 Campbell 1962, 50
50 South 2002, 55–57
51 Keynes and Lapidge 1983, 197–202
52 South 2002, 90–94
53 Keynes 1999, 330

Chapter 10
1 From *The Itinerary of John Leland in or about the Years 1535–1543*, edited by L. Toulim Smith in 1907, as quoted in Barley 1964.
2 Barley 1964
3 Barley 1981
4 Richard Hodges (1989) first coined the phrase 'first English industrial revolution' to describe the transformation in craft production in Anglo-Saxon England in the 9th and 10th centuries AD.
5 Rowe 2008; the excavations were conducted by Pre-Construct Archaeology based in Lincoln, in advance of a planned housing development.
6 Perry 2016; our work on the town at Torksey will feature in Hadley and Richards in prep.
7 The survey was undertaken by

Headland Archaeology; Harrison 2018.
8 Hadley and Richards 2016b reports on this work and provides details of the relevant unpublished reports.
9 Carver 2010, 127–32
10 Vince 2006, 528–32
11 Vince 2001; Hadley 2013
12 Sawyer 1998, 186–90; Hall 1989, 182
13 Mahany and Roffe 1983; Hall 1989, 195–96
14 Hadley 2000, 228–29
15 Kilmurry 1980; Mahany and Roffe 1983, 205
16 Whitelock 1961, 66
17 Whitelock 1961, 66
18 Mahany and Roffe 1983, 209
19 Blackburn 2001, 130–31
20 Whitelock 1961, 71
21 Rogerson and Dallas 1984, 58, 68; Blackburn and Bonser 1984, 70; Andrews and Penn 1999, 38; Wallis 2005, 38–40, 115; Atkins and Connor 2010, 40–41, 117
22 Dallas 1993, 218–19

Epilogue
1 Perry 2016; 2019

Further Reading and Bibliography

Further Reading

Brink, S. and Price, N. (eds) 2008. *The Viking World*. Abingdon and New York: Routledge.

Hadley, D. M. 2000. *The Northern Danelaw: Its social structures, 800–1100*. London: Leicester University Press.

Hadley, D. M. 2006. *The Vikings in England: Settlement, society and culture*. Manchester: Manchester University Press.

Hall, R. A. 2013. *Exploring the World of the Vikings*. London and New York: Thames & Hudson.

Higham, N. J. and Ryan, M. 2013. *The Anglo-Saxon World*. New Haven and London: Yale University Press.

Jesch, J. 2015. *The Viking Diaspora*. Abingdon and New York: Routledge.

Richards, J. D. 2004. *Viking Age England*. Stroud: Tempus. Second edition; first published by B. T. Batsford/English Heritage 1991.

Richards, J. D. 2018. *The Vikings: A very short introduction*. Oxford: Oxford University Press. Revised edition; first published 2005.

Roesdahl, E. 1998. *The Vikings*. London: Penguin Books. Revised edition; first published 1991.

Sawyer, P. H. (ed.) 1997. *The Oxford Illustrated History of the Vikings*. Oxford: Oxford University Press.

Williams, T. 2017. *Viking Britain: A history*. London: William Collins.

Bibliography

Abels, R. 1988. *Lordship and Military Obligation in Anglo-Saxon England*. Berkeley: University of California Press.

Abels, R. 2003. 'Alfred the Great, the *micel hæðen here* and the Viking threat', in T. Reuter (ed.), *Alfred the Great: Papers from the eleventh-century conferences*. London: Routledge, 265–79.

Abels, R. 2006. 'Alfred and his biographers: Images and imagination', in D. Bates, J. Crick and S. Hamilton (eds), *Writing Medieval Biography, 750–1250*. Woodbridge: Boydell and Brewer, 61–76.

Abrams, L. and Parsons, D. N. 2004. 'Place-names and the history of Scandinavian settlement in England', in J. Hines, A. Lane and M. Redknap (eds), *Land, Sea and Home: Settlement in the Viking period*. Leeds: Maney, 379–431.

Abramson, T. 2018. *Coinage in the Northumbrian Landscape and Economy, c. 575–c. 867*. Oxford: British Archaeological Reports British Series 641.

Ager, B. and Williams, G. 2014. 'North Yorkshire area: Closely associated group of Viking-period and Late Saxon objects and coins (2004 T13)', *Treasure Annual Report 2014*, Department for Culture, Media and Sport, 91–93.

Akerman, J. Y. 1867. Thursday, March 28th. *Proceedings of the Society of Antiquaries of London* 3: 460–63.

Anderson, A. O. 1922. *Early Sources of Scottish History AD 500 to 1286*. Edinburgh: Oliver and Boyd.

Andrews, P. (ed.) 1997. *Excavations at Hamwic. Volume 2: Excavations at Six Dials*. York: Council for British Archaeology Research Report 109.

Andrews, P. and Penn, K. 1999. *Excavations in Thetford, North of the River, 1989–90*. East Anglian Archaeology 87.

Androshchuk, F. 2008. 'Vikings in the East', in Brink and Price 2008, 517–42.

Arbman, H. 1969. *The Vikings*. London and New York: Thames & Hudson.

Archibald, M. 1998. 'Two ninth-century lead weights found near Kingston, Dorset', *British Numismatic Journal* 68: 11–20.

Archibald, M., Pirie, E., Wastling, L., Panter, I. and Rogers, N. 2007. 'The Anglo-Saxon coins, mensuration weights and ingots', in D. Evans and C. Loveluck (eds), *Life and Economy at Early Medieval Flixborough, c. AD 600–1000*. Oxford: Oxbow Books, 402–24.

Ashby, S. 2015. 'What really caused the Viking Age? The social content of raiding and exploration', *Archaeological Dialogues* 22(1): 89–106.

Astill, G. 1984. 'The towns of Berkshire', in J. Haslam (ed.), *Anglo-Saxon Towns in Southern England*. Chichester: Phillimore, 53–86.

Atkin, M. 1985. 'The Anglo-Saxon urban landscape in East Anglia', *Landscape History* 7: 27–40.

Atkins. R. and Connor, A. 2010. *Farmers and Ironsmiths: Prehistoric, Roman and Anglo-Saxon settlement beside Brandon Road, Thetford, Norfolk*. East Anglian Archaeology 134.

Baker, J. 2011. 'Warriors and watchmen: Place-names and Anglo-Saxon civil defence', *Medieval Archaeology* 55: 258–67.

Baker, J. and Brookes, S. 2013. *Beyond the Burghal Hidage: Anglo-Saxon civil defence in the Viking Age*. Leiden: Brill.

Barley, M. W. 1964. 'The medieval borough of Torksey: Excavations 1960–2', *Antiquaries Journal* 44: 165–87.

Barley, M. W. 1981. 'The medieval borough of Torksey: excavations 1963–8', *Antiquaries Journal* 61: 264–91.

Barrett, J. H. 2008. 'What caused the Viking Age?', *Antiquity* 82(317): 671–85.

Barrett, J. H. 2010. 'Rounding up the usual suspects: Causation and the Viking Age diaspora', in A. Anderson, J. H. Barrett and K. Boyle (eds), *The Global Origins and Development of Seafaring*. Cambridge: McDonald Institute Monographs, 289–302.

Bateman, T. 1861. *Ten Years' Diggings in Celtic and Saxon Grave Hills, in the Counties of Derby, Stafford, and York, from 1848 to 1858*. London: J. R. Smith.

Baug, I., Skre, D., Heldal, T. *et al.* 2019. 'The beginning of the Viking Age in the West', *Journal of Maritime Archaeology* 14: 43–80.

Berg, H. L. 2015. ' "Truth" and reproduction of knowledge: Critical thoughts on the interpretation and understanding of Iron-Age keys', in M. H. Eriksen, U. Pedersen, B. Rundberget, I. Axelsen and H. L. Berg

(eds), *Viking Worlds: Things, spaces and movement*. Oxford: Oxbow Books, 124–42.

Besteman, J. 2004. 'Two Viking hoards from the former island of Wieringen (The Netherlands)', in J. Hines, M. Redknap and A. Lane (eds), *Land, Sea and Home*. Leeds: Society for Medieval Archaeology, 93–108.

Besteman, J. 2006–7. 'A second Viking silver hoard from Wieringen: Westerklief II', *Jaarboek voor Munt- en Penningkunde* 93–94: 5–80.

Biddle, M. and Kjølbye-Biddle, B. 1988. *Repton 1987: Interim Report*. Unpublished report.

Biddle, M. and Kjølbye-Biddle, B. 1992. 'Repton and the Vikings', *Antiquity* 66(250): 36–51.

Biddle, M. and Kjølbye-Biddle, B. 2001. 'Repton and the "great heathen army", 873–4', in Graham-Campbell *et al.* 2001, 45–96.

Biddle, M., Blunt, C., Kjølbye-Biddle, B., Metcalf, M. and Pagan, H. 1986. 'Coins of the Anglo-Saxon period from Repton, Derbyshire: II', *British Numismatic Journal* 56: 16–34.

Biddle, M., Kjølbye-Biddle, B., Northover, J. P. and Pagan, H. 1986. 'A parcel of pennies from a mass-burial associated with the Viking overwintering at Repton in 873–4', in Blackburn 1986, 111–23.

Biddle, M. 2018. 'The Repton sculptures', in Hawkes *et al.* 2018, 51–68.

Bigsby, R. 1854. *Historical and Topographical Description of Repton*. London: Woodfall and Kinder.

Bill, J. 2008. 'Viking ships and the sea', in Brink and Price 2008, 170–80.

Blackburn, M. A. S. (ed.) 1986. *Anglo-Saxon Monetary History: Essays in memory of Michael Dolley*. Leicester: University Press.

Blackburn, M. A. S. 1998. 'The London mint in the reign of Alfred', in M.A.S. Blackburn and D. N. Dumville (eds), *Kings, Currency and Alliances: History and coinage of Southern England in the ninth century*. Studies in Anglo-Saxon History. Woodbridge: Boydell and Brewer, 105–23.

Blackburn, M. A. S. 2001. 'Expansion and control: Aspects of Anglo-Scandinavian minting south of the Humber', in Graham-Campbell *et al.* 2001, 125–55.

Blackburn, M. A. S. 2002. 'Finds from the Anglo-Scandinavian site of Torksey, Lincolnshire', in B. Paszkiewicz (ed.), *Moneta Mediaevalis: Studia numizmatyczne i historyczne ofiarowane Profesorowi Stanisławowi Suchodolskiemu w 64. rocznicę erodzin*, Warsaw: DiG, 89–101 (text), 526–27 (plates).

Blackburn, M. A. S. 2004. 'The coinage of Scandinavian York', in R. A. Hall (ed.), *Aspects of Anglo-Scandinavian York*. The Archaeology of York 8(4). York: Council for British Archaeology, 325–49.

Blackburn, M. A. S. 2007. 'Gold in England during the "Age of Silver" (eighth–eleventh centuries)', in J. Graham-Campbell and G. Williams (eds), *Silver Economy in the Viking Age*. Walnut Creek: Left Coast Press, 55–98.

Blackburn, M. A. S. 2008. 'The coins finds', in D. Skre (ed), *Means of Exchange: Dealing with silver in the Viking Age*. Kaupang Excavation Project Publication Series 2. Aarhus: Aarhus University Press, 29–74.

Blackburn, M. A. S. 2009. 'Currency under the Vikings. Part 5: The Scandinavian achievement and legacy', *British Numismatic Journal* 79: 43–71.

Blackburn, M. A. S. 2011. 'The Viking winter camp at Torksey, 872–3', in M. A. S. Blackburn, *Viking Coinage and Currency in the British Isles*. British Numismatic Society Special Publications 7. London: Spink/British Numismatic Society, 221–64.

Blackburn, M. A. S. and Bonser, M. J. 1984. 'Single finds of Anglo-Saxon and Norman coins: 1', *British Numismatic Journal* 54: 63–73.

Blackburn, M. A. S. and Keynes, S. D. 1998. 'A corpus of the *Cross-and-Lozenge* and related coinages of Alfred, Ceowulf II and Archbishop Æthelred', in M. A. S. Blackburn and D. N. Dumville (eds), *Kings, Currency and Alliances: History and coinage of southern England*. Woodbridge: Boydell, 125–50.

Blair, J. 2005. *The Church in Anglo-Saxon Society*. Oxford: University Press.

Blair, J. 2013. 'Holy Beams: Anglo-Saxon cult sites and the place-name element *Bēam*', in M. Bintley and M. Shapland (eds), *Trees and Timber in the Anglo-Saxon World*. Oxford: Oxford University Press, 186–210.

Blair, J. 2018. *Building Anglo-Saxon England*. Princeton and Oxford: Princeton University Press.

Blunt, C. E. and Dolley, R. H. M. 1959. 'The hoard evidence for the coins of Alfred', *British Numismatic Journal* 29: 220–47.

Bogucki, M. 2009. 'Two Northumbrian stycas of Eanred and Æthelred II from early medieval Truso in Poland', *British Numismatic Journal* 79: 34–42.

Borrell, H. P. and Hawkins, E. 1840–41. 'On some Saxon coins discovered near Gravesend, in 1838', *Numismatic Chronicle* 3: 14–39.

Brink, S. and Price, N. (eds) 2008. *The Viking World*. Abingdon and New York: Routledge.

Brooke, G. C. 1924. 'Beeston Tor find of Anglo-Saxon coins', *Numismatic Chronicle and Journal of the Royal Numismatic Society* 4: 322–25.

Brookes, S. 2013. 'Mapping Anglo-Saxon civil defence', in J. Baker, S. Brookes and A. Reynolds (eds), *Landscapes of Defence in Early Medieval Europe*. Turnhout: Brepols, 39–63.

Brooks, N. P. 1979. 'England in the ninth century: The crucible of defeat'. *Transactions of the Royal Historical Society* 29: 1–20.

Brooks, N. P. 2010. 'Why is the *Anglo-Saxon Chronicle* about kings?', *Anglo-Saxon England* 39: 43–70.

Brooks, N. P. and Graham-Campbell, J. 2000. 'Reflections on the Viking Age silver hoard from Croydon, Surrey', in N. P. Brooks (ed.) *Communities and Warfare 700–1400*. London: Hambledon, 69–91.

Buckberry, J., Montgomery, J., Towers, J. *et al.* 2014. 'Finding Vikings in the Danelaw', *Oxford Journal of Archaeology* 33(4): 413–34.

Budd, P., Millard, A., Chenery, C., Lucy, S., and Roberts, C. 2004. 'Investigating population movement by stable isotope analysis: A report from Britain', *Antiquity* 78: 127–41.

Cameron, K. 1998. *A Dictionary of Lincolnshire Place-Names.* Nottingham: English Place Name Society.

Cameron, K. and Insley, J. 2010. *The Place-Names of Lincolnshire. Part 7: Lawress Wapentake.* Nottingham: English Place Name Society.

Campbell, A. 1962. *The Chronicle of Æthelweard.* London: Nelson.

Campbell, J. (ed.) 1982. *The Anglo-Saxons.* Harmondsworth: Penguin.

Carver, M. O. H. 2010. *The Birth of a Borough: An archaeological study of Anglo-Saxon Stafford.* Woodbridge: Boydell Press.

Christie, E. 2004. 'Self-Mastery and submission: Masculinity and holiness in the lives of Anglo-Saxon martyr-kings', in P. H. Cullum and K. J. Lewis (eds), *Holiness and Masculinity in Medieval Europe.* Cardiff: University of Wales Press, 143–57.

Christmas, H. 1862. 'Discovery of Anglo-Saxon coins at White Horse, near Croydon', *The Numismatic Chronicle and Journal of the Numismatic Society, New Series* 2: 302–4.

Coates, R. 2008. 'Reflections on some Lincolnshire major place-names, Part 1: Algakirk to Melton Ross', *English Place-Name Society Journal* 40: 35–95.

Cole, R. E. G .1906. 'The royal borough of Torksey, its churches, monasteries and castle', *Ass Architect Soc Rep and Pap,* 29: 451–530.

Cole, A. 1992. 'Distribution and use of the Old English place-name *mere-tūn*', *English Place-Name Society Journal* 24: 30–41.

Colgrave, B. and Mynors, R. A. B. 1993. *Bede's Ecclesiastical History of the English People.* New York: Oxford University Press. First published by Clarendon Press in 1969; revised edition first published by Oxford University Press in 1991.

Coupland, S. 1991a. 'The rod of God's wrath or the people of God's wrath? The Carolingian theology of the Viking invasions', *Journal of Ecclesiastical History* 44: 535–54.

Coupland, S. 1991b. 'The fortified bridges of Charles the Bald', *Journal of Medieval History* 17: 1–12.

Coupland, S. 1998. 'From poachers to gamekeepers: Scandinavian warlords and Carolingian kings', *Early Medieval Europe* 7(1): 85–114.

Coupland, S. 2001. 'The coinage of Lothar I (840–855)', *Numismatic Chronicle* 161: 157–98.

Coupland, S. 2003. 'The Vikings on the Continent in myth and history', *History* 88(2): 187–203.

Coupland, S. 2006. 'Between the devil and the deep blue sea: Hoards in ninth-century Frisia', in B. Cook and G. Williams (eds), *Coinage and History in the North Sea World, c. AD 500–1250: Essays in Honour of Marion Archibald.* Leiden: Brill, 241–66.

Cowie, R. 1988. 'A gazetteer of Middle Saxon sites and finds in The Strand/Westminster area', *Transactions of the London & Middlesex Archaeological Society* 39: 37–46.

Craig, G. 1991. 'Alfred the Great: A diagnosis', *Journal of the Royal Society of Medicine* 84(5): 303–5.

Cubitt, C. 2000. 'Sites and sanctity: Revisiting the cult of murdered and martyred Anglo-Saxon royal saints', *Early Medieval Europe* 9(1): 53–83.

Crawford, B. 1987. *Scandinavian Scotland.* Leicester: Leicester University Press.

Dallas, C. 1993. *Excavations in Thetford by B. K. Davison between 1964 and 1970.* East Anglian Archaeology 62.

Darlington, R. R. (ed.), McGurk, P. P. (ed. and trans.) and Bray, J. (tr.) 1995. *The Chronicle of John of Worcester.* Oxford: Clarendon Press.

Dass, N. 2007. *Viking Attacks on Paris: The Bella Parisiacae urbis of Abbo of Saint-Germain-des-Prés.* Paris: Peeters.

Daubney, A. J. 2016. *Portable Antiquities, Palimpsests, and Persistent Places*: *A multi-period approach to Portable Antiquities Scheme data in Lincolnshire*. Leiden: Sidestone Press.

Dobat, A. S. 2017. 'From Torksey to Füsing and Hedeby: Gambling warriors on the move?', in B. V. Eriksen, A. Abegg-Wigg, R. Bleile and U. Ickerodt (eds), *Interaction Without Borders: Exemplary archaeological research at the beginning of the 21st century*, Volume 2, Schleswig: Stiftung Schleswig-Holsteinische Landesmuseen, 597–605.

Downham, C. 2007. *Viking Kings of Britain and Ireland: The Dynasty of Ívarr to AD 1014*. Edinburgh: Dunedin Academic Press.

Dunning, G. and Evison, V. 1961. 'The Palace of Westminster sword', *Archaeologia* 98: 123–58.

Edgeworth, M. 2008. 'The Tempsford project: An interim report', *South Midlands Archaeology* 38: 8–16.

Edwards, J. F. and Hindle, B. P. 1991. 'The transportation system of medieval England and Wales', *Journal of Historical Geography* 17(2): 123–34.

Ekwall, E. 1930. 'How long did the Scandinavian language survive in England?', in N. Bøgholm, A. Brusendorff and C. A. Bodelsen (eds), *A Grammatical Miscellany Offered to Otto Jespersen on His Seventieth Birthday*. London and Copenhagen: Levin & Munksgaard, 17–30.

Eriksen, M. H. 2013. 'Doors to the dead: The power of doorways and thresholds in Viking Age Scandinavia', *Archaeological Dialogues* 20(2): 187–214.

Evans, J. 1866. 'Discovery of Anglo-Saxon coins at White Horse, near Croydon', *The Numismatic Chronicle and Journal of the Numismatic Society, New Series* 6: 232–40.

Everson, P. and Stocker, D. 2007. 'Two newly discovered fragments of pre-Viking sculpture: Evidence for a hitherto unsuspected early church site at South Leverton, Nottinghamshire?', *Transactions of the Thoroton Society of Nottinghamshire* 111: 33–49.

Evison, V. 1969. 'A Viking grave at Sonning, Berks.', *Antiquaries Journal* 49: 330–45.

Fell, C. 1986. 'Old English *wicing*: A question of semantics', *Proceedings of the British Academy* 73: 295–316.

Fell, C. 1987. 'Modern English Viking', in T. Turville-Petre and M. Gelling (eds), *Studies in Honour of Kenneth Cameron*. Leeds Studies in English, New Series 18. Leeds: University of Leeds School of English, 111–22.

Fellows-Jensen, G. 1968. 'Scandinavian personal names in Lincolnshire and Yorkshire', *Navnestudier* 7, Copenhagen: Akademisk Forlag (DBK).

Foot, S. 1996. 'The making of *Angelcynn*: English identity before the Norman Conquest', *Transactions of the Royal Historical Society*, 6th series, 6: 25–49.

Gardela, L. 2015. 'Vikings in Poland: A critical overview', in M. H. Eriksen, U. Pedersen, B. Rundberget, I. Axelsen, and H. Berg (eds), *Viking Worlds: Things, spaces and movement*. Oxford: Oxbow Books, 211–32.

Giles, J. A. 1849. *Roger of Wendover's Flowers of History, Volume I*. London: Henry G. Bohn.

Gotfredsen, A. B., Primeau, C., Frei, K. M. and Jørgensen, L. 2014. 'A ritual site with sacrificial wells from the Viking Age at Trelleborg, Denmark', *Danish Journal of Archaeology* 3(2): 145–63.

Graham-Campbell, J. 2000. 'On the non-numismatic silver in the Croydon (Whitehorse) hoard, Surrey', in N. P. Brooks (ed.), *Communities and Warfare, 700–1400*. London: Hambledon Press, 92.

Graham-Campbell, J. 2001. 'Pagan Scandinavian burial in the central and southern Danelaw', in Graham-Campbell *et al.* 2001, 105–23.

Graham-Campbell, J. 2002. 'The dual economy of the Danelaw: The Howard Linecar Memorial Lecture 2001', *British Numismatic Journal* 71: 49–59.

Graham-Campbell, J. 2004. 'The archaeology of the "Great Army" (865–79)', in E. Roesdahl and J. P. Schjødt (eds), *Beretning fra treogtyvende tværfaglige vikingesymposium,* Højbjerg: Aarhus Universitet, 30–46.

Graham-Campbell, J. and Batey, C. 1998. *Vikings in Scotland: An archaeological survey.* Edinburgh: Edinburgh University Press.

Graham-Campell, J., Hall, R. A., Jesch. J. and Parsons, D. N. (eds). 2001. *Vikings and the Danelaw. Select Papers from the Proceedings of the Thirteenth Viking Congress, Nottingham and York, 21–30 August 1997.* Oxford: Oxbow Books.

Groothedde, M. 2004. 'The Vikings in Zuphten (Netherlands): Military organisation and early town development after the Viking raid in 882', in R. Simek and E. Engel (eds), *Vikings on the Rhine: Recent research on early medieval relations between the Rhinelands and Scandinavia.* Vienna: Fassbaender, 111–32.

Guilbert, G. 2004. 'Borough Hill, Walton-upon-Trent: If not a hillfort, then what?', *Derbyshire Archaeological Journal* 124: 242–57.

Hadley, D. M. 1997. 'And they proceeded to plough and to support themselves', *Anglo-Norman Studies* 19: 69–96.

Hadley, D. M. 2000. *The Northern Danelaw: Its social structure, 800–1100.* London: Continuum.

Hadley, D. M. 2006. *The Vikings in England: Settlement, society and culture.* Manchester: Manchester University Press.

Hadley, D. M. 2013. 'Whither the warrior in Viking-Age England', in D. M. Hadley and A. Ten Harkel (eds), *Everyday Life in Viking Towns: Social approaches to towns in England and Ireland, c. 800–1100.* Oxford: Oxbow Books, 103–17.

Hadley, D. M. 2020. 'The archaeology of migrants in Viking-Age and Anglo-Norman England: Process, practice, and performance', in W. M. Ormrod, J. Story and E. M. Tyler (eds), *Migrants in Medieval England, c. 500–c. 1500.* Proceedings of the British Academy. Oxford: Oxford University Press, 175–205.

Hadley, D. M. and Hemer, K. 2011. 'Microcosms of migration: Children and early medieval population movement', *Childhood in the Past* 4: 63–78.

Hadley, D. M. and Richards, J. D. 2000. (eds) *Cultures in Contact: Scandinavian settlement in England in the ninth and tenth centuries.* Studies in the Early Middle Ages 2. Turnhout: Brepols.

Hadley, D. M. and Richards, J. D. 2016a. 'The winter camp of the Viking Great Army, AD 872–3, Torksey, Lincolnshire', *Antiquaries Journal* 96: 23–67.

Hadley, D. M. and Richards, J. D. 2016b. 'The Viking winter camp and Anglo-Scandinavian town at Torksey, Lincolnshire: The landscape context', in V. E. Turner, O. A. Owen and D. J. Waugh (eds), *Shetland and the Viking World: Papers from proceedings of the Seventeenth Viking Congress,* Lerwick: Shetland Heritage Publications, 127–39.

Hadley, D. M. and Richards, J. D. 2018. 'In search of the Viking Great Army: Beyond the winter camps', *Medieval Settlement Research* 32: 1–7.

Hadley, D. M. and Richards, J. D. 2020. 'Changing places: Tracing the Viking Great Army in the Anglo-Saxon countryside', in A. Pedersen and S. Sindbæk (eds), *Viking Encounters: Proceedings of the 18th Viking Congress.* Aarhus: Aarhus University Press, 108–29

Hadley, D. M. and Richards, J. D. in prep. *The Viking Great Army: From tents to towns.* Oxford: Oxford University Press. (forthcoming)

Hadley, D. M., Willmott, H. B., Crewe, V. A. and Howsam, C. L. 2016. *Fieldwork in West Halton, Lincolnshire, from 2003–09.* Unpublished report, University of Sheffield.

Haldenby, D. and Richards, J. D. 2016. 'The Viking Great Army and its legacy: plotting settlement shift using metal-detected finds', *Internet Archaeology* 42: https://doi.org/10.11141/ia.42.3 (unpaginated).

Hall, M. A. 2016. 'Board games in boat burials: Play in the performance of migration and Viking Age mortuary practice', *European Journal of Archaeology* 19(3): 439–55.

Hall, R. A. 1989. 'The Five Boroughs of the Danelaw: A review of present knowledge', *Anglo-Saxon England* 18: 149–206.

Hall, R. A. 1994. *Viking Age York*. London: B. T. Batsford Ltd / English Heritage.

Hall, R. A. 2001. 'Anglo-Scandinavian urban development in the East Midlands', in Graham-Campbell *et al.* 2001, 143–56.

Hall, R. A. 2011. 'Recent research into early medieval York and its hinterland', in D. Petts and S. Turner (eds), *Early Medieval Northumbria: Kingdoms and communities, AD 450–1100*. Turnhout: Brepols, 71–84.

Hall, R. A. and Williams, G. *et al.* 2020. 'A Riverine Site Near York: A possible Viking Camp?', in Williams 2020, 3–102.

Halsall, G. 2000. 'The Viking presence in England? The burial evidence reconsidered', in Hadley and Richards 2000, 259–76.

Halsall, G. 2003. *Warfare and Society in the Barbarian West, 450–900*. Abingdon: Routledge.

Hamerow, H. 2007. 'Agrarian production and the emporia of mid Saxon England, *c.* AD 650–850' in Henning, J. (ed.), *Post-Roman Towns, Trade and Settlement in Europe and Byzantium*, vol. 1. Berlin and New York: Walter de Gruyter, 219–32.

Harrison, D. 2018. *Torksey Embankment, Lincolnshire: Geophysical survey for Arcadis*. Unpublished report by Headland Archaeology.

Hawkes, J. and Sidebottom, P. with Biddle, M. 2018. *Derbyshire and Staffordshire: Corpus of Anglo-Saxon Stone Sculpture XIII*. Oxford: Oxford University Press, for the British Academy.

Hennius, A. 2018. 'Viking Age tar production and outland exploitation', *Antiquity* 92(365): 1349–61.

Heywood, N. 1884. 'Saxon coins found on the site of Waterloo Bridge, London', *Numismatic Chronicle* 4: 349–50.

Hines, J. 1991. 'Scandinavian English: a creole in context', in P. Sture Ureland and G. Broderick (eds), *Language Contact in the British Isles*. Tubingen: Niemeyer, 403–27.

Hodges, R. 1989. *The Anglo-Saxon Achievement: Archaeology and the beginnings of English society*. London: Duckworth.

Holm, P. 1986. 'The slave trade of Dublin, ninth to twelfth centuries', *Peritia* 5: 317–45.

Hooper, N. 1989. 'Some observations on the navy in late Anglo-Saxon England', in C. Harper-Bill, C. Holdsworth and J. L. Nelson (eds), *Studies in Medieval History Presented to R. Allen Brown*. Woodbridge: Boydell, 203–13.

IJssennagger, N. 2013. 'Between Frankish and Viking: Frisia and Frisians in the Viking Age', *Medieval Scandinavia* 9: 69–98.

Jagodziński, M. F. 2010. *Truso between Weonodland and Witland*. Elbląg: Archaeological and Historical Museum in Elbląg.

Jarman, C. 2018. 'Resolving Repton: Has archaeology found the great Viking camp?', *British Archaeology* March–April 2018, 28–35.

Jarman, C. 2019. 'Resolving Repton: A Viking Great Army winter camp and beyond', *Current Archaeology* 352, 18–25.

Jarman, C., Biddle, M., Higham, T., and Bronk Ramsey, C. 2018. 'The Viking Great Army in England: New dates from the Repton charnel', *Antiquity* 92(361): 183–99.

Jennbert, K. 2004. 'Sheep and goats in Norse paganism', in B. S. Frizell (ed.), *Pecus: Man and Animal in Antiquity. Proceedings of the conference at the Swedish Institute in Rome, September 9–12, 2002*, Rome: The Swedish Institute in Rome, 160–66.

Johnson, P. G. 2002. *Cemetery Excavations at Village Farm, Spofforth, North Yorkshire: Archaeological post-excavation assessment*. Unpublished report by Northern Archaeological Associates.

Johnson South, T. 2002. *Historia de Sancto Cuthberto*. Anglo-Saxon Texts 3. Woodbridge: Boydell and Brewer.

Jørgensen, L. 2008. 'Manor, cult and market at Lake Tissø', in Brink and Price 2008, 77–82.

Kelly, E. 2015. 'The *longphort* in Viking Age Ireland: the archaeological evidence', in H. B. Clarke and R. Johnson (eds), *The Vikings in Ireland and Beyond*. Dublin: Four Courts Press, 55–92.

Kershaw, J. 2013. *Viking Identities: Scandinavian jewellery in England*, Oxford: Oxford University Press.

Kershaw, J. 2016. 'Scandinavian-style metalwork from Southern England: New light on the "First Viking Age" in Wessex', in R. Lavelle and S. Roffey (eds), *Danes in Wessex: The Scandinavian impact on southern England, c. 800 – c. 1100*. Oxford and Philadelphia: Oxbow Books, 87–108.

Kershaw, J. 2017. 'An early medieval dual-currency economy: Bullion and coin in the Danelaw', *Antiquity* 91(355): 173–90.

Kershaw, J. and Røyrvik, E. C. 2016. 'The "People of the British Isles" project and Viking settlement in England', *Antiquity* 90(354): 1670–80.

Kershaw, P. 2000. 'The Alfred-Guthrum treaty: Scripting accommodation and interaction in Viking Age England', in Hadley and Richards 2000, 43–64.

Keynes, S. 1997. 'The Vikings in England, c. 790–1016', in P. H. Sawyer (ed.), *The Oxford Illustrated History of the Vikings*. Oxford: Oxford University Press, 46–82.

Keynes, S. 1999. 'The Cult of King Alfred', *Anglo-Saxon England* 28: 225–356.

Keynes, S. and Lapidge, M. 1983. *Alfred the Great: Asser's Life of King Alfred and Other Contemporary Sources*. Harmondsworth: Penguin.

Kilger, C. 2008. 'Wholeness and holiness: Counting, weighing and valuing silver in the early Viking period', in D. Skre (ed.), *Means of Exchange: Dealing with silver in the Viking Age*, Kaupang Excavation Project Publication Series 2, Aarhus: Aarhus University Press, 253–326.

Kilmurry, K. 1980. *The Pottery Industry of Stamford, Lincs., AD 850–1250*. Oxford: British Archaeological Reports, British Series 84.

Langdon, J. 1993. 'Inland water transport in medieval England', *Journal of Historical Geography* 19: 1–11.

Leonard, A. 2015. *Nested Negotiations: Landscape and portable material culture in Viking-Age England*. Unpublished PhD thesis, University of York.

Leslie, S., Winney, B., Hellenthal, G. *et al.* 2015. 'The fine-scale genetic structure of the British population', *Nature* 519: 309–14.

Loveluck, C. P. 1996. 'The development of the Anglo-Saxon landscape, economy and society "On Driffield", East Yorkshire, 400–750 AD', *Anglo-Saxon Studies in Archaeology and History* 9: 25–48.

Loveluck, C. P. 2007. *Rural Settlement, Lifestyles and Social Change in the Later First Millenium AD: Anglo-Saxon Flixborough*. Excavations at Flixborough 4. Oxford: Oxbow Books.

Lund, N. 1986. 'The armies of Swein Forkbeard and Cnut: *leding* or *lið*?', *Anglo-Saxon England* 15: 105–18.

Lund, N., Crumlin-Pedersen, O., Sawyer, P. H., and Fell, C. E. 1984. *Two Voyagers at the Court of King Alfred*. York: Sessions.

Mac Airt, S. and Mac Niocaill, G. (eds and trs). 1983. *The Annals of Ulster, to AD 1131*. Dublin: Dublin Institute for Advanced Studies.

Macdonald, A. 1929. *A Short History of Repton*. London: Ernest Benn.

MacGregor, G. 2009. 'Changing people changing landscapes: Excavations at The Carrick, Midross, Loch Lomond', *Historic Argyll* 8: 8–13.

Mahany, C. M. and Roffe, D. R. 1983. 'Stamford: The development of an Anglo-Scandinavian borough', *Anglo-Norman Studies* 5: 19–219.

Mainman, A. 2019. *Anglian York*. Pickering: Blackthorn Press.

Malcolm, G., Bowsher, D. and Cowie, R. 2003. *Middle Saxon London: Excavations at the Royal Opera House 1989–99*.

MoLAS Monograph Series 16. London: Museum of London Archaeology Service.

Mays, S., Harding, C. and Heighway, C. 2007. *Wharram: A Study of Settlement on the Yorkshire Wolds XI: The Churchyard*. York University Archaeological Publications 13. York: University of York.

MacLean, S. 2009. *History and Politics in Late Carolingian and Ottonian Europe: The Chronicle of Regino of Prüm and Adalbert of Magdeburg*. Manchester: Manchester University Press.

McLeod, S. 2006. 'Feeding the *Micel Here* in England, *c.* 865–878', *Journal of the Australian Early Medieval Association* 2: 141–56.

McLeod, S. 2014. *The Beginning of Scandinavian Settlement in England*. Turnhout: Brepols.

Metcalf, D. M. 1958. 'Eighteenth-century finds of medieval coins from the records of the Society of Antiquaries', *The Numismatic Chronicle and Journal of the Royal Numismatic Society* 18: 73–96.

Montgomery, J. E. 2000. 'Ibn Fadlān and the Rūsiyyah', *Journal of Arabic and Islamic Studies* 3: 1–25.

Morris, R. 1989. *Churches in the Landscape*. London: J. M. Dent & Sons.

Morton, A.D. (ed.) 1992. *Excavations at Hamwic Volume 1: Excavations 1946–83, excluding Six Dials and Melbourne Street*. Council for British Archaeology Research Report 84. London: Council for British Archaeology.

Naismith, R. 2005. 'Islamic coins from early medieval England', *Numismatic Chronicle* 165: 193–222.

Nelson, J. L. 1991. *The Annals of St Bertin*. Manchester: Manchester University Press.

Nelson, J. L. 1992. *Charles the Bald*. London: Longman.

Nelson, J. L. 1997. 'The Frankish Empire', in P. H. Sawyer (ed.) *The Oxford Illustrated History of the Vikings*. Oxford: Oxford University Press, 19–47.

Nelson, J. L. 2003. 'England and the Continent in the ninth century: II, the

Vikings and others', *Transactions of the Royal Historical Society* (6th series) 13: 1–28.

Nicolaysen, N. 1877. 'Udgravninger i Fjære 1876. Foreningen til Norske Fortidsmindesmerkers bevaring', *Aarsberetning 1876*, 117–39.

O'Connor, T. 2000. *The Archaeology of Animal Bones*. Stroud: Tempus.

Ó Cróinín, D. 2013. *Early Medieval Ireland, 400–1200*. London and New York: Routledge.

Ó Floinn, R. 1998. 'The archaeology of the early Viking Age in Ireland', in H. B. Clarke, M. Ní Mhaonaigh and R. Ó Floinn (eds), *Ireland and Scandinavia in the Early Viking Age*. Dublin: Four Courts Press, 131–65.

Owen, D. M. 1971. *Church and Society in Medieval Lincolnshire*. Lincoln: Lincolnshire Local History Committee.

Pagan, H. 1965. 'Coinage in the age of Burgred', *British Numismatic Journal* 34: 11–27.

Pagan, H. 1966. 'The Gainford hoard', *British Numismatic Journal* 35: 190–91.

Pagan, H. 1986. 'Presidential Address 1986', *British Numismatic Journal* 56: 207–9.

Page, R. I. 1971. 'How long did the Scandinavian language survive in England? The epigraphical evidence', in P. Clemoes and K. Hughes (eds), *England before the Conquest*. Cambridge: Cambridge University Press, 165–81.

Pedersen, U. 2008. 'Weights and balances', in D. Skre (ed.), *Means of Exchange: Dealing with silver in the Viking Age*, Kaupang Excavation Project Publication Series 2, Aarhus: Aarhus University Press, 119–95.

Pelteret, D. 1980. 'Slave raiding and slave trading in early England', *Anglo-Saxon England* 9: 99–114.

Perry, G. 2016. 'Pottery production in Anglo-Scandinavian Torksey (Lincolnshire): Reconstructing and contextualising the *chaîne opératoire*', *Medieval Archaeology* 60(1): 72–114.

Perry, G. 2019. 'Situation vacant: Potter required in the newly founded Late

Saxon Burh of Newark-on-Trent, Nottinghamshire', *Antiquaries Journal* 99: 1–29.

Pestell, T. 2013. 'Imports or immigrants? Reassessing Scandinavian metalwork in late Anglo-Saxon East Anglia', in D. Bates and R. Liddiard (eds), *East Anglia and its North Sea World in the Middle Ages*, Woodbridge: Boydell, 230–55.

Pestell, T. 2019. *Viking East Anglia*. Norfolk Museums Service. Shaftesbury: Blackmore Group.

Pettersson, A. (ed.) 2009. *The Spillings Hoard: Gotland's role in Viking Age World Trade*. Visby: Gotlands Museum.

Pirie, E. J. E. 2000. *Thrymsas, Sceattas and Stycas of Northumbria: An inventory of finds recorded, to 1997*. Northumbrian Numismatic Studies 2. Llanfyllin: Galata Print.

Price, N. S. 1991. 'Viking armies and fleets in Brittany: A case study for some general problems', in H. Bekker-Nielson and H. F. Nielson (eds), *Beretning fra Tiende Tværfaglige Vikingsymposium*. Højbjerg: Hikuin, 7–24.

Price, N. S. 2019. *The Viking Way: Magic and mind in late Iron Age Scandinavia*. Revised edition. Oxford: Oxbow Books. First published by Department of Archaeology and Ancient History, Uppsala, 2002.

Price, T., Peets, J., Allmäe, R., Maldre, L., and Oras, E. 2016. 'Isotopic provenancing of the Salme ship burials in pre-Viking Age Estonia', *Antiquity* 90(352): 1022–37.

Purcell, E. 2015. 'The first generation in Ireland, 795–812: Viking raids and Viking bases?', in H. B. Clarke and R. Johnson (eds), *The Vikings in Ireland and Beyond*. Dublin: Four Courts Press, 41–54.

Raffield, B. 2014. '"A river of knives and swords": Ritually deposited weapons in English watercourses and wetlands during the Viking Age', *European Journal of Archaeology* 17(4): 634–55.

Raffield, B. 2016. 'Bands of brothers: A re-appraisal of the Viking Great Army and its implications for the Scandinavian colonization of England', *Early Medieval Europe* 24(3): 308–37.

Raffield, B., Price, N. and Collard, M. 2017. 'Male-biased operational sex ratios and the Viking phenomenon: An evolutionary anthropological perspective on late Iron Age Scandinavian raiding', *Evolution and Human Behaviour* 38(3): 315–24.

Ravn, M. 2016. *Viking-Age War Fleets: Shipbuilding, resource management and maritime warfare in 11th-century Denmark*. Maritime Culture of the North 4. Roskilde: Viking Ship Museum.

Raxworthy, C. J., Kjølbye-Biddle, B. and Biddle, M. 1990. 'An archaeological study of frogs and toads from the eighth to sixteenth century at Repton, Derbyshire', *Herpetological Journal* 1: 504–9.

Reuter, T. 1992. *The Annals of Fulda*. Manchester: Manchester University Press.

Richards, J. D. 1999. 'Cottam: An Anglian and Anglo-Scandinavian settlement on the Yorkshire Wolds', *Archaeological Journal* 156: 1–110.

Richards, J. D. 2000. 'Identifying Anglo-Scandinavian settlements', in Hadley and Richards 2000, 295–309.

Richards, J. D. 2004. *Viking Age England*. Stroud: Tempus.

Richards, J. D. *et al*. 2004. 'The Viking barrow cemetery at Heath Wood, Ingleby', *Antiquaries Journal* 84: 23–116.

Richards, J. D. 2013. 'Cottam, Cowlam and environs: An Anglo-Saxon estate on the Yorkshire Wolds', *Archaeological Journal* 170: 201–71.

Richards, J. D. and Hadley, D. M. 2016. *Archaeological Evaluation of the Anglo-Saxon and Viking site at Torksey, Lincolnshire*. York: Archaeology Data Service. http://dx.doi.org/10.5284/1018222

Richards, J. D. and Haldenby, D. 2018. 'The scale and impact of Viking settlement in Northumbria', *Medieval Archaeology* 62(2): 322–50.

Richards, J. D. and Naylor, J. 2012. 'Settlement, landscape and economy in early medieval Northumbria: The contribution of portable antiquities', in D. Petts and S. Turner (eds), *Early Medieval Northumbria: Kingdoms and communities,* Studies in the Early Middle Ages 24, Turnhout: Brepols, 129–49.

Richards, J. D., Naylor, J. and Holas-Clark, C. 2009. 'Anglo-Saxon landscape and economy: Using portable antiquities to study Anglo-Saxon and Viking Age England', *Internet Archaeology* 25: http://dx.doi.org/10.11141/ia.25.2

Robinson, C. H. 1921. *Anskar: The Apostle of the North, 801–865.* London: The Society for the Propagation of the Gospel in Foreign Parts.

Rogers, N. S. H. 1993. *Anglian and Other Finds from 46–54 Fishergate: The small finds,* Archaeology of York 17/14, York: Council for British Archaeology.

Rogerson, A. 1995. *A Late Neolithic, Saxon and Medieval Site at Middle Harling, Norfolk.* East Anglian Archaeology 74.

Rogerson, A. and Dallas, C. 1984. *Excavations in Thetford, 1948–59 and 1973–80.* East Anglian Archaeology 22.

Rollason, D. (ed.) 2000. *Symeon of Durham: Libellus de Exordio atque Procursu istius hoc est Dunhelmensis Ecclesie. Tract on the Origins and Progress of this the Church of Durham.* Oxford: Oxford University Press.

Rowe, E. 2008. *Land to the North of the Railway, Torksey, Lincolnshire: Archaeological evaluation report.* Unpublished report by Pre-Construct Archaeology.

Russel, I. R. and Hurley, M. (eds) 2014. *Woodstown: A Viking-Age settlement in Co. Waterford.* Dublin: Four Courts Press.

Sawyer, P. H. 1958. 'The density of the Danish settlement in England', *University of Birmingham Historical Journal* 6: 1–17.

Sawyer, P. H. 1962. *The Age of the Vikings.* London: Edward Arnold.

Sawyer, P. H. 1998. *Anglo-Saxon Lincolnshire.* History of Lincolnshire 3.

Lincoln: History of Lincolnshire Committee.

Schoenfelder, M. and Richards, J. D. 2011. 'Norse bells: A Scandinavian colonial artefact', *Anglo-Saxon Studies in Archaeology and History* 17: 151–68.

Scull, C. 2009. *Early Medieval (Late 5th– early 8th centuries AD) Cemeteries at Boss Hall and Buttermarket, Ipswich, Suffolk.* Society for Medieval Archaeology Monograph 27. Leeds: Society for Medieval Archaeology.

Sheehan, J. 2008. 'The longphort in Viking Age Ireland', *Acta Archaeologica* 79: 282–95.

Sherlock, R. J. 1956. 'A nineteenth-century manuscript book on coins', *British Numismatic Journal* 28: 394–9.

Short, I. (ed. and tr.) 2009. *Geffrei Gaimar: History of the English.* Oxford: Oxford University Press.

Simpson, L. 2005. 'Viking warrior-burials: Is this the *longphort?*', in E. Duffy (ed.), *Medieval Dublin Symposium 2004.* Dublin: Four Courts Press, 11–62.

Sindbæk, S. 2008. 'Local and long-distance exchange', in Brink and Price 2008, 150–57.

Sindbæk, S. 2009. 'Routes and long-distance traffic: The nodal points of Wulfstan's voyage', in A. Englert and A. Trakadas (eds), *Wulfstan's Voyage: The Baltic Sea region in the early Viking Age as seen from shipboard.* Maritime Culture of the North 2. Roskilde: The Viking Ship Museum: 72–78.

Sindbæk, S. 2018. 'Thousands of objects discovered in Scandinavia's first Viking city', *Science Nordic* https://sciencenordic.com/archaeology-denmark-researcher-zone/thousands-of-objects-discovered-in-scandinavias-first-viking-city/1458765. Accessed 23 Dec 2019.

Skre, D. (ed) 2007. *Kaupang in Skiringssal.* Kaupang Excavation Project Publication Series 1. Aarhus: Aarhus University Press.

Skre, D. 2008. 'The development of urbanism in Scandinavia', in Brink and Price 2008, 83–93.

Smart, V. 1986. 'Scandinavians, Celts, and Germans in Anglo-Saxon England: The evidence of moneyers' names', in Blackburn 1986, 171–84.

Sloane, B., Swain, H. and Thomas, C. 1995. 'The Roman road and the river regime', *London Archaeologist* 7(14): 359–70.

Smith, R. A. 1925. 'The Beeston Tor Hoard', *Antiquaries Journal*, 5(2): 135–40.

Smyth, A. 1999. 'The effect of Scandinavian raiders in the English and Irish churches: A preliminary reassessment', in B. Smith (ed.), *Britain and Ireland 900–1300: Insular responses to medieval European change.* Cambridge: Cambridge University Press, 1–38.

Somerville, A. A. and McDonald, R. A. 2014. *The Viking Age: A reader.* Toronto: University of Toronto Press.

South, T. J. 2002. *Historia de Sancto Cuthberto.* Woodbridge: Boydell.

Speed, G. and Walton Rogers, P. 2004. 'A burial of a Viking woman at Adwick-le-Street, South Yorkshire', *Medieval Archaeology* 48: 51–90.

Stafford, P. 1980. 'The "farm of one night" and the organisation of King Edward's estates in Domesday', *Economic History Review* 33(4): 491–502.

Stamper, P. A. and Croft, R. A. (eds). 2000. *Wharram: A study of settlement on the Yorkshire Wolds VIII: The South Manor Area.* York University Archaeological Publications 10. York: University of York.

Steedman, K. 1994. 'Excavation of a Saxon site at Riby Crossroads, Lincolnshire', *Archaeological Journal* 151: 212–306.

Stein, S. 2013. 'The geoarchaeology of Viking overwintering camps in England: Preliminary results of a radiocarbon dated palynological sequence at Brampton in Torksey, Lincolnshire', *Quaternary Newsletter* 131: 51–4.

Stein S. 2015. *Understanding Torksey and the Viking Winter Camp of 872–3: A geoarchaeological and landscape approach to Viking overwintering camps.* Unpublished PhD thesis, University of Sheffield.

Stenton, F. M. 1943. *Anglo-Saxon England.* Oxford: Clarendon Press.

Swanton, M. J. 1999. 'King Alfred's ships: Text and context', *Anglo-Saxon England* 28: 1–22.

Tester, A., Anderson, S., Riddler, I. and Carr, R. J. M. 2014. *Staunch Meadow, Brandon, Suffolk: A high status Middle Saxon settlement on the Fen Edge.* East Anglian Archaeology 151.

Thomas, C., Cowie, R. and Sidell, J. 2006. *The Royal Palace, Abbey and Town of Westminster on Thorney Island: Archaeological excavations (1991–8) for the London Underground Limited Jubilee Line Extension Project.* MoLAS Monograph Series 22. London: Museum of London Archaeology Service.

Townend, M. 2000. 'Viking Age England as a bilingual society', in Hadley and Richards 2000, 89–105.

Townend, M. 2014. *Viking Age Yorkshire.* Pickering: Blackthorn Press.

Tummuscheit, A. and Witte, F. 2018. 'The Danevirke in the light of recent excavations', in J. Hansen and M. Bruus (eds), *The Fortified Viking Age: 36th Interdisciplinary Viking Symposium.* Odense: University Press of Southern Denmark, 69–74.

Tweddle, D., Moulden, J. and Logan, E. 1999. *Anglian York: A survey of the evidence.* Archaeology of York 17/14. York: Council for British Archaeology.

Vince, A. 2001. 'Lincoln in the Viking Age', in Graham-Campbell *et al.* 2001, 157–79.

Vince, A. 2006. 'Coinage and urban development: Integrating the archaeological and numismatic history of Lincoln', in B. Cook and G. Williams (eds), *Coinage and History in the North Sea World, c. AD 500–1250.* Leiden and Boston: Brill, 525–44.

Wade, K. 1988. 'Ipswich', in R. Hodges and B. Hobley (eds), *The Rebirth of Towns in the West AD 700–1050.* Council for British Archaeology Research Report 68. London: Council for British Archaeology, 93–100.

Wallis, H. 2005. *Excavations at Mill Lane, Thetford.* East Anglian Archaeology 108.

Walther, S. 2004. 'The Vikings in the Rhinelands according to Latin sources', in R. Simek and E. Engel (eds), *Vikings on the Rhine: Recent research on early medieval relations between the Rhinelands and Scandinavia.* Vienna: Fassbaender, 165–77.

Webster, L. 1991. 'The Age of Alfred: Metalwork, wood and bone', in L. Webster and J. Backhouse (eds), *The Making of England: Anglo-Saxon art and culture AD 600–900.* London: British Museum Press.

Whitelock, D. (ed.) 1961. *The Anglo-Saxon Chronicle.* London: Eyre and Spottiswoode.

Whitelock, D. (ed.) 1979. *English Historical Documents, Vol. I.* London: Routledge.

Williams, G. 2008. 'Burgred "Lunette" type E reconsidered', *British Numismatic Journal* 78: 222–27.

Williams, G. 2011. 'Silver economies, monetisation and society: An overview', in J. Graham-Campbell, S. M. Sindbæk and G. Williams (eds), *Silver Economies, Monetisation and Society in Scandinavia, AD 800–1100.* Aarhus: Aarhus University Press, 337–72.

Williams, G. 2013. 'Towns and identities in Viking England', in D. M. Hadley and L. Ten Harkel (eds), *Everyday Life in Viking Age Towns: Social approaches to towns in England and Ireland, c. 800–1100.* Oxford: Oxbow Books, 27–49.

Williams, G. 2014. 'Coins and currency in Viking England, AD 865–954', in R. Naismith, M. Allen and E. Screen (eds), *Early Medieval Monetary History: Studies in memory of Mark Blackburn.* Abingdon: Ashgate, 13–38.

Williams, G. 2015. 'Viking camps and the means of exchange in Britain and Ireland in the ninth century', in H. B. Clarke and R. Johnson (eds), *The Vikings in Ireland and Beyond.* Dublin: Four Courts Press, 93–116.

Williams, G. 2019. *Weapons of the Viking Warrior.* Oxford: Osprey Publishing.

Williams, G. (ed.) 2020. *A Riverine Site Near York: A possible Viking Camp?* British Museum Research Publications 224. London: British Museum Press.

Williams, G. and Naylor, J. 2016. *King Alfred's Coins: The Watlington Viking hoard.* Oxford: Ashmolean Museum.

Willmott, H. and Daubney, A. 2019. 'Of saints, sows or smiths? Copper-brazed iron handbells in early medieval England', *Archaeological Journal* 177: 63–82.

Wilson, D. M. 1965. 'Some neglected Anglo-Saxon swords', *Medieval Archaeology* 9: 32–54.

Wilson, D. M. 1976. 'The Scandinavians in England', in D. M. Wilson (ed.), *The Archaeology of Anglo-Saxon England.* Cambridge: Cambridge University Press, 393–403.

Wilson, D. and Blunt, C. 1961. 'The Trewhiddle Hoard', *Archaeologia* 98: 75–122.

Winterbottom, M. (ed. and tr.) 1972. *Three Lives of English Saints.* Toronto: Pontifical Institute of Mediaeval Studies.

Woods, A. in prep. 'Viking economies and the "Great Army": Interpreting the precious metals from Torksey, Lincolnshire', in J. Shepard, M. Jankowiak and J. Gruszczynski (eds), *Silver, Slaves and Gotland: Cogs and drivers in Viking Age trade.* London: Routledge. (forthcoming)

Wrathmell, S. (ed.) 2012. *Wharram: A study of settlement on the Yorkshire Wolds XIII: A history of Wharram Percy and its neighbours.* York University Archaeological Publications 15. York: University of York.

Acknowledgments

We are grateful to Colin Ridler, of Thames & Hudson, for encouraging us to write this book. We would also like to thank Ben Hayes, Flora Spiegel, Rowena Alsey, and Anabel Navarro for their support throughout the writing and production process, and Drazen Tomic for working with us on the illustrations. Many others have contributed to the story told here. Firstly we should acknowledge the contribution of the metal detectorists who have shared information about their finds with us, and with the Portable Antiquities Scheme (PAS). For Torksey they include Dave and Pete Stanley, and Neil Parker, as well as others who prefer not to be named. Roger Thomas took us to see his find-spots at Catton, with other members of Witan Archaeology. Ian Briggs and Ricky Brelsford provided information about Spofforth; Paul Robbins, Paul Greenwood and other members of the Grimsby and District Metal Detecting Club discussed their finds from Swinhope and Binbrook with us. Geoff Bambrook, Richard Bourne, Gary Johnson, Jon Mann and Lee Toone provided invaluable information about finds from Aldwark, which Mark Ainsley showed Julian around, many years ago. We would like to thank Dave Haldenby for his invaluable finds recording at Cottam, as well for his observations on the Torksey finds, and we are grateful to him and his contacts for additional information about East Yorkshire sites. We are also grateful to Michael Lewis for permission to use data from the PAS; as well as a number of Finds Liaison Officers, notably Martin Foreman, Adam Daubney, Wendy Scott, Rebecca Griffiths and Amy Downes. In more traditional academic circles, Andrew Woods of the Yorkshire Museum discussed the Flixborough stycas with us; Tessi Loeffelmann, PhD student at Durham University, shared her Heath Wood animal cremation stable isotope results; James Graham-Campbell drew our attention to a possible gaming piece from the Kiloran Bay burial; Andres Dobat told us about the gaming pieces from Füsing; and Michel Groothedde shared information about those from near Zutphen. Over the course of our research the Torksey project team members Andrew Woods, Sam Stein, Hannah Brown, Andrew Marriot, Gareth Perry and Lizzy Craig-Atkins all gave generously of their time and expertise. Ben Robinson and Tim Allen of Historic England have supported our research in Torksey, granting Scheduled Monument permission for survey south of the village, and Steve Dean of the Environment Agency shared their Torksey Lock geophysical survey results with us. Numerous landowners and farmers have also allowed access at Cottam and Torksey, including Robert Bannister, Rodger Brownlow, Derrick Small, Dick Denby and Edward Dickinson. We have been fortunate to receive funding for our research at Torksey and other sites visited by the Great Army from the British Academy, the Society of Antiquaries of London, the Robert Kiln Trust, the University of Sheffield and the University of York. Last, but not least, we owe a debt of gratitude to the late Mark Blackburn for putting us on the trail of the Great Army at Torksey. While none of the above are responsible for any remaining errors, we hope they will enjoy reading this story.

293

Sources of Illustrations

Index